THE APE HAS STABBED ME

A Cocktail of Reminiscences

Vincent Poklewski Koziell

The Ape Has Stabbed Me
A Cocktail of Reminiscences

by Vincent Poklewski Koziell

ISBN 978-0-9568735-7-6

A CIP catalogue record for this book is available from the British Library.

First published in Great Britain by The Write Factor, 2014
www.thewritefactor.co.uk

Printed in the UK by TJ International, Padstow, Cornwall

THE APE HAS STABBED ME

Contents

Foreword

FIRST OF ALL, I would like thank and acknowledge the myriad people, from bus conductors to bishops, who have – for seconds, or years – entered, helped or altered my life in some way. After all, unless one has spent one's life contemplating on top of a pillar, one has been part of the world and been affected by it in some way, for better or worse.

Pray, dear reader, do not treat this as full memoirs, but merely a few hopefully amusing reminiscences of a somewhat unusual life. It is, I hope, reasonably discreet as I cannot claim too many successes in either sexual or financial matters. However I have always confined myself to the opposite sex in the former matters, but sadly not entirely to the honest, in the latter ones. My contact with crooks has however sometimes caused me amusement and added to my experiences – however painful.

On a more serious note, I owe special thanks to Charlotte Wilkins who inspired and guided me in writing this book. The sweat – and sometimes tears – of digging into one's past was much alleviated by a series of long and pleasant lunches. When she moved to France, the task was bravely taken over by my beloved daughter Sophie.

Finally, excuses for excess of 'I's. I have made great attempts to include some other people as well, but pray excuse me if I have failed, thank God, to achieve a book of biblical proportions. On this note I will hand you over to Dennis O'Driscoll's poem:

MEMOIR

It has been
absolutely
fascinating
being me.

A unique
privilege.

Now my
whole life

lies ahead
of you.

No thanks
at all are

called for,
I assure you.

The pleasure
is all mine.

- Dennis O'Driscoll

Notes About My Family

MY MOTHER WAS born a de Stoeckl: an Austrian family who were in Russian service. In those days – and in fact until the revolution – Russians had no objections to employing foreigners as diplomats or courtiers. My mother's father was Baron Sasha de Stoeckl, the son of Baron Edouard de Stoeckl who, in 1850 became Chargé D'Affaires of the Russian Embassy in Washington, and in 1854, assumed the post of Minister. He was responsible for selling Alaska (which at that time was known as Russian America) to the Americans in 1867. As his sole surviving descendant, I was invited to the centenary celebrations in Anchorage, which were unfortunately cancelled due to an earthquake.

Apparently he had quite a lot of trouble with the sale as nobody wanted Alaska – being as it is, such a vast landmass consisting mainly of tundra, ice and permafrost. Nobody was aware of the valuable gas and oil reserves at that time, and whoever held Alaska simply had to support the native population there, and defend it. This meant there were vast numbers of troops that had to be kept at various garrisons right across Alaska and God knows how many tens of thousands of horses to drag supplies to all the far-flung outposts.

Anyway, my great-grandfather managed to negotiate the sale of Alaska for $7,200,000 and there's a picture of him in the New York Central Library together with US Secretary of State, William

H. Seward, 'doing the deal'. This deal became known in America as 'Seward's Folly' as rumour had it that de Stoeckl had to bribe a number of congressmen to vote for the purchase. It makes me think that nothing much has changed in politics, but in the light of the ensuing years it turned out to be a brilliant folly.

Edouard de Stoeckl's son, my grandfather, Sasha, chose to live in Paris and he became Controller to the Grand Duke Michael of Russia who was exiled from Russia for committing a morganatic marriage with Countess Torby. As Equerry and Controller of the Household his work combined several different functions: he was responsible for arranging all visits and appointments, but he had staff to support this role. This meant that as the Grand Duke Michael spent his life mostly between England and France, my grandfather did too. His wife, my grandmother Agnes, had no duties: she was just simply his wife, though she was obviously expected to play a part in courtly social life. Eventually, my grandfather's job came to an end and in 1909 he was offered a new role as Equerry to the Grand Duchess George, who lived in a vast palace in St. Petersburg. So, my grandparents and Zoia, my mother, moved to St. Petersburg for this new adventure. The whole family used to go with the Grand Duchess George to Harex, close to Livadia, the Emperor's palace on the Black Sea, where life could be relaxed and less formal as there wasn't the court etiquette to be followed. My mother became a court favourite – by all accounts, she was amusing, pretty and had the cheek of a canal horse.

It was through this connection that my mother Zoia became maid-of-honour to the last Empress of Russia, Alexandra Feodorovna, and as such became engrossed with Imperial family life – she must have been all of 18 or 19 at the time. One of the oft-remembered incidents involving my mother Zoia was at Harex during one of the Emperor's biweekly visits for dinner. The entire table was discussing a fancy headdress ball to be given by the Mayor of Yalta, and the Emperor turned to my mother and asked, "What are you going to wear on your head Zoia?" My mother replied without hesitation, "I thought of asking you to lend me your crown, Sire." Silence reigned around the table among the shocked guests, because in spite of my mother's reputation of getting away with treading where angels dared not fly, this was clearly too much. Everyone glanced at the Emperor to see how he was taking this, but he just looked at her sadly and answered, "My dear child, I would gladly do so, but I fear that you would find it too heavy for your shoulders." Needless to say this gentle snub was never forgotten by my mother.

ON MY FATHER'S side we were what might be termed, 'run-down Polish nobility' living on our estate near Połock (now Belarus) in a part of Poland that was occupied by Russia more or less since the beginning of the 19th century, right until the end of the First World War. So we were treated as if we were just another part of Russia.

Our family had hit upon hard times, being apparently down to fifty-six peasants on the estate, which was by no means excessive as many estates had thousands. I don't know why the family fortunes declined but the Polish aristocracy were not notable for indulging in business. They acquired their money either by fighting or by marriage which were the only two ways of making money for 'gentlemen' – apart from gambling, but clearly their gambling wasn't that successful.

So my great-grandfather at the age of twenty-something was sent off to St. Petersburg. He may not have had a lot of cash but he had rather a lot of good social connections, so he joined St. Petersburg society under the wing of various smart friends. I detail his escapades in Chapter Twelve, so will not repeat them here. Suffice to say that he was an extraordinary entrepreneur and amassed a huge fortune. His son Vincent (who was my grandfather) and his brothers were known as 'The Siberian Rockerfellers'. All their immense wealth and properties disappeared overnight in the Russian revolution.

My father Alfons (Vincent's son) was brought up in St. Petersburg in the winter and in Siberia in the summer, where the family went for 2 or 3 months to their estates. He was educated at school in St. Petersburg, and then at a university there which prepared young men for the guards and Corps des Pages. From there he joined the Imperial Grodno Hussars and subsequently escaped during the revolution as part of the White Army, a confederation of anti-Bolshevic forces. Meanwhile my grandfather, grandmother, uncle and aunt escaped from their Siberian house, Talica, to England via Japan, having being tipped off by their loyal staff the night before the Bolshevics entered the house. Goodness knows what might have befallen them had they not fled. My father eventually ended up in England where he was introduced to my mother Zoia de Stoeckl at a weekend party of Lady Cunard's. They were subsequently married in London in 1919.

The revolution was a total tragedy for our family, as with so many others, whose entire wealth was wiped out overnight. My father became commercial counsellor at the Polish Embassy in London, but after a while he had to give up this poorly paid diplomatic position of £350 per annum, as opposed to his Russian annual allowance of £50,000! He moved to Poland where he obtained a good position running a mining and smelting business, and managed to fit in shooting and other country pursuits with his friends. Then, in September 1939, his life was finished again when the Germans invaded. At that time we lived in Katowice, Silesia, only a few kilometres from the German border, and my father had the presence of mind to send my mother, brother and myself to London to my grandmother Agnes de Stoeckl – a week before the Germans marched into our house. He was able to rejoin us in London after some harrowing months during which we had no news of him. Sadly his own mother and sister were stuck in Warsaw. They survived – they had to – but there was no getting out once the border had closed.

After the war, in 1946, my aunt was arrested by the (then) communist government of Poland. She was put on trial with twelve other people just for being anti-government: like being guilty these days for simply voting Labour or Conservative. Four people were executed on trumped-up charges, and she was sentenced to twelve years in prison at the age of fifty-seven. It was awful for my father after the war, having finally got to England, knowing that his beloved sister was incarcerated in this terrible jail in freezing cold Poland while he was living comfortably in London – but he couldn't do anything about it. My aunt spent ten years in the most appalling Polish prison until 1956. Then with a change of government (although still communist), some of the political prisoners were released. She was let out of jail but only lived for three months: she was riddled with cancer and of course had never seen a doctor in all those years in prison.

I was only ten when we left Poland, and I was fairly sheltered from world events. To me it was just an exciting trip to London; the potential war horrors were screened off. We left on a first-class train to Brussels via Berlin. My outstanding memory was that there was a cow on the line, which made the train late.

CHAPTER ONE
Take The Little Angel Out

I WAS BORN by caesarean section in a bathroom in St. John's Wood, London, on the 30th June 1929. I know that it was the year of the Wall Street crash, but poverty was not the reason for being born in this fashion. It has to be explained to my younger readers that, in those days, the smart thing to do was to be operated on at home; a surgical team would arrive and scrub out a suitable room – usually the bathroom – and install a temporary operating theatre. It's quite possible the surgeon could even have worn a morning coat under his white apron. The mind boggles in this day and age at the very thought.

The first four years of my life were spent in London where my father, Alfons Poklewski Koziell (known by all as 'Alik') was commercial counsellor at the Polish embassy. As mentioned in 'Notes About My Family', we had lost all our possessions in Poland and Russia during the war, and my father's income had dramatically declined. This does not seem to have affected my parents' lifestyle too much at first as my father continued to patronise the best tailors, hotels and clubs. When the family landed in England via Paris after the revolution they moved into Claridges as an 'economy measure', together with their ladies' maids and valet. Like all refugees they lived on credit, believing that they would get

1

everything back in due course.

My early memories of London are very vague, and undoubtedly some are not memories at all, but family stories passed on to me from relatives now long gone. A memory I do have, which I certainly shared with no one, is being told by nanny to face the wall in bed while she was undressing, and stealing a peek at her naked body. The shock was such that it put me off the opposite sex for a long time and I have always blamed that incident for the fact that I was a late starter with women. I have not studied the statistics on these matters, but hope that it will contribute to me being a late finisher also.

At around the age of three I remember two occasions that stand out among the endless nursery meals, baths, "Stop doing that!" and so on. One was when I was taken to Mass by Mama, in the local church in St John's Wood. Sermons seventy-nine years ago were about as exciting as they are today, so I was naturally bored, and distracted myself by climbing the empty pews nearby. All might have been well were I not impersonating a steam train, with all the accompanying noises, such as loud puffs of steam and frequent hoots. The poor priest finally interrupted his sermon – upon which the congregation awoke – and he addressed my mother from the pulpit saying, "Would someone please take the little angel out?" whereupon my poor mother, scarlet in the face, proceeded to drag me down the aisle, fortunately cursing in one of her languages that was unlikely to be understood by the congregation.

The other memory was of The Ritz. I had apparently heard talk among the grown-ups about the food there. As I was greedy, interested in food, and slightly tired of cold shepherd's pie, I asked granny Agnes – whom we were living with in Edgware – if she might take me to The Ritz. Penniless but, as always, undaunted, she agreed – and off we trundled on the Number 53 bus to the lunch counter at Woolworths in Oxford Street. That evening at my normal six o'clock audience in the drawing room, all the grown-ups asked me in unison how I had enjoyed The Ritz. Apparently, arms akimbo, I made it quite clear that I did not find either the food or the atmosphere at all overwhelming.

After a while, my father had to give up his ill-paid diplomatic position and face up to his debts. Fortunately he was highly intelligent: he spoke and corresponded in five languages and had acquired a gold medal at St. Petersburg University prior to entering the Corps des

Pages and the Imperial Guard – the Grodno Hussars. Thus, unlike some other refugees he did not have to drive a taxi for a living. He went to Poland and got a job in a coal and zinc concern in Katowice, the capital of Polish Silesia, an appallingly polluted city of remarkable ugliness. It must have been an awful shock for him to have to live there in a rented house while all his friends moved back to their beautiful chateaux and broad acres. Our own two estates were now no longer in Poland but in Belorussia, and together with our vast properties in Siberia, safely in communist hands. However, he stuck it out and by the beginning of the Second World War, had succeeded in becoming managing director, only to lose everything again in September 1939, when Poland was invaded by the Germans.

When my father went off to Poland, my mother, brother, and myself moved in with my maternal grandmother, Agnes de Stoeckl, who was living in reduced circumstances in London having also fled Russia and lost her husband the year I was born. She decided for some unknown reason to buy a new semi-detached house on a ribbon development near the metropolitan station of Edgware. I believe her mortgage was something like 2 shillings and 6 pence a week. The cook (a very bad one) was 25 shillings a week and the maid 5 shillings.

My brother and I had some sort of keeper, but I cannot remember whether it was still nanny Howard or the first of a ghastly line of governesses who never stayed, usually because brother Alex, five years older than me, was so badly behaved. There was a particularly nasty one who forbade us to drink anything during meals. Eventually in desperation, we hid granny behind the curtains in the dining room so she could hear the sadistic order and send the monster away to some other victims.

In general, granny had very old-fashioned and continental views on nursery staff. I always remember her telling me that when they first moved the household to London from Paris in 1893, she brought over, among the other servants, a Normandy wet nurse, for my mother. The wet nurse would follow the nanny and pram, and promenade in Hyde Park in full traditional Normandy costume complete with black lace cap, flaunting her immense bosoms, on standby for a feed. It apparently caused much shock, disapproval and comment from the other nannies in Hyde Park, but clearly left my mother well satisfied and with a lifetime appetite of serious proportions.

There was a story about my brother when he had just started in the kindergarten and was proudly paraded in front of my mother's friends at tea time, kitted out in his first grey flannel jacket and shorts. Needless to say, as always with young children, the shorts and sleeves were far too long (to allow for growth), and he must have presented a lugubrious figure, rather diminutive and very thin, with no hands or knees showing. He had walked back with the governess, and one of the ladies asked him how they coped when it was raining, upon which he bent his elbows, and taking up a very serious standing stance, pronounced that "actually some of the chaps arrive in prams."

Other memories of Edgware were of a boy called Ernest, who was a neighbour of my age whom I adulated, but who for some reason or another, was frowned on by Mama and granny. Poor Ernest always had dreadful colds, and on one famous occasion, my grandmother, who was never short of imagination, determined to put him off coming to tea with me in case I caught the cold. She rang his parents to say that unfortunately she had to put him off as Queen Mary was coming to tea. They must have swallowed the story, although Edgware tea parties were not usually on the Queen's list.

My hero who looked as if he was the original inspiration for *Just William* was eventually banned from my life after it was discovered that he had staged a very illuminating afternoon in the bushes, during which, with the aid of his sister and a friend, he initiated me into the mysteries of how girls pee.

The other part of the 'semi' was bought by my great uncle Otho Barron, who was granny's brother. He was married to a very excitable Mexican lady called aunty Lucita, who always spoke in very fast and totally incomprehensible English. The family never forgot an incident many years later during the Second World War when her son, my cousin Harry Barron, was serving in the airborne forces and poor aunty Lucita was in permanent fear of him becoming a casualty. At that time, I was spending Easter at school at Downside. For some reason, I had taken it into my head to make a meritorious gesture for Holy Week, and decided to send telegrams to the few members of my family in England, saying "Happy Easter, love from Vincent." Aunty Lucita was one of the recipients. No one sent telegrams at that stage of the war, except for the most serious of reasons. The Barrons in their quiet wartime existence in Edgware, certainly never did. When the telegraph boy appeared with my telegram, Lucita opened the door and started wailing, knowing it had to be announcing that her son Harry had been killed in action. She could not face opening it, and when uncle Otho returned in the evening from his job as censor, he found his wife practically lifeless on the floor, sobbing uncontrollably over a very moist unopened telegram. The poor man opened it with trembling fingers, only to read "Happy Easter, love from Vincent." The incident was immediately reported back to Mama who met me on my return home for the holidays with a thundering "You bloody fool!" So much for charitable gestures and "It's the thought that counts," I thought to myself.

WHEN THE TIME finally came in 1933 to join my father in Poland, we set off in the Berlin Express with our luggage. I was four and my brother was ten. The only memory I have of the journey was of a large canvas bag falling down from the luggage rack. There was a metal potty in one of the outside pockets. I remember thinking it a little strange, as I was already four and well past the potty-training stage, but in those days my family never travelled without an immense number of emergency articles, "just in case my dear."

Finally we arrived in Katowice, a bustling and polluted city in Silesia, in southern Poland. The city was surrounded by coalmines and steelworks, which belched dust and noxious fumes. We lived in a rented house with a tiny garden in which nothing grew due to the pollution. The initial shock for me at the age of four must have been quite something. There I was in a 'foreign' country, without a word of Polish to my name, in a city bilingual in German, which I did not speak either. A temporary English keeper, whose name and appearance escape me, accompanied my brother and I, and it must have been equally confusing for her, as she could not speak a word either. The domestic arrangements were pretty chaotic, as the staff were all Polish but my mother didn't speak the language, only English, French and Russian. It must have thrown quite a strain on my father, and it was no wonder he spent a long time at the office or travelling to Berlin, Paris, or London where he always had an amazing number of 'meetings'. I remember my mother remarking that, "these business trips must be very tiring."

My father also enhanced his quality of life with endless shooting parties on his friends' estates. He was very popular – with the ladies because he waltzed divinely, and with the men because he was a first class shot. I believe he was regarded as one of the four best shots in Poland but fortunately it was never actually put to the test, as being descended from a long line of hot-blooded Poles they would undoubtedly have shot each other after the results were announced.

After a while I acquired a Polish governess called 'Pani' (Polish for 'Miss') Slava. She was a wonderful person who had a great influence on me. We all adored her. With her help my Polish was perfected, to the extent that, in 1939, when I returned to England, I spoke English with a thick Polish accent. (I subsequently slaved to acquire King's English with a plummy upper class accent, only to eventually find myself living in Ireland through 'The Troubles' with quite the wrong accent, and being called a "fucking Brit" in pubs).

The only aspect of my life which darling Pani Slava was not able to influence, was my eating habits. I was greedy by nature and very tubby, as the family had absolutely no tradition of exercise – or sport of any kind – apart from my father's continuous shooting. In fact I have no idea whether either of my parents could swim and I could certainly never imagine them in swimming costumes, although my maternal grandmother told me that they used to bathe from great wooden machines at Deauville when they were young.

As a result of all this, I took enthusiastically to Polish eating habits, and grafted them quite happily on to my English eating regime. My mother insisted that we had a full English breakfast – as Polish breakfast was a snack only – after which I happily plunged into Polish 'elevenses' which consisted of yards of garlic sausage, bread and dripping. This kept me going until lunchtime, and so on to a proper English tea, and then a good solid cooked supper. I suspect that my mother – who at aged eighteen had a nineteen-inch waist at the Russian court, but had since become comfortably round – surveyed me proudly as a farmer might, watching his piglet grow rosy and fat.

I remember being rather fussy about food, and taking an immense liking to a form of cutlet, 'Pojarski', minced chicken in breadcrumbs, fried in butter. My mother tried to cure me of this obsession and decreed that I should have these cutlets seven days a week for lunch. This regime continued for six months during which I was blissfully happy, after which my mother finally realized her scheme hadn't worked and I was slowly weaned onto other kinds of food.

Our kitchen was at first run by a chef, a Silesian called Max Popluc, who was always chasing me out of the kitchen, which needless to say I found the most interesting room in the house. He once disappeared for a while because of either illness or holiday, I forget which, and in the emergency his duties were taken over by a young maid, Marysia. She had no formal training at all and did not even like eating (I can never remember her ever eating more than a sandwich in the forty years I knew her). She proved, however, to be a quite sensational cook, and Max Popluc was never seen again.

The nearest German town to Katowice was Beuthen, now Polish again and called Bytom. We used to make frequent shopping expeditions there, as the quality of certain things was much better than in Poland, and prices sometimes better. The Germans excelled in toymaking at which they were undoubtedly world leaders. This, needless to say, interested me immensely. The problem was that the Polish Customs on the border were relentless in preventing any smuggling. However, most of the Customs Officers got to know our chauffeur, our car, and our mother, so they did not bother us too much, but there were exceptions.

I remember just before Christmas, Mama, Miss Probyn (our very prudish English governess), brother Alex and I were making the 'big' Christmas shop, well equipped with fur rugs to hide the spoils. We duly returned to the Polish border post, to realise to our horror that there was something different about the usual scene. A very important Customs Officer from Warsaw had arrived to do an inspection and as a result the whole home team were lined-up, pretending that they had never seen us before. Horror and dismay! Everyone was made to get out of our car and march to the Customs House. Mama, having stuffed half the goodies down her chest, which was normally thin and bony, now looked like Dolly Parton. She tottered across the yard, leaning dangerously forward.

The main problem was a toy sewing machine, which I had asked for as a Christmas present. It was a working model, so although small, it was substantial. Poor Miss Probyn was in a panic, and asked Mama what to do. "Put it down your bloomers," Mama barked at her. When Miss Probyn objected, Mama hissed, "Shut up and get on with it, otherwise we'll find ourselves in jail, and miss dinner." Miss Probyn obliged by pushing the sewing machine down her ample bloomers, which she achieved in secrecy under the mountain of rugs in the car. She then, poor thing, had to cross the yard under the eyes of the Polish Customs Force, saying the Lord's Prayer in English under her breath, waddling with spread legs, the dreaded metal sewing machine dangling between her thighs, having to suffer my mother's imprecations of "Hurry, you fool! Keep quiet and keep your legs closed." Fortunately this extraordinary procession totally unnerved the customs and we were finally waved on.

What may have finished them was my mother, who on being asked whether she had anything to declare said, "Yes, I have a ham." This electrified the Poles, as ham was one of their main home products, and they shouted with one voice, "Show us!" To which she lifted her skirt and slapped her ample thighs. "Oh, go on," they shouted, "you and your jokes." Needless to say the unfortunate Miss Probyn got a new pair of bloomers, and I serenely turned the handle of my mini sewing machine with pride.

When I had acquired sufficient Polish I was enrolled in the Adam Mickiewicz day school down the road, where all the children of the 'haute bourgeoisie' of Katowice attended. In the first few days I ran into a problem. I must explain that my Polish acquired from Pani Slava, was quite good by then, but my mother's – having been acquired from our chauffeur Reihel, and various odd-job men – was quite appalling and extremely vulgar to boot. I imagine that my father was unaware of this, as they always communicated in a mixture of English and French (or Russian when they did not want me to understand).

At school the class of six-year-olds were asked in turn to stand up and tell a story. When my turn came, I recounted a fairy tale that Mama had concocted for me recently, and which for some reason she had told to me in Polish. The conclusion was that the young knight who, being refused the hand of the princess by the king, reacted by kicking the king. My mother said, "in the dupa" which is an even more vulgar term than 'arse'.

Confusion reigned: the schoolmistress fainted, and I was taken out of the class and interrogated by the headmistress as to where I had picked up this unspeakable vulgarity, to which I replied, "It was one of mummy's bedtime stories." My poor Mama was sent for the next day by the head and, to her shame, had to promise never to do likewise again.

One event stands out in Katowice. I must have been five or six, around 1936 when the whole anti-Semitic movement was getting into full swing in Germany. One day there was a big anti-Jewish demonstration rally by a large crowd of German thugs going down the street howling "Zyd! Zyd!" ("Jew! Jew!"), smashing the windows of Jewish shops. I was on my bike followed by my governess, when turning a corner we were confronted by this mob. Seeing this little fat, well-dressed boy with black curly hair, the crowd took me to be a Jew, and threw stones at me. One of them knocked me off the bike, but I was only slightly injured and was somehow saved by the governess, having endured my first political lesson.

I also remember my first Holy Communion at the age of nine. I marched down the main street of the town with the other communicants, all of us dressed in smart new blue suits. I was holding a large lit candle and proudly sporting a white carnation in my buttonhole. During this time my brother Alex was suffering from leukemia, causing my parents deep distress as they had already lost their first-born son, Romek, to the same disease at the age of six (in 1926, before I was born). I was kept unaware of Alex's illness but I remember that my mother made me promise to give my first communion for a very important but secret cause of hers. This I duly did with all the solemnity the occasion deserved.

Alex had been taken to every known doctor and institution by my desperate mother, but to no avail. Finally, he was taken in by Professor Groer in Breslau, Germany, who experimented on him with a totally new procedure (now common) of bone marrow transfusion. In spite of this treatment being interrupted by the outbreak of war, it turned out to save his life. Thanks must go to the eccentric Professor, or my first communion, who knows? Probably both, but I claim no merit as my part was after all an unknowing intention, albeit reinforced by the innocence of childhood.

THE HIGHLIGHTS OF our Polish life were our frequent visits to the 'zamek' of Lançut, which belonged to Count Alfred Potocki, a very close friend of my parents. Zamek literally means 'castle' in English and Lançut was undoubtedly the most luxurious and eccentric residence in Poland. Fenced-off by post and rail from the little town of Lançut, with gate lodges giving access to the drives, the castle was surrounded by a moat and a magnificent park which included a golf course, polo grounds and tennis courts. There was also a large stable complex, for the famous Arab horses, and a unique collection of carriages, phaetons, broughams, shooting brakes and sleighs – numbering over a hundred assorted vehicles.

The castle was large with an inner courtyard and orangery. We stayed in the children's quarters, which were above the orangery and connected to the castle by a long 'flying corridor' over an arch. There we were looked after by a governess, Nanny Howard, a nursery footman and dedicated maids. Life in the nursery was strict, albeit comfortable and fun. At certain times of the day we would go to the main house, and I can still remember being pursued by a bat down the long, dark connecting corridor, running screaming with terror, as we had always been told that bats would settle in our hair and would be impossible to remove.

There are so many childhood memories I have of that magical place, made all the more special because of the contrast with grubby, smog-ridden, coal dust-covered Katowice. Certain incidents do however stand out in my memory. When I was still very young, say five or six, a liveried groom would arrive mid-morning bringing with him a small model Rolls Royce, which had an electric motor. I would pack my pudgy bottom into the seat and set off down one of the garden avenues at 4mph crying, "Poop Poop," just like Toad of Toad Hall. In case of accidents I was well equipped with followers: an anxious groom in Potocki livery and a waddling nanny, and the rear was brought-up by a gardener carefully raking over the tracks. On rainy days I could bicycle up and down the vast corridors, also carefully supervised in case I crashed into a cabinet of special porcelain, inevitably from some central European court or a Field Marshall's travelling 'canteen'.

At an equally early age, I remember appearing on stage in the castle theatre. This was part of the ground floor reception rooms, a beautifully decorated real theatre, with stage curtains, orchestra pit, fitted stalls and gallery. My mother Zoia was usually chosen to write the plays, always in French in view of the international make-up of the house parties, and also so that the servants who were sitting in the gallery should not understand the play (which was inevitably witty and vulgar, containing quite a lot of *pas devant* language). The play in question was performed on New Year's Eve at midnight, and I was fished out of bed and dressed up, appearing as someone's illegitimate child. I can remember having a terrible earache and remonstrating with Mama, but to no purpose: "What trash my dear, the play must go on!" I was given a shot of something, undoubtedly alcoholic, and having been shoved onto the stage, I swayed dangerously.

Another episode I remember was setting out to the little town to the area full of Jewish shops. I was clutching a ten groszy coin in my hand (about tuppence-halfpenny equivalent in those days). The gatekeeper, a great friend, asked me where I was going. I said that I had ten groszy to buy myself a little penknife, which I had hankered after for some time. In reply to this, he said, that he was coming with me, as, "Those Jews would cheat you out of your money!"

Thus accompanied by the fearsome looking gatekeeper, at least six foot high and eighteen stone in his uniform, I entered one of the ghetto shops. It was a small dark hovel where the ancient, tiny Jewish shopkeeper hovered anxiously with his long *pejsy* (curly side locks), glancing uneasily at the magnificent gatekeeper, holding the hand of the small fat boy clad in clothes from Daniel Neale in London. Much bargaining ensued, the knife was finally mine and I left holding my change of one grosz, with the self-satisfied gatekeeper nodding his head, and the poor old Jew looking shifty and beaten. Let us not forget that I had saved a tenth of two and a half pennies after all!

The main part of the castle was immensely grand, with a procession of great salons, a ballroom, library and billiard-room, not to mention a real Turkish bath in the basement, chapel, theatre and God knows what else. As far as I can remember, there was one grand dining room, but others as well. I was always told there were eleven, so that a house party never dined in the same one twice. Apart from the central heating, there were wood fires everywhere, as the old, beautifully-tiled stoves built into the walls were no longer used. I remember that a medium-sized lorry used to trundle into the rear of the castle twice a day full of logs, which had been dried for at least a year, to feed the fires. I cannot remember the number of staff, but there must have been over fifty indoor staff in livery, apart from the log carriers, laundry maids, gardeners, coachmen, stable lads and chauffeurs.

There was also the Lançut brass band, formed mostly out of the staff, plus a few permanent professional musicians, and the conductor. All the liveried staff were dressed in the Potocki livery of yellow and blue, as were the entire band, except that the band had a separate summer and winter uniform. The band had many functions, but the one I remember, being too young to attend the dinners and balls, was their Sunday duty.

On Sunday the entire house party would assemble in front of the castle and solemnly walk to church behind the brass band, who were playing in full regalia. The whole procession was watched by the Jews and peasants outside the gates. We would then enter through a side door, into the family box, which was totally enclosed in glass, with the exception of a small window, which was opened so that one could receive communion through it. The reason for this arrangement was explained to me as, "avoiding the smell of peasants, especially on a damp day." After Mass, the procession would return, led by the band, to the stable complex, where the house party would sit down in the main yard in which the sand had been beautifully raked into the design of the family crest. After that the liveried grooms would appear with baskets of washed and trimmed carrots to follow the guests who would admire and feed the beautiful Arab horses in their stalls. Then back outside again, where the guests would sit with drinks in hand and four heralds would duly appear – one standing at each of the four corners on the roofs surrounding the courtyard – and perform a fanfare on long trumpets each with heraldic flags hanging on them. This was immensely impressive especially for the English guests, whose Sunday mornings on their own country estates were possibly less dramatic. The said trumpeters also featured at the shooting lodge, called Julin, about an hour's drive from the castle, in the middle of the woods. At dusk, when the guests were having pre-dinner drinks on the lawn, fanfares would suddenly sound from four directions – half a kilometre apart – answering each other. Slightly theatrical no doubt, but it apparently went down well with the amazed guests, who by that time were happily replete with champagne, dry martinis or white ladies.

The other great source of pride which Alfred Potocki couldn't resist showing off was his carriage driving. He loved it, and was an excellent whip. Every morning at about eleven, a 'four-in-hand' was brought to the main doors, and Alfred would gallop down the drive, often with me by his side – a little frightened, but excited – through the villages with two grooms hanging on behind blowing their horns to warn anyone in the way. I shall always remember going through those villages at what seemed incredible speed, and the sparks flying from the metal rims of the wheels on the cobble stones – no tarmacadam in that part of Poland then.

His master-trick however would take place in the late afternoon in the summer, usually when there was a large house party of international guests. They would all be assembled for tea in the main arrival hall of the castle, which had great doors each end. All the tables and chairs were arranged carefully, just slightly away from a wooden lane that ran down the middle of the hall, between the two great doors. Alfred's mother, who was also the chatelaine of Lançut (as Alfred was unmarried), would be pouring tea out of a great silver tea pot with footmen hovering with cucumber sandwiches and various pastries. Suddenly the sound of horns would explode outside the doors, against which two footmen threw themselves to open them, and Alfred would gallop through, four-in-hand, while Sèvres teacups shook perilously close by. He never hurt anyone, or made a mistake. Only once did he try to take an eight-in-hand through the hall – this time without guests holding quivering teacups. I remember witnessing the occasion at a safe distance, held back by a disapproving governess. Alfred without any outriders, holding eight spirited horses in his two hands could not quite control them, and as a result a large piece of masonry was broken off one of the entrance pillars. No harm done to human or to horse, only to his deep purse, but he confined himself to four horses at a time after that.

One of the most memorable occasions was in 1938, when my parents had brought the Duke and Duchess of Kent to stay at Lançut. They had stayed in our house at Katowice overnight, the Duke having driven at great speed across Germany in his Rolls, the Duchess in the front seat with him, and Field his head chauffeur spread comfortably in the back, behind the glass screen. It was always that way, as the Duke preferred to drive. The Kent party, including my mother, were met at the station by

Alfred. The cortège consisted of three open carriages with outriders and a standing groom at the rear. They then drove to the castle, to be greeted by the band playing God Save The King as the carriage drove over the moat, and all the house party and senior servants stood in greeting at the main doors. Not being too impressionable at that age I started playing with one of the dogs just as the carriage was crossing the moat, and I clearly remember my father behind me, taking me by the shoulders, pointing me towards the scene, and saying, "Look carefully, because I doubt if you will ever witness a similar occasion again!" How right he was, as the clouds of war were already gathering over Europe.

The shooting parties and accompanying picnics at Lançut were tremendous affairs with rows of carriages and horse-drawn sleighs, depending on the season. Apart from the gamekeepers and grooms who were all in the Potocki livery, there were crowds of beaters, who in the winter would stand around in frost-covered long beards, wearing fur hats and coats – not quite from the furrier in the Avenue Montaigne, but highly colourful all the same. My main memories, especially from the winter shoots, were of endless bloody corpses – wild boar down to hares – laid out in the snow, the steamy breath of the beaters reeking of vodka, and the guests clad in splendidly cut sheepskin fur coats standing about, also tippling vodka, but from silver Asprey flasks. I think that everyone – high and low – enjoyed these occasions. I certainly did, in anticipation of an excellent picnic, which usually included potatoes roasted in their jackets in the ashes of a bonfire, consumed with masses of butter.

The subject of butter reminds me that once, just before the footmen and grooms started to serve the picnic, one of the sporting dogs was seen licking at the large and suitably embossed hunk of butter. Shrieks of alarm followed – I suspect mostly from the non-Polish guests. Alfred Potocki immediately arranged for the fastest conveyance to gallop back to the castle for new butter, which eventually returned (I suspect having been licked back into shape by the grooms round the corner). The only person out of this enormous crowd who did not enjoy these events was my mother, who was particularly unsporting as far as outdoor activities were concerned. She was always remembered, sitting on a sleigh, well away from the noise and blood, dressed in at least three fur coats, murmuring one of her favourite phrases, I think from Voltaire, "Comme la vie serait agreeable sans les plaisirs."

14

APART FROM LAŃCUT, Alex and I spent time most summers on the estate of one of my father's closest friends, Witold Morawski. He was a towering figure of a man, with tremendous charm, except when he was in a rage, and then he was terrifying. Witold was a Colonel in the regular army and unmarried, but rumour had it he was a man highly interested in pursuing the opposite sex. He was, I suspect, dedicated to offering a discreet service to certain aristocratic ladies whose husbands were over-attentive to shooting, cards and claret, leaving little time or energy to satiate their spouse's not unnatural demands. His estate, Oporowo, in the district of Poznan was in the depths of the country, where he had a typically substantial, though not enormous, country house, with a fairly wild small park, stables and large farmyard next door. There were no motorcars there and all transport was by horse or pony, carriage or trap. I suppose he must have had a car and a fast one at that, but I cannot remember seeing it, and in any case it would not have been much use on most of the lanes, and forest 'roads' which were made largely of sand.

For us it was heaven, running wild, surrounded by all the agricultural activities on the doorstep: wagons of wheat rolling in on small rails, horse-drawn from the distant fields. There was no need to be particularly clean or tidy, especially as our host and our parents were frequently away, visiting friends' estates. This always took some days, due to the primitive transport and a civilised outlook on the purpose of holidays. We were left with the charming staff, of whom I remember a maid called Kasia, who seemed at the time to be terribly old but was probably no more than thirty. What amazed me the most about Kasia was that she had never been on a train in her life, although the nearest station on the little country branch line could not have been more than twelve kilometres away.

I was also devoted to Walenty the coachman who supervised us in the pony trap, which once to my horror ran away with me, and tipped me into a ditch, fortunately deep and muddy and wet. I have always believed – like my mother – that one should 'get over' as many sports as possible, when one is young, so that one can concentrate on those that really give pleasure. By now, mine are confined to walking, swimming, bicycling and eating (not to mention drinking).

One activity of which one cannot be proud in this politically correct day and age, but which was considered great fun by my brother and me, was driving along muddy roads through tiny villages throwing sweets behind the carriage. These were then scrabbled over by little children in the mud, while we sat cosseted on cushions.

Another vivid memory of staying there was the night a cyst on my back burst and I had to be taken to the doctor in Poniec, which was the nearest small town. This caused great excitement in the stables as the horses were harnessed and Walenty the coachman rushed around with lanterns. We galloped through the night with me lying on the governess's lap while she staunched the blood. The doctor in his dressing gown sewed me up, and then we trotted home again.

I remember my governess well. For some reason my parents called her 'The Penguin'. Maybe it was her shape or her walk. All I can say is that whatever it was, it appealed to the taste of my brother's horrible tutor Mr. Sadowski (rather aptly named as he was sadistic). During the long, hot summer afternoons when the grown-ups were all away somewhere, he and The Penguin used to lock us up with our books, pens and paper while they walked hand in hand, and presumably got on with their more adult homework. This would have been bad enough, but on their return Mr. Sadowski used to thrash Alex with all the strength remaining after his afternoon's exertions – for not doing his maths properly. When finally we complained to Mama about being locked up, she ignored it as exaggeration and so the Sadowski/Penguin reign continued throughout the whole summer. My eccentric mother eventually sacked Sadowski, not because he beat Alex, but because he smelt badly.

My great chum was the son of the church organist, and speaking a mixture of Polish and English, I always amused the company by saying that I was going to play with the organist's "sin". I never knew why they laughed so uproariously, but now understand that it was the simple pun of misplacing the Polish for son, which is *syn* and pronounced 'sin'. In retrospect, considering my parents communicated with each other in English, French and Russian – all intermingled – it is a miracle that I speak at least one language decently.

Another more eccentric member of the staff was the night watchman. He was a small gnarled man of strange appearance who prowled round all night with a posse of chained, wild, slavering dogs.

These beasts had somehow been trained into total savagery, and would attack and attempt to devour any being, animal or human, if let off the chain by their master. Unlike English police dogs, which are trained to seize a person's arm, these dogs would have simply consumed it. We were terrified of them, as we saw them being led out at sunset, starving (they were not fed until daybreak and I suspect none too generously at that to keep their appetites at fever pitch). Anyway the result was that there were no burglars as the 'pack' was well known and respected in the neighbourhood, and performed the duty of the rather negligent police force that scarcely existed in those remote parts.

We spent happy summers at Oporowo, and loved our imposing host. My father and Witold often went away for 'business' weekends together to Berlin, returning somewhat drained. My father told a wonderful story about when they were travelling by night on a train, and finding an empty 'Ladies Only' carriage lay down and slept there. They were woken by a very officious conductor who tried to chuck them out, whereupon Witold rose to his full immense height and told the conductor to, "Go to Hell!" The man got his notepad out, and announced that he was going to make a report to the railway directors. Wittold replied, "By all means do. I am Colonel so and so, commanding regiment so and so – you can put all that down in writing, and you can also kiss my arse. The former you can do by hand, and the latter by mouth!" and slammed the door on the unfortunate man. Needless to say, nothing further was heard as a pre-war Polish Colonel was treated like God.

Poor Witold fought the Germans but eventually ended up in the Malthausen concentration camp, where being a Colonel, and well known at that, he was murdered by a bullet through the back of his head.

CHAPTER TWO
War is Declared and Dinner is Served

BY THE SUMMER of 1939 war was brewing, with the might of the German army's storm troops and panzer divisions massed at the border only a few kilometres from Katowice. My father in his wisdom sent both of us boys and Mama to London, to my grandmother who lived there. People frequently asked then, as now, how I escaped from Poland only a week before the Germans invaded. Most expected some hair-raising tale of deceit, bravery and luck, but instead received a sheepish reply that my exit was by way of first class on the Berlin Express and on to Brussels. My father had to remain but managed, through great fortune and bravery, to escape some months later through Romania. It must have been a terribly anxious time for my mother but I was kept in ignorance of the gravity of the situation. Instead I was in awe of the daily pleasure of travelling on top of a double-decker bus and the sights of London, not to mention the glow at night from the bombed and burning docks.

That autumn, as the war began, I found myself being sent to a prep school called Ladycross in Seaford, Sussex. At the age of ten, having left behind a milieu of governesses, nannies, cooks, chauffeurs and so on, it

19

was a tremendous shock. It must have also been a tremendous shock to my friends too, but they had obviously all heard of prep, or private boarding school, where incidentally nothing at all was private, including one's privates. In any case, it was an English tradition, which they knew they had to go through. I, on the other hand, was quite unprepared, and of course neither of my parents had ever been near one, or had the slightest idea of the conditions.

The 'delivery' took place in the headmaster's wife's drawing room, with an excellent tea – the last one I had for three months – and lots of insincere chat. Then the moment came for matron to sweep me up, the headmaster's wife wisely telling my mother that these things were better done quickly, and I found myself in a cold beige and green painted stone passage at least ten degrees lower in temperature than the 'salon'. The décor from then on did not change much throughout the school, and it was quite clear that they had not wasted any money on Colefax and Fowler. Not having as yet heard of concentration camps, I thought that I was quite simply in prison and on punishment rations at that. No cheese soufflé, but stale cheddar on even staler bread and margarine. The dormitory featured long lines of beds with red blankets and 'hospital corners', which we were meant to maintain on the pain of the dreaded 'tolly' (of which more later). The windows were all healthily open to the sea air and occupied more space than the walls, presumably to save money and ensure our health, toughness and endurance. The school motto was *Mens sana in corpore sano* (A healthy mind in a healthy body). No comment on either as this is meant as a book for all the family.

After being woken by the bell the first morning, I was led by the head boy to the showers, told to strip and shoved under a cold shower. I thought that this must have been a punishment of some kind, but discovered that all the boys had to have one every morning. This, I learned much later, was part of the 'healthy body, healthy mind' motto. I suppose it kept my body clean but my mind at that age did not dwell either on my own body, or even matron's, so that part of the shower was wasted.

The night before I arrived, apparently the headmaster's wife addressed the whole school and told them that there was this poor little Polish refugee coming the next day, having escaped the German

invasion, and that they should all be kind to him. This, needless to say
was a disaster, as they were all of the age where they found it quite
natural to tear the wings off live flies, to see what happens. The result
was that they invented a game called 'Poles vs. Germans'. They decided
to be Germans. Not much fun really, especially as far as I was concerned
because when they finally captured me, I was flogged with nettles.
However, under English boarding school laws, at least the unwritten
ones, there was no question of 'sneaking' about the bullying otherwise
you would be 'sent to Coventry' by the other boys.

I finally solved the problem with a bit of clearly in-built, or inbred,
sense of bribery. At the time the supreme school bully, or 'Capo', was a
Bolivian boy called Suarez. A great big thug, physically well advanced
beyond his 12 or 13 years, who already had to shave twice a day while
the rest of the school had cheeks like babies' bottoms. I discovered that
his great weakness, apart from one of the scullery girls, was big boiled
sweets known as gobstoppers, of which we were issued with one each
day. This was quite inadequate for Suarez who would get the weaker
boys to hand over their daily ration in order to avoid a fierce Bolivian
kick between the legs. I personally settled protection money with him
by giving him two gobstoppers a day. I achieved this by somehow
reaching my mother at Claridges from a forbidden telephone box.
We were not allowed to ring home, or anywhere at all for that matter,
without permission, which was only granted after a serious excuse, and
was, naturally, listened-in to. Security was such that on completing our
compulsory weekly letter home on Sundays, we were made to leave it
open with the envelope on our desks. The official line was that it was to
check our spelling, but of course it was actually to ensure that there was
no hint of any kind to the effect that we were not living in pure heaven.

The result of my secret communication with Mama, who after all
was already a refugee twice over and understood survival by underhand
methods, was the following. She sent me a parcel every ten days or
so, of a paperback book of either juvenile tales or junior history. These
were hollowed out and packed with gobstoppers then firmly strapped
together to pass matron's customs inspection. Thus I achieved, or rather
bought, protection from Suarez who, like most crooks and mercenaries
was good for his word while payment was kept up.

By the next term I had shed half a stone in weight by keeping goal at football (I was not too good at running yet) and had learned where to kick small English schoolboys, either to achieve my ends or protect myself. By that time the Capo Suarez must have returned to his parents in Bolivia to learn how to shoot accurately, tend the family poppy fields, and pleasure the maids.

When I joined Ladycross I was seen as being somewhat obese, and as a result was put on a special diet of a boiled egg and Ryvita for breakfast, which compared to the horrors that the rest of the boys were eating, I regarded as excellent fare. The only upsetting part that I can remember was being refused my ration of a slice of cold deep-fried white bread for elevenses. To this day I still dream of fried bread. As a result of my being so fat I was allowed to wear long trousers a year ahead of my time, as I had great difficulty cramming my thighs into 'Daniel Neal's' best flannel shorts.

Breakfast for non-dieters commenced with a tepid porridge the consistency of Blu-Tac, except that it was grey. In later life I understood why there were so many remedies on offer for constipation in England. This was clearly a subject that totally engrossed the school authorities, as mid-morning we were all lined up by 'Sister' the nurse who was matron, and our names were called out one by one. One had to answer 'Plus' or 'Minus', meaning whether one had what sister called a 'bowel movement' or not. The result was that anyone in their right mind answered 'Plus' because if you answered 'Minus' you were immediately in for a very large spoonful of revolting syrup of figs. However the problem was that if the whole school chanted 'Plus' sister would conclude correctly that we were lying and the entire school would get dosed. In order to avoid this unpleasant digestif after breakfast, it was decided that at least one or two of the boys would have to declare a 'Minus'. Thus two of the most submissive and frightened boys were told, under threat of torture and a tanning in the dorm, to chant the dreaded 'Minus'. I hope now in my benevolent old age that they survived, although I do remember them as being rather thin by the end of term.

So, my first term at Ladycross ended, and somehow my constitution survived the physical abuse and my innards the consumption of English school food – the latter before the arrival of food rationing as well! After Christmas, Ladycross was evacuated to Salperton Park in Gloucestershire, a large country house, which had presumably been either commandeered or leased for the purpose. It was totally chaotic to start with, which suited us boys perfectly although it must have driven the staff mad. The teachers were all lodged in the village; the ballroom or drawing room had been converted into a chapel and the garage into a gym. The teachers had almost all changed due to call-ups. The result was that we were taught by either physically or mentally-disabled people who had been considered wholly unsuitable for even the lowliest form of military service.

One very civilised master, who wore a corset, was considered gay. However, some of us thought that he was quite actively playing 'masters and mistresses' in the village with the French teacher (charming but we thought her very old – in retrospect probably well short of the menopause). Then there was a new gym instructor who had a glass eye and had worked at a borstal, which he had left, it was said, under a cloud (the mind boggles). I remember him holding us enthralled during a break in the gym class explaining the punishment they meted out at the borstal, as opposed to our spoilt establishment. To quote him, "We would bend the lad over the gym horse, head and arms well over the side – bare bum – and give him a Japanese sunset on his rear." At this he could be seen to be slavering slightly at the mouth, presumably out of excitement. The oldest master, well beyond retirement age, was a sinister little moustached man called Mr Herbert, known universally as Bert (but not to his face). He taught science and basic physics, rather well actually, although he was horrid to the boys he disliked. I remember he used to make a friend of mine stand on a chair and shout at him saying that he had "deceitful Irish eyes" – all this in return for an incorrect answer about some obscure experiment. We were all terrified by him, although he did not pick on me and I kept jolly quiet about my Irish grandmother.

The house, large as it was, was clearly inadequate to house sixty boys plus staff. To start with, in true English country house tradition, there were very few 'lavs' and they had to be supplemented by four 'Elsans' – chemical lavatories – placed in a loose box. By that time, any sense of privacy had long been abandoned so we just got on with it. Baths were twice a week only and very shallow to save on hot water. In addition, four boys had to use the same water. I, being foreign and regarded as hyper-hygienic among other eccentricities, always managed to suck up to matron and get first bath while the fourth boy, clearly less fussy than me, had to get into something that resembled minestrone. The food was awful with sugar, butter and jam at an increasing premium. The games however, every afternoon were heaven. During the early terms at Salperton, in view of uneven fields, lumps and hillocks, anything in the nature of organised games was clearly out of the question. So we were loosed-off into the woods to play Cowboys and Indians, build tree houses and listen to hidden crystal radio sets.

So life continued with increasingly worse food as the war progressed and of course there were no half-term holidays, or visits from parents, due to there being no petrol, and public transport being unreliable. It must have been wonderful for my parents, as I simply cannot imagine my father playing in the father's cricket team on sports day. The only time my mother came to evacuated Ladycross was when she was pressurised by the extremely snobby headmaster's wife to bring the Duchess of Kent to our Sports Day, in return for which I was made, to my great horror, head boy of the school – a role I was totally unfit for. (I have subsequently been told in frequent interviews and jobs, that among the many qualities I undoubtedly possess, leadership is not among them.) The result was that I was totally unable to get any boy to obey me as I was much too wet – or perhaps too charitable – to have him beaten by the headmaster, Mr Roper.

Mr Roper was jolly enough in a way but wielded a thick leather strap, consisting of several layers of cow hide sewn together, purpose-made by the ESC (Educational Supply Company). This was the dreaded 'tolly' which Mr Roper administered on the open palm, on alternate arms, while holding a boy's hand up to ensure perfect connection between leather and flesh. It stung like hell. I cannot truly say whether the headmaster enjoyed beating us. Whatever pleasure he gained from it was cunningly concealed, but he never showed any pain himself, however efficiently he administered it on us. I remember well when he took the Latin lessons on unannounced days and would ask every boy in turn a question from the Latin translation. If you were unable to suggest an answer or offered an incorrect reply (which most of us 'non-swat' brigade did), you were called up to the front, open hand out and given a strong, sharp swipe from the tolly. One could always tell when one of those lessons was going on from the steady sound of thwacks, like a threshing shed at harvest time. Finally the class would end and a long queue of boys with red, swollen palms would emerge and run to the washbasins to alleviate the pain under cold water. The usual punishment for ordinary offences was two, three or four strokes on each hand. For more serious offences, like stealing a jar of jam from the larder, the tolly would be applied to the bare bum. No joking matter that.

The most heinous crime I committed, but which went physically unpunished was when I cheated doing the Boy Scouts' Mile. I was in the scouts in Peewit Platoon, and was taught to shout, "Peewit, Peewit" to identify my troop. I was taking part in the Scouts' Mile, which we did individually, walking and running a hundred paces alternately. Not being, as usual, particularly fit, I knew that I could probably not achieve the mile in the ten minutes allocated. I therefore arranged for a friend to stand-by in the woods with his bike, so I could hitch a lift, after which I appeared, panting heavily at the finish. Someone in authority (or was it a sneak?) gave the game away. Shock, horror, and public disgrace for my action, which apart from being unsporting, was certainly considered un-English. However I was not beaten with the tolly, as being publicly denounced as un-English was considered severe enough. All this delivered by an old wrinkly, kinky, scoutmaster who certainly should never have worn shorts. I did not mind the sporting and racial insults, being well accustomed to them, but did resent the smug titters and satisfaction of the assembled twerps who only condemned me for being caught, especially as they had not thought up the ruse themselves.

Apart from the threat of physical exercise, the filthy food, cold showers, bullying and the tolly, I also learned to dread the school train leaving at the beginning of term. A crowded platform and assembled fussing parents: the new young boys trying to hold off their tears, their mothers failing to. Then the overexcited crush of older boys, eager for school, the first eleven, authority and bulling *ad infinitum*. In the meantime I was trying to pretend that I had nothing to do with my mother who lacked anything of a stiff upper English lip. She would either hug me like a parting lover, in a very un-English way, or start publicly clowning about to try and cheer me up, much to my embarrassment and disapproval of the other 'normal' parents. After the first few times I begged her not to see me off again, and so she sent the housekeeper instead, much to our mutual relief.

MEANWHILE, AS I was enduring the best of the British preparatory school system, my parents had been taken under the wing of their friends, the Duke and Duchess of Kent and were living with them at Coppins, in Iver, Buckinghamshire. We initially stayed in the main house before moving into one of the 'courtesy' cottages at the end of the garden. The cottage was originally built for the head chauffeur Field, who was much too grand to live there, luckily for the Poklewski family, who all managed to cram in somehow. There were six of us, including Marisia the cook and Kasia the maid. I hesitate to think how little, if anything, the poor things got paid, but I was reassured by Mama that "they were both lucky and happy."

Marisia had 'escaped' with Papa from Poland. I don't think, being of a local Katowice family, that she had the slightest desire to be 'rescued' but would never have dared to defy my father whom she adored. As for him, the very idea of running away without the superb cook, who also doubled as his valet, would not have even entered his mind. When eventually they arrived they had all his clothes and none of my mother's, as my father regarded his as more important because, "of course, ladies' fashions change."

Thus downsized and in 'reduced circumstances' with "only two staff" my parents lived really quite happily. I still, after all these years, cannot work out how we all managed to fit in, as Mama and Papa firmly slept in separate bedrooms, owing I was told, to my father's ferocious snoring. It was not for any other reason, as they adored each other for forty-five years, and after all produced three children.

Life was peaceful on the whole, except when my parents had a row, which was fairly frequent, totally inconsequential, and much enjoyed by them both – but not by the other inhabitants of the tiny house. I can hear them now, with my father saying in quiet measured tones, "You are shouting now," and Mama yelling back, "No I'm not," and slamming the door of her room loudly. All this took place in a mixture of English, French and Russian, the latter language being employed for the most foul of swear words so that I should not understand. Of course I learned them off by heart. The finale of these exchanges would be Marisia rushing out of the kitchen, arms akimbo, shouting, "Madam you should not be shouting like that." Needless to say she would not dare to address her adored boss like that, always claiming that it was Mama's fault.

The reply to Marisia from Mama at the top of the stairs was a shout of "And you shut up too", followed by the slamming of kitchen doors and bedroom doors, and then total calm.

In spite of rationing, the cuisine was excellent at Coppins Cottage. This was in part due to assistance from Marisia's hens and Blossom the cow, who was shared with the big house. At the beginning of our occupation of Coppins Cottage we had a Polish cook called Jadwiga, who was incredible in the kitchen, but also an awful bitch, ugly to boot with a huge, greasy nose. While Jadwiga's cooking was divine, her English was appalling, and one day she was overheard ringing the village greengrocer saying, "Ees that vegetable? Poklewski here, I vant von cocking beetroot!" My parents put up with her for quite a while for the sake of her sauces, then she left unlamented to some other cocking job. Meanwhile Marisia had acquired her culinary skills and took over as cook – just as well, as my mother was quite incapable of boiling an egg, and even the thought of it would certainly not have passed through my father's mind.

Eventually Kasia left us, owing no doubt to pressure for space in bedrooms and beds, and was replaced by a daily, who was shared with Coppins. She was treasured by both the Kent family and us for her formidable character, remarks and music hall northern accent. In spite of confining her working hours to leaning on brooms and brushes, rather than using them, Mrs Rodenight was a pure thespian treasure. Her immortal remark, to this day remembered by myself and my friend Edward, the present Duke, was as follows. When my mother asked Mrs Rodenight why she hadn't produced more children (other than one rather podgy daughter) she replied, "You see Modom, Mr Rodenight wasn't very lusty."

The middle cottage at Coppins was occupied, in much less cramped a style by Mr Bysouth the butler at Coppins, and his wife. They had no children and were very pleasant neighbours. One had the impression that Mrs Bysouth, who was not employed at Coppins, was somewhat the social superior of the two, having started life as a personal lady's maid to some very grand personage.

Bysouth himself had started his working life as a young boy in a rather lowly position: sitting on the box of the carriage next to the coachman. There he would perch on his open seat, exposed to the elements, having completed his duty of loading the luggage, tucking his mistress into a carriage rug with a pottery foot-warmer and winding up the steps. I remember him telling me of the day he was sitting in front, in the pouring rain, when his mistress tapped loudly on the glass in front of her. The carriage stopped and he jumped down. He thought that she had taken pity on the poor young boy and was going to offer him shelter in the otherwise empty carriage, instead of which she said sternly, "Henry, the buttons on the back of your coat are out of line!" I never asked him which political party he voted for.

The third cottage was occupied by granny Agnes and my old nanny, nanny Howard, who had looked after us in Edgware before the war. Like many old-fashioned nannies, she never really left us, and frequently returned to look after granny, when we were settled at Coppins cottage. She would occasionally leave in a huff after a terrific confrontation over the gastronomic properties of a rice pudding and would be temporarily replaced, only to be begged to return soon after.

One of granny's eccentricities was her cats. She started with one, a very common ginger specimen called Peter whom we all loved. He became as eccentric as his owner, as pets tend to do. His main eccentricity was that the only way he would eat his meals was off the *Daily Express* and if by any chance he was served on *The Times*, *Telegraph* or *Mail* he would not touch his food. Unfortunately granny then took to feeding strays and ended up with around twenty-four cats prowling outside her cottage waiting for their *table d'hôte*.

All this performance began to annoy my father, her son-in-law, who thought that it was quite mad (as it was) and gave a bad example to the public, who were constantly tightening their belts as rationing increased. It all ended when granny's eccentricity went too far. On this occasion she convinced herself that there was a cat hiding in a bonfire being prepared by the jobbing gardener. She spent every day undoing the bonfire with her stick when the poor man had left. Eventually my parents had the whole bloody thing spread out when no one was around to prove to her that there was no cat there. After that my father got some cat-catcher to dispose of the colony behind granny's back, and she was left with Peter and the *Daily Express*. Eccentric as she was, she started writing her fascinating memoirs, the first volume called *Not All Vanity*, the second *My Dear Marquis*, followed by four further historical books, all published by John Murray. Not bad, considering that she started writing at the age of seventy-two.

Granny had an elder sister, Constance Baring (the widow of the banker Thomas Baring), who lived in Bracknell in Berkshire. I will always remember her as an imposing figure dominating the dining table at her house, being served by an amazing staff, even more eccentric than her. After lunch, she would don white gloves and light a cigarette, the only one of the day. One day my father was present there at a lunch party of rather important guests, including a number of MPs and a top civil servant. It was when the war in Africa was going rather badly for the allies, and someone remarked that the problem was that we did not have a really good general (that was before Monty). Aunt Constance drew herself up and scathingly pronounced to an astonished audience, "But what about Rommel?"

On another occasion she was asked by the village authorities to give the school children a lecture on road safety. She returned home proudly and on being asked how it went, she said, "Very well, I told them firmly never to play on the pavement, but always in the middle of the road." History does not relate the consequences.

School holidays, when the war allowed, were spent at Coppins where life was always very glamorous and fascinating even to a ten-year-old boy as I was then. In the ensuing years, I attended many lunches and dinners and evenings of intellect, politics and international royalty: Winston Churchill, King George of Greece, Cecil Beaton, Chips Channon, Peter Coates, Malcolm Sargent, Noel Coward, Douglas Fairbanks, not to mention Princesses Elizabeth and Margaret, George Galitzine and other colourful exiles and émigrés. I did not at that stage take part in the conversation, but listened carefully.

Dinners were always grand, served with gleaming silver and porcelain, served by the redoubtable Bysouth in white tie and tails, and a likewise-clad current footman, who as far as I can recall was always called 'Charles' regardless of his real name. This was the habit in upper class houses before the war as butlers usually stayed a long time (as there was no higher position to aspire to), whereas footmen changed more frequently due to promotion to another house, drink, or impregnating a maid. Thus, butlers were always called by their surname, whereas the footman was called by his Christian name – but as Bert or Ron would have been out of the question, it was always Charles or George.

Some incidents stand out in my mind when we were all staying at the main house at Coppins at the outbreak of war. The first one was when the housekeeper, a rather sombre lady, splendid in black bombazine, entered the nursery sitting room to draw the curtains and in doing so quietly announced, "War has just been declared," showing no emotion, followed by, "Dinner is served."

Almost immediately after the declaration of war we had air-raid warnings although in the first weeks they were false ones. Anyway on police advice, the Duchess and the household repaired to the wine cellar, where we were all rather crushed sitting on crates while the Duchess and mother sat on chairs both looking distinctly unrelaxed, pressed rather too closely to the chattering crowd. Monsieur Maioux, the French chef, looking distinctly nervous silenced the maids by saying, "Quiet, the enemy might hear us." The cellar experience was altogether too much for the Duchess and my mother, the result of which was that an air-raid shelter was swiftly erected for them in the garden. This consisted of a steel cylinder of about eight feet diameter tapering like an Indian tepee and packed outside with sandbags. The entrance was a sort of steel hatch, about three feet above the ground and not too generous in size.

During the subsequent siren warning, my brother and I popped into the shelter, whereupon the Duchess pushed my rather stout mother through the hatch shouting "Vite, idiote, les Boches arrivent!" All of this performance took place in dressing gowns in the cold, with a partially-dressed footman following with blankets and a thermos – then mother got stuck halfway through the hatch with the Duchess pushing her and me pulling. A distinctly uncomfortable three hours or so were spent in the steel tepee until the all-clear sounded and our comfortable beds were reoccupied. The two ladies subsequently decided that the thought of the butler snoring soundly in his comfortable bed in the cottage at the end of the garden was altogether too much, and they settled for chancing air raids in their beds.

During the war, the entire royal domestic staff were taken out of their fancy and formal attire, and put into dark blue battle dress, modelled on the army, with the Royal Crown sewn onto the breast pocket. Our dear Duchess did not approve of this, "They look so common my dear, poor things, quite unsuitable." She calmly insisted on her staff continuing in morning dress with their stiff collars until the afternoon, when they would change into full evening tails. No one seemed to worry or criticize her, regarding her Greek upbringing as foreign and different, I suppose.

Meanwhile, Monsieur Maioux was called up into the British army and, being a famous cook, was naturally assigned to an Officers' Mess. There disaster struck as "les brave Anglais" rose up in revolt because the food was considered far too rich. The poor man had probably served sauce tartare instead of brown sauce with the fried fish. The result was that he ended up in the lower ranks of the catering corps and probably spent the war stirring vast vats of porridge with an entrenching tool.

One of the sacred ceremonies at Iver was on Sundays, when Mr. Weatherley the garage owner would arrive in an ancient large Daimler to collect all of us for church in Uxbridge. I remember it cost five shillings return for about seven miles, including a wait of one hour. I would sit in front on the sunken leather seat, while the ample Mr. Weatherley did the same, blowing the air out of his even more sunken seat with a regular, loud exclamation for my ears only (as there was a glass partition behind us) of, "Oh, me bleeding piles!" On returning from church we stopped at Platts' Stores, which was the grocery store. It was closed, naturally as it was a Sunday, but the manager Mr. Gathergood would dart out after eyeing the street left and right and hand us a large box of black market food, marked 'MAD POP'. Everything in the village was always delivered to 'MAD POP' as they could not manage Madam Poklewski. Mother, not being pompous, especially about black market goods, could not care less. I once queried her on the patriotism of indulging in the black market and she replied, "Balls, mon cher, il faut vivre tôut de meme," the Poklewski dietary requirements being evidently different to the rest of the nation.

Small as the cottage was, we entertained the Duchess at least once or twice a week, and then dined at Coppins equally frequently. I often met our present Queen, then Princess Elizabeth, and her sister Princess Margaret at Coppins' dinners and parties where we had great fun with charades and other games. Naturally my mother and I cheated when we could, which was somehow accepted by some, but not quite all: Princess Margaret being the exception. She was always rather correct, putting me in my place, which as I was younger and she HRH and all, was very easy.

One day my mother had a brilliant idea, when Princesses Elizabeth and Margaret, King George of Greece and others were invited for a buffet dinner to our cottage. The sitting/dining room was tiny, so my mother turned it into a canteen, which was a new wartime phenomenon. None of the guests had ever been in a canteen, of course, and each were issued with a tray and made to stand in line by my mother. She was dressed as the manageress and was acting in character, being short and rude to the customers. Alex and I were the kitchen boys and Marysia, dressed in Polish national costume, slapped the food out onto their plates. The guests absolutely adored it – they shouted and pushed past each other in the queue. Sometimes it is very simple to amuse very important and sophisticated people, and my mother knew how to do it. Father always stood by, amazed and slightly shocked, but I suspect proud underneath.

The Duke had a wonderful sense of humour, as did the Duchess. My mother, who was one of her best friends and a constant companion, suffered – as did her mother, my grandmother Agnes de Stoeckl – from a very infectious and sometimes dangerous sense of humour. One near disastrous example was when Mrs Eleanor Roosevelt, the wife of the American president, came to tea at Coppins. She was representing her husband, President Roosevelt, who was young Prince Michael of Kent's godparent. Prince Michael was born on July 4th – American Independence day – and it was considered a politic gesture to ask the President to be a godparent.

The Duchess hadn't met Mrs Roosevelt yet – due to the war – and in view of the latter's reputation as a severe and savvy figure on the international scene, the Duchess was slightly apprehensive about dealing with her over tea. Hence my mother was sent to join them and help out. The three of them were sitting stiffly in the drawing room, when in entered the formidable butler Bysouth in morning tails wheeling the trolley with silver kettle boiling, followed by the footman carrying a tray of sandwiches and cakes. Bysouth prepared to retire with the footman and said, "Will that be all your Royal Highness?" to which the Duchess replied, "Yes, thank you Bysouth." The procession duly left and the door closed. The nervous Duchess turned round to Mrs Roosevelt, and asked, "Do you take sugar Mrs Bysouth?" upon which my mother collapsed in tears of laughter, and raced from the room before she wet the sofa, leaving a furious and highly embarrassed hostess. Of course the story was told at dinner to howls of laughter and entered Coppins history from then on.

Until he was killed flying in the RAF in a tragic accident in Scotland on his way to Iceland in 1942, I saw quite a lot of Prince George, the late Duke of Kent. He was an immensely attractive, raffiné and cultured character. Everybody loved him, his taste, sense of humour and generosity. I remember my parents describing a dinner party given by the Kents at their London house in Belgrave Square before the war. Glittering company, of course, with a table laden with crystal, silver and gold, a butler in attendance and endless footmen. A relatively young man, apparently not well known, was among the guests and was remarked by my parents as seeming nervous in the august company. He slowly turned from ivory to pale green in the middle of the main course. They realised that he was clearly about to be sick, but was too terrified to leave the room. Suddenly a tsunami of sick swept across the polished table, sweeping the Fabergé cruets and candlesticks all before it. The wretch fled the room, while the Duke with immense *sang froid*, quietly rose to his feet and said, "Shall we all leave now?" and led the way to the drawing room. Memory does not relate the rest of the evening, nor the fate of the *plat sucré*, but the young man was evidently not asked again poor chap, and in the event of his writing his memoirs, is unlikely to include this particular dinner.

I will always remember the Duke's dog, a chow called 'Muff' who adored him and was likewise adored by his master. Muff always waited outside the front door of Coppins for the Duke, even after his absence of several days. Everyone was particularly upset by Muff's solitary and despairing wait for weeks outside the front door after his master was killed, until he was finally persuaded to come inside.

Talking about Belgrave Square – where the famous Chips Channon had a house about two away from the Duke and Duchess of Kent, and where he had installed his famous Nymphenberg dining room – I shall always remember two of his more amusing remarks. One was when his son – later to become a well-known politician – Paul Channon, apparently had a dream which he recounted to Chips, and which Chips recounted with great pride (Paul then being very young but, clearly with his breeding, not unsophisticated). The dream went as follows: Chips said that Paul dreamed that he was giving a dinner party for the twelve

Apostles, and was trying to work out the seating order. Chips then asked him whom he had finally decided to put on his right, to which Paul replied, "Jesus Christ." "Brilliant," said Chips, "I am so proud of him… he will go far."

The other 'Chips' episode that I personally heard was when he declared during the fifties, after the medical consequences of smoking were discovered, that he had given up smoking, but, "My dear, what am I going to do with all my Fabergé cigarette cases?" It was for me, one of those learning moments in life, that whatever or whoever one is, we all have our problems from time to time.

War is Declared and Dinner is Served

CHAPTER THREE
The Upsides of Downside

AT THE END of my last term at Ladycross, my parents chose to send me to Downside the Benedictine public school near Wells in Somerset. They had considered sending me to Eton, but decided against it. I never discovered why, but it was either because in those days Catholic families rarely sent their children to Eton, or because my parents had met too many of its products. On the other hand, it may have been because of the fees, or the fact that it was only down the road from home, which would have meant them attending school matches and worse, parents matches. I imagine that it was more likely to have been the latter of the two reasons.

During the war, due to transport restrictions, there were no half-terms and no visits from parents. Instead, once a term we had a whole day holiday spent at the nearest town (in our case Wells). No petrol, and fathers either in uniform, Whitehall, or down mines. Likewise mothers were Wracs, Wrens or land girls. My father being too old for the army – having been in the Russian White Army as a young officer in the Imperial Guard Hussars in the first great war – was running the Polish Red Cross in London, while mother was busy running the unpaid staff and trying to stop granny feeding all the cats in Buckinghamshire. My mother was also supporting the whole Coppins set-up, especially the poor Duchess who was widowed with three children.

Downside, being a public school, was a totally different cup of tea to the dreaded Ladycross. I knew a few boys there, who had been at Ladycross before me; as a matter of fact, one of my friends McSweeny who had left Ladycross a term before me was tragically killed in his first term at Downside, together with eight or nine others, when an RAF trainee crashed his plane into the cricket pavilion during a match.

On the whole, during my four years at the school I had a happy time, except for the dreaded wartime food, and the totally unnatural concentration on sports, which however, I soon learned to modify to reasonable proportions.

The school was almost entirely run by monks who were mostly civilised, cultured, caring and not overly sadistic. The prep school tolly had been replaced by the cane, which kept us in reasonable order, as in those days we could not complain to the police, or for that matter to our parents (as that presumably was the main reason they sent us to these institutions). Anyway, I survived my fairly infrequent punishments without catching a lifetime dose of English upper class masochism.

The food was appalling. At the best of times English school food has never been mentioned in the *Guide Michelin*, but under wartime conditions it hit undreamt of depths. For a start, every institution was meant to grow its own vegetables if it had land. Cabbage and carrots were fine, if no different, after hours of boiling, but the soil was totally unsuitable for growing potatoes. As a result we had to live off spuds that were half purple in colour when boiled and already soft before that.

Menus were not necessary as the food was always the same on the particular day of the week. I remember that on Thursdays we always had what we called 'Cab Horse Pie' (probably more fact than fiction) followed by an equally revolting tapioca pudding which we used to stretch like a piece of rubber. This was known as 'period pud' due to a blob of ersatz red jam in the middle. For supper on Sunday, which was after evening Benediction in the Abbey, we always had a big chunk of cheese, supposedly cheddar, but with a 'special' flavour. To this day when I hear the singing of *O Salutarius Hostia*, I always remember that taste.

Sadly nowadays, for some reason, Benediction is a rather rare ceremony in the Catholic church. It's a great pity I think because I always found it the most spiritual of all the services in our beautiful Abbey church, apart from the fact that it was the shortest. Strangely enough, although on Sundays we went to the Abbey three times, for Low Mass, High Mass and Benediction, I never found the religious part of our education tedious or unnecessary and got on with the singing in my totally flat but loud voice. When not praying, which let's face it is quite difficult to keep up for long periods unless you are in an enclosed Order, I read the Bible, which I found fascinating. My neighbour in the Abbey, on the other hand, I can remember reading *Forever Amber* in black covers. When I reflect on my life I don't suppose he will be far behind me on the day of judgement.

Among the popular – if faintly non-religious – occasions in the Abbey, was volunteering to serve at one of the early morning Masses. These were celebrated by a monk in one of the many side chapels. As a server, one prepared all the instruments for Mass in the empty vestry and carried them to the allocated side chapel. The preparation involved filling the communion wine jug, and gave one the opportunity to take a swig on the way to the chapel and on the way back if there was any left. The result was that one entered the refectory for breakfast on a truly high note, having had a belt of shaky sweet wine on an empty stomach.

It was in the refectory, run by mostly Irish maids, where our only contact with the opposite sex occurred. The maids were very jolly, but not overly tempting – even to sex-starved sixteen-year-old boys. Most were red-haired, some with sadly hirsute upper lips. I remember one of the younger ones, who was Irish and our favourite tease. One boy in the middle of the long refectory table would shout out when she was some way away and ask for a fork. The poor girl would then return and go up and down the table shouting, "Who of yez wants a fock?" to which we replied in unison, "Me!" Fortunately the poor girl never quite got the joke.

Most of the other servants in the school were male and known as 'Johns': they were of an advanced age, and unadvanced faculties. I remember one, whose name escapes me, who was dressed in his brown overalls carrying an enormous, laden tray, and when stopped in the hall and asked the time, being unable to cope with two duties at the same time answered, "Twelve o'clock father," and simultaneously dropped the tray.

As mentioned previously, one of my problems was that Downside, like all English public schools, laid great importance on sport. Rugger was the most trying sport, and being totally shortsighted without my specs, I was harnessed together with some other unathletic types to form a rugger scrum, against which the first and second fifteen teams could practice. Thus I found myself bent over with my head lodged between some malodorous fatso's thighs for most winter afternoons, being kicked from behind by some muscular brute to push harder. I managed however to keep my ears until I had worked out an alternative afternoon occupation. I thus joined the Downside pack of beagles. This of course involved a tremendous amount of running round in circles hunting hares. My solution was to volunteer for the least popular occupation, to sit in the kennels with a big stick and supervise the breeding of the hounds, and either encourage them or prevent them from overtiring themselves. This ensured a relatively peaceful afternoon with a book, avoiding the running, panting and farting hordes on the muddy fields. Among other advantages it meant that I did not have to fall back on the birds and bees to learn the facts of life. Anyway thanks to those sweet beagle hounds I learned all the basics at leisure, and as a result have never been 'stuck', unlike the poor hounds, who frequently were.

The only activity that prevented these contented afternoons was when the weather was really too filthy for either rugger or hunting, and we all had to do a school run. Utter horror, as this consisted of running around roads and muddy fields in the pouring rain with a school prefect herding us behind with a menacing stick and an extra drill for the last one home – guess who? The summer was of course cricket and either hitting or catching balls. Having inevitably not being selected for the first eleven I took up the delightful career of scorer to the team, and spent many a peaceful afternoon sitting, pen and book in hand, only occasionally being aroused by an unnecessary shout of "Howzat!!" to which I learned not to reply, "Fine." As far as I was concerned, not playing cricket had only benefits: firstly I avoided having my private parts imprisoned in a steel box on a long hot afternoon; and secondly, as scorer, I still travelled with the teams for away matches and could enjoy the excellent tea, competitively prepared by rival schools.

The other activity was the OTC, or Officers' Training Corps, which I enjoyed and somehow felt that I was participating in the war effort. I liked wearing full military kit with rifles and bayonets, and was particularly proud to be allowed to wear a white and red 'Poland' badge sown on to my battle dress, like the Polish army in England. I managed most tasks, including staggering around with a heavy military wireless and massive batteries strapped to my back. The only incident that could have caused my dismissal was when the annual inspection by a real army Colonel took place in the quad. We were standing in ranks, pressed and polished, ready to be carefully gone over. The soldier to my right stood to attention, rifle on shoulder, when suddenly he sneezed just as the Colonel passed by him. An enormous gob of phlegm flew out of the unfortunate chap's mouth and landed on the end of his rifle. There it hung, swinging up and down like a trapped oyster, in front of the amazed Colonel's eyes while my unfortunate companion froze motionless with horror. The Colonel stared uncomprehendingly while I burst into uncontrollable giggles, doubled over and eyes running. Fortunately, the Colonel was too embarrassed to report the incident, or my reaction to it, and I remained a soldier for the rest of my stay at Downside.

I have on the whole many very pleasant memories of my time at Downside, both of fellow pupils and monks. My two closest friends among the community were Father Meinrad Geoghegan and Father Coelfrid O'Hara. Father Meinrad took a great part in the school life. I cannot remember quite what it was – as I do not think he taught – but was always around us, chain smoking and involved in parties. He was a very human and divine person, if highly eccentric and intellectual, with a wonderful sense of humour. He was reputed to keep his bedroom door permanently locked and no staff or fellow monk was ever allowed in. The mind boggles at what state that room must have been in, ceiling high with books, letters and pictures by the time he died.

Father Coelfried O'Hara, a housemaster by the time I left, was instrumental in forming the Downside Beagles, on whose premises we would brew the most terrifying Somerset scrumpy, which must in retrospect have been responsible for my high use and tolerance of alcohol. Through his connection with the farming community he organised an annual summer harvest camp, which I always attended and have the most wonderful memories of riding on horse-drawn carts, piled high with stooks of wheat with me swaying dangerously on top.

The evenings were largely attended outside the Seymour Arms, slurping cider, followed by deep sleep on mattresses spread on the floor of the local village school. After he retired as housemaster he became a parish priest in one of the Catholic parishes which Downside used to man, in Norfolk. He has since been 'gathered' as the Irish say and I think of him fondly chasing beagles in the sky, mug of cider in hand, caring for lost animals and humans, with the same skill he was blessed with on Earth.

The Upsides of Downside

THE APE HAS STABBED ME

CHAPTER FOUR
Steam's Up, Vincent!

HAVING LEFT DOWNSIDE, I applied for a scholarship to Cambridge. In those days it was necessary to secure a scholarship as neither government nor banks – not to mention my parents' dangerously empty pockets – would finance higher education. Having failed the scholarship, I had to face the prospect of the army or work.

Conscription being in existence in 1947, I duly went off for a medical. My father had decided that being Polish, and reasonably polished, the only suitable regiment for me would be the Irish Guards, the Colonel of which was a friend of his, and a number of the officer cadets being friends and contemporaries of mine at school. However this was not to be – for better or for worse – who knows? I went off for the army medical, which took place mid-winter in a hall, either church or municipal, I cannot remember which. However, I can remember the discomfort and cold, being paraded round stark naked for a good couple of hours in the company of fellow youths. They suffered more than me as they came principally from, what in those days, was termed 'the working classes', and unlike the pampered youth that I was, had not had the privilege of frequently appearing naked in public. They had not of course been through the English boarding school system, which always seems to have involved much naked display in front of fellow scholars, assistant matrons, occasional dodgy masters and PE instructors. Anyway, after much shuffling around, purple with cold and much coughing to order and fondling, they decided to turn me down on the grounds of bad eyesight. I can't say that I was totally disappointed, not being by nature a military man.

After missing out on the culture and fun of Cambridge, and the grandeur of the Officer's Mess at Chelsea Barracks, I set about finding a job. I began by grandly seeking an occupation in the film business through a famous director called Del Giudice who, being an intimate member of the Coppins set, offered to help. He was a very colourful and plump Italian, who had just had a great success with Laurence Olivier in Hamlet, which he pronounced "Omlet" when excited. I was naturally going to start at the bottom as a clapper boy, but alas was not able to get into the Film Worker's Union, which was an extremely closed shop in those days for reasons that escape me, but either because I was 'dead foreign' (this, of course, did not apply to directors or producers), or because my grandfather had not bedded Mary Pickford. Thus, through the influence of my father's best friend, Harold Wernher (who was the chairman of Electrolux), I got the much sought after position of office boy in the branch office of Electrolux in King Street, Hammersmith, at three pounds a week.

My first shock was that I only got two pounds fifteen shillings net, after deductions of five shillings a week for government dues – a pension or something, which I don't seem to get. My darling grandmother Agnes decided, seeing my disappointment and shock, to make it up and gave me a banker's order for £13 a year. This, I might say, went on forever, and I fondly remembered her when I received it at Christmas – I am ashamed to say without reminding her that it was no longer totally necessary.

I started work, my main duties being to make tea for the two secretaries, to answer the telephone and to do the filing. I can still remember the senior secretary, who was not a great advert for her sex, very spinsterish and well past her prime, that is if she ever had one, poor thing. After I had been told to put the kettle on the gas ring and I was busily filing my hundredth invoice of the morning, she would shout loudly, "Steam's up Vincent" and I proceeded to make the tea, as numerous nannies and governesses had taught me. This was a frequent occurrence, which broke the tedium of the filing, but meant that she suffered from permanent tea-halitosis. The younger secretary, though no temptress either – rather short, with over-dimpled rayon-clad legs and inadequate length of skirt (clothes rationing was still on) – was definitely jolly, but suffered from a very genteel accent: "Heow, Neow, Vincent" being her favourite phrase for whatever was required.

One of the two district managers was my favourite. Of humble origin, and with a strong regional accent, he was astute and very brave. He had lost both legs below the knee while serving in the merchant navy, as a result of sitting too long in a lifeboat in freezing conditions, having been torpedoed on an Arctic convoy. My accent, which embarrassingly stood out among the three thousand employees of the company, the vast majority of whom had not had the doubtful privilege of an English public school education, was no barrier at all to our firm friendship. This we constantly cemented in the local pub with either brown or bitter ale. In view of the difference in our pay, I fear that most of the rounds were on him.

It was from this rat hole of an office that I had to ask for the day off to attend the future Queen's wedding in Westminster Abbey. Eyebrows were raised but by that time I had been accepted as being rather eccentric, if not different. As I did not own a morning coat, but it being winter I managed to get away with wearing my black overcoat for the ceremony, and as the reception was some days later in Buckingham Palace (to which I was not invited), my suit sufficed, and the Moss Bros hire fee was saved.

This reminds me of an embarrassing occasion some two years later, while I was working at the Electrolux head office, still employed in a very junior position, when my good friend the Duke of Kent, himself still junior in the army hierarchy, rang the office and asked to speak to "Mr Vincent", which was my official name in the firm. When asked who was ringing he replied, "The Duke of Kent" whereupon one of my fellow clerks who had taken the call replied, "and I'm the Archbishop of Canterbury" and put the phone down.

AFTER GALLONS OF tea, my day at Hammersmith ended, via the underground to Uxbridge and the bus to Iver. At Coppins, I would go to granny's cottage for a bath as she had a gas geyser and we only had what was rather hopefully called an 'Ideal Boiler' which had to be stoked by hand and had given up by the evening. Dinner as always, cooked by Marisia, was excellent and about three times a week I dined very grandly with the Duchess at Coppins.

An alternative evening, as opposed to underground, bus and shower under granny's geyser, was either an evening in louche London with my brother Alex (and his highly varied, but always fun friends) or a deb dance. These usually occurred twice or three times a week during the London 'season', or even up to four times if one had been asked to all of them, and if one's liver (and stiff shirts) could last out the week. It was an extraordinary system for exposing one's daughters to the eligible members of the opposite sex. Of course not all of us were in the financial sense eligible, but if the accent and background were passable, the fingernails clean, the manners good and the line of chat handy, one found oneself on the list.

Deb dances were most handy for impecunious youths like me, as one did not have to know one's hostess or even her daughter to be asked, and the whole evening was delightfully free apart from the laundry bill. Even if one did not know the people who had asked one, one knew lots of other fellows 'on the list' and one's favourite debs also. Of course those like me, who did not have castles coming to them, broad acres, or fat portfolios, never had the first dance. Castles in the air, or in Siberia for that matter, did not really get one high on the waiting list, and as for yachts which some of the chaps had the use of – forget it.

The evening always started with a large dinner party, usually given by a friend of the principal hostess, either at their home, or with luck in the Savoy or Claridges, where the food and drink were more copious and of a higher quality. Then on to the ball, either in a grand house, hotel ballroom, or hired grand house (like Londonderry House): up the steps, grab a glass, greet the hostess, and sum up the scene quickly.

Sometimes the castles, titles and broad acres had not yet arrived, and one had the chance to get in a quick one on the dance floor with one of the chosen ones and find out if there were any particularly grand and amusing weekend country parties coming up. Then the polite rule was to dance with one's dinner hostess and, if she had evidently enjoyed it, one could get by without a repeat performance. Then it was one's duty to dance with the wallflowers, by no means to be sniffed at, but usually pitied as they were mostly very shy if not a bit dumpy, dowdy, or downright ugly, and they, poor things, would rather have been anywhere else if they had not been sent there by their pushy mothers.

In any case I usually had great fun, lots of booze and made up for the one-twoing on the floor with the dumplings, by dancing with some of the more attractive mothers. Mind you, they were usually 'old bags' of forty or fifty, but well dressed, and exuded an air of sophistication, and in some cases great experience. However in those days, it was not usually done or acceptable to take advantage of the experience, which I don't mind admitting I could have done with. The older mothers were rather grand and terrifying, and one could not hold them too closely or whirl them about too much, because of the pearls, diamonds, brooches, tiaras and diadems – disturbance of which could cause one to be removed from the list instantly. I shall never forget two elderly dowagers regarding a young fellow guest, foreign I think, who was darting around lighting girls' cigarettes. "Rather a nice looking young man don't you think, but just a little too handy with his cigarette lighter," said one to the other. I made a mental note to leave the odd cigarette unlit.

On the most important subject of sex, there was not too much of it around the deb dances among either generation. In any case those few who 'did' confined themselves to the castle and lolly set. I remember years later meeting a friend of a friend who confessed to me that she used to absolutely love it and the only way she could prevent herself from succumbing after a Pimms or two was by wearing a dirty bra, as she knew she would be too ashamed to undress. It struck me as being a novel form of birth control, but quite effective all the same, especially as it was well before the pill.

The country deb dances were rather different and lasted one or two nights in a country house. These usually consisted of great splendour, food, terrific cellars and splendid gardens. Also, there were more opportunities for post-ball kissing and cuddling, which in London had to be confined to a taxi (considered somewhat vulgar, not to mention uncomfortable). In the country there was usually a park or garden with plenty of leafy camouflage, or a ha-ha. I remember an excursion between waltzes at the Guards' Boatclub at Maidenhead, in an electric canoe with a rather magnetic girl, which nearly ended in disaster when my hand strayed from the tiller, and we nearly went over the weir.

The downside of the country dances was the dreadful cold, and I can well remember sleeping in large draughty rooms with the bedside carpet on top of my bed, listening to the hissing and gurgling of an ancient heating system which had not been turned on in the guest wing since before the war. Also, there was the terrible worry of how much to tip the servants. Some houses had closed boxes in the hall for the purpose, which provided blissful anonymity for yours truly and the other less well-off youth.

The country parties remind me of an occasion my wife Vicky has never forgotten, of a lovely girl coming back from the garden through the French windows, in a white ball gown to the strain of romantic violins. It was not until she had turned round that Vicky noticed the green grass stains on her behind and elbows. The deb scene holds many happy and funny memories for me and certainly enabled me to live well above my financial station, which otherwise would have confined me to pubs and draught beer with my less well-connected and sophisticated workmates. Mind you, I enjoyed that equally and always feel sorry for people who have spent their entire lives in only one milieu. Variety is after all one of the more important spices of life.

It was Princess Marina's birthday, I think in 1947, when I had just left Downside and was a not over-worldly seventeen-and-a-half years old. Princess Marina had arranged a small dinner party buffet in her suite at the Dorchester, which she used when staying or entertaining in London. In those days of post-war austerity, the Dorchester was a sort of upper-class club, full of people like the Wernhers and Nancy Cunard who had permanent apartments there. It was all Madame Vernier's hats and Hardy Amies' outfits, faintly austere and not using too much material in view of cloth rationing.

Being the youngest present I was put in charge of the bar after dinner, which, alas, turned out to be a mistake. There were, as far as I can remember, about twenty guests including my brother Alex, my mother and a few of her intimate circle, plus Princess Elizabeth (in 1947 not as yet on the throne) together with her sister Princess Margaret. I had been liberally helping one and all to drinks, unfortunately not forgetting myself, as I let myself rip on the Dorchester's varied supply, not available in those days at home in Coppins Cottage.

Games – as was usual in those days – started after dinner. As the party warmed up it was decided to play Blind Man's Bluff. I can remember being selected to be the blind man, and boy was I blind from the cocktails by then. In fact the blindfold was quite unnecessary except to explain my inability to either walk or stand straight. I was needless to say, a great success, everyone thinking what an excellent show I was putting on. The last thing I could remember was trying not very successfully to negotiate the revolving doors in the hall and being carried into a taxi by my brother and David Milford Haven, who then went out of his way to mention the incident ("How sad that Vincent was so drunk...") in his letter of thanks to the Duchess who until then was happily unaware of my state. She, being a tolerant and totally loving person merely passed the letter on to my mother with a shrug, who then subsequently passed it on to me with another sad shrug. I never forgot or forgave him for that totally unnecessary gesture.

I can remember waking up in my brother Alex's girlfriend's house the next morning with a hangover, which still stands out in a long string of quite memorable ones. Alex, Penny and one or two of the casual denizens of 22 Moore Street, then took me out for lunch to a Chinese Restaurant in Soho, the contents of which still remain in my memory, and is perfectly illustrated by the East End description of a bookmaker's lunch as "sweet and sour pork each way."

Penny Power's house at 22 Moore Street deserves some description. The top floor was reserved for Penny and her then resident lover Alex, while the rest could only be described as a home of repose for 'casuals'. Principal among those was Professor Desmond Williams of Cambridge University, a famous historian and equally famous drinker. I can remember, on more than one occasion, being asked by him to send a telegram to Cambridge explaining his absence at an important gathering – usually on an extremely sunny day – by the message, 'Return to Cambridge unfortunately delayed by fog'.

Other 'occasionals' were Colin Welch, Peregrine Worsthorne, and an assortment of intellectuals, but first and foremost there were *bon viveurs*. One indelible and frequent memory was mid-morning shouting from the upper storeys in shaky voices, directed to the basement, which was inhabited by a splendid Irish housekeeper, whose main occupation was washing glasses, having first ensured they were truly empty. In reply to these shouts there would frequently come the shout from Bridie, as the indomitable lady was called, of, "There's noe food and noe muney!" followed by groans and the odd pound note floating unwillingly down the stairwell.

Another famous occasion was when we all gave Desmond Williams a farewell party on his leaving for Berlin. He had been co-opted into the British army of administration, which was then responsible for running the British sector of Berlin after the end of the war. He was, being among other things a German scholar, employed in researching and editing the secret Nazi archives. As there were no foreign civilians allowed in Berlin at the time, he had to be given the rank of Captain complete with the various uniforms. We tried them on him, and the result was a figure of tremendous fun. He was very podgy with a gammy leg. By the time we had to dress him for his departure with the RAF, we only just managed to get him into his uniform – including the Sam Browne belt, incorrectly fitted. As it was quite impossible to locate the khaki trousers, we were obliged to send him off clad in a pair of grey flannel trousers which had certainly seen better days. We managed to manoeuvre him into a taxi, reeking of stale alcohol, juggling his officer's stick with his walking stick, which we managed to find only at the last moment. Thus saluting loudly, we dispatched our beloved Captain Williams to Berlin.

History does not relate what his arrival was like, but could well be imagined. However, with his immense intellect and crazy body, he managed an amazing task, as once sitting down (with sufficient booze of course) he was capable of working through several days without sleep. He gave us much fun, and splendid company after he was demobbed, and was given an even more splendid welcome home party, and by that time he was even more eccentrically clad. I am sure that he would have received an important decoration could the powers that be have possibly risked his appearance at Buckingham Palace, even if he had got the day right. Finally, alas, his various trends of mind and body finally met head on, and as his fellow Irishmen put it, he was sadly 'gathered'.

I remember long before the Jamaican immigration in the 1950s there was an established black community, mostly in Soho, who had a splendid nightclub not surprisingly called 'The Sunset Club'. It was pretty exclusive, in the sense that white faces were not welcome unless well known – and very few at that. We used to gain entrance through one of my brother's friends, who like a lot of them could hardly be described as a stereotype and was unlikely to be found at the bar of Whites or Boodles. He was far more likely to be propping up the bar at the Coach & Horses with Eddie Chapman *et al*. However, we seem to have passed his 'companionship test' and he introduced us to The Sunset Club where we were accepted as his guests, but naturally on condition that we paid. In fact that was where I originally learned the true meaning of the English expression 'PG'.

The atmosphere of the club was sensational: very dark, clouds of pot and the most wonderful live Jamaican music to be heard outside of Kingston. Our little group, not having graduated to marijuana, used to smuggle in miniatures to mix with the disgusting jugs of cordial served at disgustingly high prices, as the club had no alcohol licence.

I have two distinctly clear memories of The Sunset. Once, when I had smuggled in Mary Moore (later Manners), and in the midst of a Caribbean clutch on the dance floor, asked her to marry me. She, not unsurprisingly, but with immense charm, declined my offer, and the Polish Caribbean reggae merrily continued.

On another occasion we were there with Alex's best friend, Casimir Stamirski, whom he had been to school with in Poland before the war. Cas, or 'The Pixie' – as he was called – was small, Jewish, multilingual, international and experienced. He adored my brother, but being as we would say these days, as gay as a cricket, did not get his admiration returned in the way he would have wished (my brother by that stage was providing constant and untiring service to the opposite sex). Suddenly, to the loud noise of whistles, the club was filled with London's best: uniformed rozzers on a police raid. I am not quite sure what they were looking for. As there was no alcohol there it must have been drugs, mafia or murderers, or perhaps all three. Cas, immediately alert like a pointer, swept us into the Gents' loo saying, "I don't think it's very healthy to stay here in view of my application for a British passport." (He had recently left the RAF and had a good chance of getting citizenship). He went through the window like a rat but neither Alex nor I could fit, having been better fed than him, and firmly stood to attention in the urinal while the boys in blue politely waited for us to conclude. We thus had a short time to get mentally prepared to answer any questions in our plummy English accents. Having explained what we were doing there, we were honourably discharged into the Soho night.

MY DAYS OF making tea at the Hammersmith office came to an end, and I walked out of the door and towards Hammersmith station with the entreaty "Steam's up, Vincent!" echoing in my ears for the last time. Electrolux cuppas were behind me, and a thousand brown ales and bitters being pulled to the sound of a legion of "cheers" and "tas" lay ahead – for I had been sent to the factory and head office in Luton. There I sat, ensconced at a desk in a vast office containing some hundred men and young female clerks and typists.

At the head of the room sat an elderly ex-serviceman, like an invigilator at school exams. Mr Scott was a kind and gentle soul, having risen though the ranks to the heady position of Captain in the Service Corps. Many people who had neither perished or been wounded did not regret the armistice, but some like my boss the invigilator, regretted every glamorous and intoxicated moment (duty free) in the Officers' Mess in Gibraltar and other reasonably safe and well supplied billets. He now found himself back in the dull and grey environs of lower middle class Luton, with, I suspect a dull and grey wife who was also equally missing the flirty years of manning a mobile tea van safely away from her everyday man.

Anyway, Mr Scott singled me out by my plummy Officers' Mess accent, and put me just below his desk, where I had to endure long hours of wartime reminiscences, which consisted of endless pink gins, and alas, no slit German throats. However this was altogether a lot less taxing than having to examine and inspect returned vacuum cleaners in order to ascertain what the matter was with them, and what parts needed replacing or fixing under the guarantee. Never having acquired (to this day) any mechanical ability, I found this task quite difficult, that is, until some lowly floor sweeper tipped me off to open the motor and smell it. It was thus easy to detect a burned out motor, which in most cases was the correct assessment.

The only moment of panic that occurred was when I was assigned a typist to take down my letters; the problem being that I had never dictated before. The girl was just as nervous as me and only about sixteen. I was all of eighteen-and-a-half. She held her shorthand notebook on a rayon-clad somewhat fulsome thigh – which due to the space was crammed against me – and blushed like a ripe tomato. I managed to dictate my letter with many throat clearings, coughs and awkwardness. The four lines of, "Dear Madam, having unassembled your model 26L cleaner we have come to the conclusion that the motor has accidentally burnt out, and we shall immediately replace it. With many apologies, etc." must have taken eight minutes, and then on to the other nine identical letters.

Luton meant living in the first of a long line of dreaded digs including those I was sent to in Wales, Glasgow and Birmingham. My first digs cost £3/10 for bed, breakfast, high tea and two baths a week. I occupied half a room separated from the other half by a plywood partition, which stopped six inches short of the ceiling. The other side was occupied by the under manager of Hector Powe, the chain of tailors. He was always to be found in the over-pressed, shiny, excrement-brown, Hector Powe, five-guinea suit and sported a thin Cary Grant moustache. Alas for him, he was never taken for the matinée idol he so desperately impersonated. Suffice to say that in view of the ill-partitioned room we were unable to conceal any olfactory odours or noises from each other. He won hands down and bottoms up. So on to the next digs for me, a frequent occurrence as I could not digest the sometimes very 'high' tea, or because I was asked to leave as I took too many baths.

My training at the Luton office eventually finished, by which time the blushing typist and I were polishing off the "Dear Madam, your motor is burnt out," at a rate of two a minute.

Sexual discrimination in the office was healthy and strong. The female typists and secretaries were forbidden to smoke and had to look on longingly while the male employees chain-smoked. Smoking was considered unladylike, and there was also the risk of ash falling onto the typewriter. Sexual relations except for 'queer' male ones were permitted, providing they did not interfere with the sale of vacuum cleaners. As for lesbian relationships, they were never even mentioned, and I spent my youth in happy ignorance of their existence and mechanics, thinking that it was something that went on in the distant past in Bloomsbury. However, I was shocked and disabused at a Christmas office party in Regent Street, when fired by a number of sweet sherries washed down by brown ales, I persuaded a rather attractive blond Canadian girl from the office to join me in a kissing tryst in the privacy of the basement lift shaft.

In the middle of a tight embrace, with the certainty that I was doing my bit for Commonwealth unity, I asked her what type she really fancied. (In the light of later life experience it was a stupid question to ask, and subsequently I always kept my mouth shut, automatically assuming that I was the type desired). Anyway my delightful young Canadian friend in answer to my question, panted out in a breath overladen by Bristol Cream sherry, with hints of lift engine oil, that she worshipped blondes. The first blow was that I was dark-haired, the second blow was that she meant girls. Oh dear! Back upstairs to the brown ale and the fat filing clerk with a squint.

That was when I was promoted to London Head Office at 153 Regent Street as an assistant dogsbody to a particularly sadistic and unpleasant contracts manager called Craig. He would press a bell on his desk every time he wanted a pencil sharpened, a report copied, or a cup of tea – which seemed like every five minutes – and I would enter his office with raised and inquisitive eyebrows and say, "Yes sir?"

I clearly remember returning ten minutes late from a lunch break to find a purple-faced Craig waiting with his door open, the buzzer full on. "Lost in the fog I presume, Mr Vincent?" was his sardonic challenge (it was a sunny day). Of course in those far off days, office discipline was very strict, and there were no committees you could appeal to against immediate dismissal on any grounds the employer chose to select.

I was probably returning from lunch with my life-long friend Kenelm Digby Jones, who at that time was working for even less money than I was for a wine merchant nearby. My late appearance could have been due to our finishing off a bottle that Kenelm had judiciously found 'corked' in the absence of his boss. We used occasionally to lose our heads and go to a little Italian restaurant in Soho which served reasonable food for reasonable prices. I remember one lunch that stands out in my memory, when somewhat to my surprise he only had one course. When the bill came for two lunches at three shillings and sixpence each he went quite pale when he realised he could have had three courses for the same price. I found it funnier than he did, but we shrugged our shoulders and promised ourselves better days.

Sometime after joining the head office at Regent Street, at the wrong end of the buzzer, I got friendly with the office manager, by the slightly odd name of Chegwidden. Mr Chegwidden figured in some not unimportant post in the London Auxiliary Fire Brigade. I was rather fascinated by this having – like most normal boys – always fancied myself riding a vast ladder fire appliance rushing through red traffic lights to jangling hand-rung bells, wearing one of those splendid fireman's helmets. I thought that as having been declined (thank God) by the army, and war being over and the Air Raid Precautions (ARP) disbanded, I would give my services to my adopted country in the part-time fire brigade. Having arranged it through the kind offices of Mr Chegwidden, I was shown the ropes, or rather the ladders.

Disillusion and disappointment followed. To start with the auxiliary brigade did not ride those glamorous fire engines, but went around in tiny red vans, like postal workers. Secondly, instead of those glamorous 'warrior' helmets we wore little round military helmets, that carried no sex appeal at all. Thirdly, ladder practice consisted of sitting on a windowsill and pulling a ten foot ladder up between one's legs, then turning it round – no mean feat on anything above the first storey – and having hooked it in to the windowsill above, turning round and mounting it, and so on up one of those practice towers. My vertigo having set in at about twelve feet, I descended, pleading cramp.

I then tried a different tack and inquired about the giant mechanical ladders, which used to be called 'steam ladders' in the old days. So I was sent to Lambeth London Fire Brigade HQ some days later, strapped on to the end of one of these monsters, and shot into the sky with a large brass cannon between my legs. Having reached an enormous height the jet was switched on, and having totally forgotten my instructions I waved the hose around in the air under the pressure of the jet, suffering from vertigo and seasickness. I think I probably soaked the commander and crew, instead of the target, and was within seconds of throwing-up on them as well. However, in their wisdom they had pressed the emergency descent button, and then politely intimated that I was not really brigade material. I did not challenge their advice and came to the conclusion that I would in future devote my loyalty to England in a civilian manner.

THE NEXT PART of my Electrolux training was to spend a few weeks with the service department in Wimbledon where I made calls with the service rep in his van, trying unsuccessfully to learn about the innards of a vacuum cleaner and fridge. Two memories stand out. When passing a tree-lined residential street in Wimbledon, the service rep pointed out No 53 and said, "I remember that house well... I was making my second call to check the good-looking lady's fridge, when she pushed me against it and tried to go about her business. I remembered from my previous call that she lived with her mother and so nervously enquired about the old lady. To which she replied: 'It's OK, Mum's upstairs with the man that's come to fix the radio.'"

I remembered this incident when calling in the same neighbourhood to replace a motor in a vacuum cleaner. The lady of the house was clearly very bored, the afternoon was very warm, and halfway through my taking apart the motor, and swallowing my third cup of tea, I suddenly realised that she was aiming to share more than a biscuit with me. In a controlled panic I started to hurriedly reassemble the machine and pack up my tool kit saying, "Thank you, Madam for everything, but I'm afraid that I must rush as I am behind with my calls."

Looking distinctly disappointed she suddenly pointed to a pile of screws and springs behind me that in my rush I had failed to notice and replace and asked, "What about those?" To which I quickly replied, "Spares, Madam" and promptly dashed for the door. It was only then that I realised that milkmen, window cleaners, service reps and postmen did not always acquire their exhausted appearance purely from their dawn starts.

I was then moved on to the sales section, the inaugural training being similar to Pirbright or Sandhurst. For it was here that I found myself endlessly vacuuming a carpet on a raised stand at the Ideal Homes Exhibition at Olympia, and other similar venues. In order to accomplish a proper 'dem' one had to spill flour, sand or some other substance on the carpet and then effortlessly vacuum it up, then open the dust bag and spill it out onto the carpet again. This is when I realised how hard it must be to hold an audience enthralled during a matinée on a rainy summer's afternoon at a seaside resort.

However this particular audience was at Olympia at 9.30 in the morning, with the 'entertainer' suffering a dreadful hangover and hoping against hope that he had tied his tie on straight. If any passing person or couple showed the slightest interest in my sleight of hand, it was my duty to ask them whether they would like a private demonstration in one of the hot little cubicles surrounding my raised platform. I would then have to sit them down and go through all the attachments. The one that was always guaranteed to make me gag slightly was called a 'crevice nozzle', designed to clean between radiator slats (as if anyone ever did). By this time I was on my knees, as the demonstration tents were very low, and I felt like a hooker at a Nevada brothel. At least, they probably got a tip, whereas, my young couple, having rested themselves for twenty minutes, got up saying "Ta, we'll think about it," leaving me with a limp order form in my hand.

Eventually I got cute at spotting wedding rings (there was a chance there, whereas young lovers or fiancés never bought), and somehow I still managed to sell two cleaners a day at £27.50 each with a ten bob deposit, and kept my job. Since my friends had heard about my presence there, they would come to witness my act. I, of course, tended to ham it up a bit, while they quietly took the piss out of me.

Olympia was an exhausting stint of 9.30am to 7pm, but the Brighter Homes Exhibition at Manchester was more fun. The public did not seem to quite understand my diction, and as for me, I could not take in a word they were saying, but somehow my target of two sales a day was always reached. The Manchester nights on the other hand were heaven, unlike London, as the 'lady demonstrators' and the 'male demonstrators' were both in digs – segregated naturally to keep one's energies for the daily platform. But like all segregations – be they Oxford colleges, Russian Gulags, or novice cloisters – it was not quite watertight. The 'ladies' as I remember, resided at the Shrubbery Hotel, where we crept in through the polluted laurels after our poached eggs, and had ourselves a ball. In the morning, back to the dreaded exhibition with throbbing

heads and happy memories, being eyed by a dour sales manager, sour
and red-eyed from his dowdy wife's snores and lack of brown ale.

Onto the next promotion: this elevation was to being a true
travelling salesman. Thus I set out on my rounds, no longer on public
transport, but in my first car, a beige Ford Prefect, which I proudly
bought secondhand for £180 with a loan from the company. I repaid
the money from my mileage allowance, fiddled in a far more skilful
fashion than that employed by present day members of Parliament. I
was so proud of my car and drove it round London – full of booze as
one did in those unbreathalysed days – to show it to friends, who must
have been really thrilled…

My job was to sell 'built-in' refrigerators for council flats, which on
the whole were not provided with adequate larders. The movement
to install fridges was aided by the post-war socialist realisation that
food can go off, and that factory workers were more efficient on a full
stomach rather than on a queasy one. One must remember that this was
the day before supermarkets, vacuum packs and deep freezing.

It was quite a tough job on the whole, as having turned my
unacceptable surname into 'Mr. P.K. Vincent' for commercial purposes
(until 5.30pm), there was little I could do about my carefully honed
public school accent. However, apparently being a born salesman – after
all, everyone has to be born to something – I made the grade, and the
expected sales targets.

Having flogged myself to death with built-in fridges, I was given a new
product of Electrolux to sell, which was a communal laundry consisting
of a giant washing machine, and a separate hydro-extractor which took
the water out of the clothes by spinning. These were for commercial
laundries on housing estates and launderettes. I therefore spent the next
few years immersed in suds, water and steam, showing the stout ladies of
Wandsworth, Brixton and Lambeth how to do their smalls.

By that time I had every possible trick that can be achieved with a
vacuum cleaner attachment, and how to pack a 1½ cubic foot fridge to
magically contain a vast amount of food. However, it was then realised
that my knowledge of washing was probably limited. So I was sent with
two colleagues to the washing 'University' at Port Sunlight, Liverpool,
run by Lever Bros. Here I was to learn how to handle smalls and so on,
and obviously afterwards recommend their 'whiter than white' powders.

Our knowledge of smalls (being limited to persuading the opposite sex to remove them), took some improvement.

After three days out of an unbelievably dull course of five days, we had a very boozy lunch in a pub, and got to the lecture late, as a result of which the only seats left were in the front row. The afternoon was warm, the lecturer was a stout lady (who these days would be described as having seriously surpassed her 'body mass' index) clad in a straining white overall with tightly permed curls on her head. The subject was handwashing, which for the purposes of demonstration, was carried out in a translucent glass basin. For a start, we were into machine washing, secondly we were drunk, and thirdly, it was very hot, and the movement of her fat fingers in permanent clockwise motion in the see-through basin was too much for us and we dozed off as a result. This was probably one of the few adult educational courses I have ever attended but at least I have never had a problem with my personal laundry.

Whilst covering the southern counties flogging laundry equipment, not totally successfully, I remember one particularly null-and-void sales call. I drove proudly in my Ford Prefect into a very smart private hotel in a grand garden setting, and rang the bell. It had been snowing heavily the night before, and as a result I could not make out the drive too well. The manageress took my leaflets with reluctance (having declined to discuss in detail the incredible advantages of the establishment doing its own laundry), thanked me not over enthusiastically and just as I was driving away screamed that I had just driven over some of their famous flower beds, and not the drive. I panicked, gave a rapid apology, and drove away with spinning tyres – unfortunately over the flowerbeds on the other side of the drive. My written 'call report' stated that, "They showed great interest and would consider the matter carefully at the next management meeting." I decided to leave out the fact that I had ploughed up their garden at the same time.

Not having oversold the communal laundry equipment in south east England, I was sent to the Glasgow office to be the sole sales rep for laundry equipment in Scotland. The Scottish general manager was a fierce but lovable character called Mr. Taylor (in those days, remember, people did not have Christian names, or at least did not disclose them to their inferiors), who like many of his fellow countrymen had no suspicion of Poles, and in fact shared many of their pleasures.

I was left to my own devices and discovered that the majority of the working class areas of Glasgow were not overly interested in laundry *per se*. I remember the owner of a launderette shrugging his not particularly over-washed shoulders, and telling me in a thick – and as yet incomprehensible – Glaswegian accent, "We've nay need of your machines, so long as the laundry comes out damp, they're happy."

I settled into a boarding house in the university area of Glasgow. The lady owner – Mrs Lindsay – was very sporting and I suspect had trodden the boards in her youth. She did mention acting, but I suspect she was not referring to Shakespeare. Like many Glasgow boarding houses it had been thoroughly subdivided with the result that the only bathroom had been created out of the kitchen by a partition, the top of which was glass so that one bulb could serve both areas. I was slightly surprised during my first bath-time to find the good lady standing on a chair, clad in a loosely tied tea-gown, wiping the glass in order to inspect me performing my ablutions. I attempted to conceal my manhood with a face flannel. The only result, thank God, of these antics was that I became her favourite lodger and was allowed a nightly bath instead of the usual twice-weekly allowance. Life went on peacefully there, although I suspect the consumption of window cleaning liquid increased somewhat.

By that time, my darling little very second-hand Ford Prefect had just about given up the ghost, and its 'sticky-out' indicators could no longer reach above 45 degrees. As I was not senior enough to warrant a company car, and had not the wherewithal to buy one myself, I was reduced to covering the whole of Scotland on a 125 cc motorbike. By the time it was loaded up with me (at sixteen stone in those days), all my laundry leaflets, plus overnight necessities (pyjamas, toothbrush and Scotch), the motorcycle had the greatest trouble with the Scottish hills, not only with the Devil's Elbow – which I can well remember shoving it up – but even the Glasgow hillocks on an icy day.

I did manage one weekend away in Aberdeenshire, where we had frequently spent time at Birkhall on the Balmoral estate. It was lent to the Duchess of Kent for the holidays during the war. On the occasion that I arrived on my motorcycle, Birkhall was occupied by another member of the Royal family, and so the 'Coppins set' – the Duchess, my mother and the children – had been installed in a small house called

Allt-na-guibhsiach on Loch Muick on the estate. Due to lack of room, my brother and I were housed in Louis Mountbatten's wartime caravan, which for some untold reason had ended up in the garden there. We were very happy and comfortable in it, and decided that the Admiral of the Fleet had not deserted his luxurious life when on campaign.

On the whole I failed to persuade the Scots to buy many of my laundries and was recalled to London, which was a great relief from a lonely life and Mrs Lindsay's glassy stares.

My career proceeded commendably, apart from the odd unreported misfortune, and only ended when I was called into the sales director for a career chat. He told me that I had done very well and, young as I was, I could reasonably aspire to become the sales director in twenty years time. I left the meeting reeling with horror, having been given this glance of the heights I might reach and after due reflection, which took about three drinks, gave in my resignation the next day.

The Ape Has Stabbed Me

CHAPTER FIVE
From East Bronx to El Morroco

HAVING FINALLY DECIDED that there must be more to life than promoting "quiet vacuum cleaners and silent refrigerators", I looked round the world as I knew it, and wondered what was next for me. Firstly, I reviewed my financial position, which in view of a positive balance in the bank of some eighteen pounds, did not take me too long. I then visited my bank manager, who was also my father's, at the Midland Bank Haymarket. He sat there in his leather chair for a moment, looking at the pathetic family balances, and after shifting his buttocks slowly – whether to break wind or just to reposition himself to break the bad news to me – refused a request for a fifty pounds overdraft, and gave me a short lesson on living within my means. I decided not to mention the half of Siberia, which I was told belonged to my family, thanked him for his invaluable advice, and left firmly resolving never to live within my means.

The next day I swept down to Victoria to the much more polite Sutton & Co., the well-known pawnbrokers to the gentry, and popped-in a lovely pair of silver Georgian candlesticks I had once received from the Duke and Duchess of Kent for Christmas, for fifty quid. My very good friend Columbus O'Donnell then concocted a plan for me to join him in a new venture of his: to start a chain of supermarkets in England. His mother, and his uncle, the eccentric Huntingdon Hertford were – by inheritance – large shareholders in the Great Atlantic & Pacific Tea Stores (A&P); at that time the biggest chain of supermarkets in the States. He suggested that he could get me a position as a trainee at A&P in New York, and organised a weekly wage of $100, plus a ticket on the Queen Mary – cabin class.

This was all organised by Columbus from his luxurious flat in Pont Street where I was lodging. By that time he had floated through two marriages and a few careers whilst helping to keep a great number of divorce lawyers, nightclubs, leading hotels and famous barmen on both sides of the Atlantic going. I would have quietly stayed on there, assisting him in playing out French bedroom farces, were it not for the tiresome difference of at least three zeros in our respective incomes. However, it was fun while it lasted. He was good looking, strong, rich and madly enthusiastic for the horizontal sports. (To prove his excellence in the horizontal position he completed the Cresta Run in the winter of 2006, at the age of eighty, and without viagra at that!) At the time I was living with him, he was conducting simultaneous affairs with numerous ladies, including the American actress and singer Eartha Kitt, whom anyone would have thought would have represented a full-time job in that department. Many a morning I remember bringing her a breakfast tray and being left breathless by the sight of her magnificent body, inadequately concealed under thin white chiffon. Anyway, after a friendly pat and some banter, I would close the door behind me with a sigh and repair to the kitchen for my – by then – very hard-boiled egg. It was all tremendous fun, with episodes of high-octane drama: combating telephone calls with glib lies; not answering the front door, and arranging discreet exits by the fire escape. Life was far from dull.

So off I sailed to America on the Queen Mary. The journey passed comfortably and peacefully in cabin class, until an unfortunate incident occurred. After the first two nights on board, I realised that cabin class consisted of middle-aged and older passengers only, and no crumpet. But I discovered that there was a sufficiency of that commodity in tourist class. However, Cunard in those days was not classless – in fact the classes were kept well apart – hence no chance of seaboard romance. However on the third night, fired by generous draughts of the cheaper red wine, I managed to smuggle my way into the lower deck – away from the string quartet gently playing their way through sedate little two steps and waltzes for the stout bourgeoisie and their lady wives. There, I joined the merry throng and picked up a not unattractive young hairdresser on her way to teasing out the dyed hair of the 5th Avenue matrons in New York.

Thinking that I would give her a jolly expedition some decks above in cabin class, I managed to magic her up there, and persuaded the fatigued quartet sawing away to an empty dance floor, to play for us. The elderly and stout fellow passengers had retired to their cabins, to remove their teeth and don their hairnets. More plonk followed for us and the band, who were delighted that someone had noticed their existence and actually wanted to dance in an animated fashion. Not having as yet conquered the magic of rock and roll, (I suspect that neither had they), I persuaded them to play a blood-tingling Hungarian tune. The combination of that, the red wine, and an armful of attractive coiffeuse, caused me to pirouette too dangerously – particularly on a ship. Fired by excitement, I lifted the poor girl above my head, when a slightly stronger wave caused the Queen Mary to tilt. The result was that I am ashamed to say, the instinct of self-preservation overcame any gentlemanly consideration for the weaker sex. While I was hurled across the dance floor, holding the unfortunate damsel above my head, I let go of her, letting her fly on to the tables and chairs, while I landed safely on my hands. Huge confusion of waiters and staff followed.

Fortunately she was not badly injured, bar torn stockings and minor bruises, and the damsel, by that time thoroughly distressed, was carried down to the tourist depths, while I retired somewhat chastened to my cabin. The incident however did not end there. I was put on 'Pursers Report' the next morning, and ordered to report there. It was a bit like being sent to report to the Head at school, and as I stood there I was severely reprimanded. He said that Cunard could not contemplate carrying a passenger capable of throwing another passenger to the other side of the dancing lounge through the air, not to mention that she was purloined from the wrong class. I duly ate humble pie, but as we were in the mid-Atlantic he was unable to offload me from the ship, although judging from his rather alarming old sea dog expression, he would have gladly put me in a life boat and cast me off.

I decided that the object of my attentions last night would not welcome either my appearance or apologies in person, so I wrote a heartfelt and faintly poetic apology, and there being no flower shop, bought a pair of the most expensive stockings to accompany it. Sadly, no reply, but I am sure she still remembers the event, and I can only hope that she has had a happy life, and met more skilful girl handlers than me.

On arrival in New York, I was interviewed by the national A&P personnel director, at the head office. I took this to be quite normal, but of course the director I met did not normally interview 3rd grade clerks on $100 per week. First I had a medical, which from memory (it was the sort of medical one tends to remember) was chiefly to find out whether I had piles. I found myself naked standing in a corridor, still holding my black overcoat with astrakhan collar and Briggs umbrella, having passed the medical and been appointed the grand job-title of 'shop assistant'. Of course, in view of my introduction through the majority shareholding family while there was a tremendous boardroom struggle going on, I was taken as a company spy, and they decided to chase me back to England on the next Cunarder. They failed.

I booked into the Winslow Hotel on the corner of 52nd and Madison Avenue where I got a bedroom for $3 a night on the top floor, which must have originally been a room for travelling servants, as it was tiny and not *en suite*. However, the phone and lift worked, as did the bathroom at the end of the corridor, albeit with many steamy and leaky protests. I was first put to work on an A&P store on 3rd Avenue which was not unpleasant as I was on the meat and dairy counter which was a service one – in other words, where one actually spoke to the public. They had moved me there, as I demonstrated an inability to 'stack' having proudly built a mountain of Heinz baked beans, which I then had to watch collapse like a house of cards all over the store and the customers' feet.

The counter service was less hazardous, but a slight problem arose when the young blacks did not understand a word of what I said, and likewise, I did not understand them. I remember standing politely in my white coat behind the counter, addressing a pair of dusky seventeen-year-old maidens in long pigtails, as I imagined a Fortnum & Mason assistant would, with the words "Can I help you Madam?" They both gaped at me wide-eyed, and said, "Gee, you speak so purty." Result: no sale, only admiring glances. My experience in that store was obviously considered as too cosy and useless, as I became an object of curiosity and slowed up the sales.

As a result I was transferred to a store in Harlem, which in those days was a more or less no-go area for whites, apart from certain nightclubs. Disaster struck one day as I noticed a big black man leaning over a low meat shelf, helping himself to a large Porterhouse steak and stuffing it into his breast pocket. I thought, with triumph, "Here I go," and following company instructions which I had just learned by heart, I tapped him on the shoulder and recited, "Excuse me sir, but I believe you have property of the Great Atlantic & Pacific Tea Stores concealed about your person, unpaid for." The man wheeled round with mad red eyes and started standing up. He passed my six foot two inches like an elevator. I was looking up at a colossus, who then put a hand on my shoulder and squeezed his thumb and forefinger with such strength that I thought they would meet through my arm. "Are you accusing me of stealin' man?" he growled. I looked around desperately only to find that all the help had fled. Writhing with agony I told him that, "I may... ow! ... No! ... I am sure! ... that I have made a mistake." He replied, "That's what I thought man," and flicked his thumb, which was the size of a jackhammer, against my shoulder. I found myself flying through the glass meat case, where I landed on my backside on a pile of broken glass and steaks. He strode out. The staff miraculously reappeared, fished me out – not too seriously hurt thank God – and reprimanded me, "You shouldna done that man! He's da biggest junkie on da block... Comes in everyday for his lunch... No-one touch him... We want to live man!"

One of my final and least comfortable postings was in one of the meat plants in the Bronx. The first shock was the temperature, as we all worked in large refrigerators, sealed by thick doors with small glass inspection windows for the supervisor to look through. We had to wear about three sets of thermal underwear, regardless of the blazing heat outside. My second shock was the initiation ceremony, when the head butcher asked me over, and held out an enormous lump of cow's liver, which he told me to smell in case it was 'off'. This I dutifully and innocently did, whereupon he pushed the entire bleeding liver – and half frozen at that – into my face, to the great amusement of all the others.

Naturally, no smoking was allowed, but I noticed that several did, and I being an avid smoker, asked what to do with one's ciggie if the inspector was seen wiping the inspection window. "What do you think these are for?" they cried, shoving their butt-end up the rear of the nearest hanging pig or sheep carcass. The ladies, mostly Porto Rican, but really only Spanish speaking, were very jolly and rather too sporty for comfort. There is definitely something about handling raw meat all day that makes women randy, I decided. Once I was in the basement loading a conveyor belt to the ground floor, when a very stout black lady, innocent of any underwear, straddled the open trap door at the top and shouted at the top of her voice, "Come and get it Limey!" The temperature, however, plus the background of butchered carcasses hooked to revolving chains – like theatre scene changes – didn't do much for my sex drive.

There was one occasion however which did impress me, and fill me with national pride. I was accompanying the German inspector on that day and we paused outside one of the blast freezer rooms. As I was clearing the window for the inspector, lo and behold we saw a Polish butcher, minus his thermals, pleasuring a stout Porto Rican girl on a large meat block, with a cloud of steam arising from the encounter. It was too soon after the war to make any nationalistic jokes, so we passed on as the inspector murmured under his moustache, "I hope it freezes."

Out of Harlem, before the company had a dead limey on their hands, I was transferred to a cheese warehouse, where I carried, cut and transported giant wheels of cheddar, gorgonzola and so on. The good result was that with the amount of physical exercise I got there, and in the other stores and depots, I lost two stone in weight, which thank goodness I have never recovered. The bad news was that at the end of the day I stank of cheese. I noticed that on my return to the Winslow Hotel, my fellow passengers on the subway – accustomed as they were to the usual malodorous human excretions of their fellow travellers – tended to move away from me and my cow, goat and sheep odours. I then had to bathe and scrub-up like a surgeon before an operation to be fit to enter a Park Avenue drawing room without causing raised eyes, not to mention handkerchiefs.

Having achieved these heights of personal hygiene I would don my dinner jacket and proceed to some grand dinner, often in the company of Columbus' mother Joe Bryce, who conveyed me grandly in a huge chauffeur-driven Rolls Royce, and had much enjoyment and satisfaction in introducing me to the company as "one of my young butchers." I became quite popular retelling stories about a New York that they knew nothing about, while enjoying caviar and champagne, which made a difference after the coke and burger in the midday diner.

Often the evenings ended in the El Morocco nightclub, or the club on top of the St. Regis Hotel, where I heard Cole Porter sing frequently. Lots of dancing, buckets of drink and fun, then returning to the $3 hotel room in Joe Bryce's Rolls Royce, for four hours of sleep. In the morning, off with the black tie and on with the jeans, before a rattle to the East Bronx on the 'EL' with a crashing hangover, and back to the conveyor belts and lorries. No wonder I lost weight.

I adored New York at both extremes, and found it – and still do for that matter – extremely invigorating. Some of the apartments and private houses were amazing. I remember going to an apartment covering three floors of a towering building overlooking Central Park, the first level of which had a vast parquet floor with a double French staircase rising up to the next level with endless grand reception rooms. Also, I recall another high-up apartment with an amazing steel balcony room jutting out over the street far below, especially built to house a great Henry Moore reclining figure. I remember it was installed while I was in New York, as they had to close the whole street during the weekend for the crane to get the sculpture up. Needless to say these families all had chic weekend estates on Long Island – although I was able to enjoy those less as I found myself working most weekends. Of course, I also had many friends who drove normal cars, did not live in skyscrapers and whose incomes did not make me too uncomfortable. They looked after me well. I especially enjoyed the traditional Bloody Mary soaked brunches at the weekend, which went on forever.

Among the few expeditions from New York was one made with Columbus O'Donnell who drove his girlfriend Eartha Kitt and I to stay in Washington for a party. I was, of course, aware of the colour prejudice that still existed in the States, but had not as yet experienced the strength of it. Racism was alive and strong in the south, and

Washington, despite flaunting itself as the centre of world democracy, was definitely southern in its views. This was clearly illustrated to me at a rather grand party in a Georgetown house, to which we had brought Eartha. She caused quite a stir, as apart from being a world-class entertainer, which excited all the foreign diplomats present, she was of course also black, the fact of which stirred some of the Washington ladies. It was okay to be black on stage, but as a guest in a private house? The mood was unsure. I was talking to one of the daunting Washington ladies, happy on my third martini, when I asked her if she knew Eartha. "Certainly not," she said, "and I must confess it makes me quite sick to see one of them in the drawing room." I reeled with shock and replied, "Really? But then what about the butler and the maid?" She replied, "They are different." So are you, I thought, as I turned my back. Things are different now thank God, although Polish and Irish jokes are still much enjoyed. Being Polish I quite enjoy some of them, my favourite being, "What was the Polish pope's first miracle?" The answer is, "When he cured a ham."

HAVING FINISHED MY year in New York learning about supermarkets, I boarded the SS Saxonia sailing down the St. Lawrence from Montreal, on its way to Liverpool. I enjoyed my experience in New York but was looking forward to my return to London, family and friends – and wearing a suit during the day instead of overalls. By the time I returned the reason for my going had evaporated, but the change from fridges and washing machines to steaks and cheese had done me good, and was a not-to-be forgotten experience.

I was first class on the boat and sat at the Chief Engineer's table, which had pleasant but not over-exciting people at it. I was happy, as I could go on talking to a reasonably polite audience, who looked quite interested without trying to interrupt me with their own stories. All went well, until one evening at dinner someone raised the question of the atomic bomb. I, having obviously partaken of a couple of fairly atomic cocktails, immediately cut into the conversation, and started to explain to the table how it worked. One of the audience – a very

pleasant but not particularly talkative member of the table – raised his
hand to interrupt me. I raised my eyebrows in amazement and queried,
"Yes?" whereupon he said, "Speaking as one of the people involved in
the making of the atomic bomb, I have to correct you on a number of
details." I can only quote 'collapse of stout party' and remained chastened
and silent – I am sure to the entire table's relief – till the end of dinner.
He was charming, as was his wife, and did not take it out on me. I
remember his name was Michael Clapham, and I was pleased that he
subsequently came to head ICI. I suppose it was just another lesson in
early life, and a subject to be avoided in future. Thinking of that, there
is an immense amount of subjects, which *au fond*, one knows nothing
about, but I ask myself, does that stop one talking?

The arrival at Liverpool was rather dramatic for me. My dear friend
Gerry Albertini, with whom I was going to share a small mews house,
had decided that it would be a hell of a wheeze to greet me at the docks.
He had recruited my brother Alex and Casimir Stamirski (the Pixie)
to travel up to Liverpool with him the night before and book into the
Adelphi Hotel for the night, as the Saxonia was docking in the morning.
They then had an almighty bash of an evening in a number of Liverpool
nightclubs and, having kept the last one open with Gerry's ever-bulging
and generous wallet, decided to hire the four-piece band to continue
playing and drinking until the Saxonia docked.

As I was going down the gangway, saying goodbye to the rather
serious acquaintances that I had made in first class, I saw to my
amazement on the dockside Alex, Gerry and the Pixie. They were
clearly the worse for wear and were waving and yelling, with four
musicians behind them in dinner jackets playing their drunken hearts
out. Delighted as I was by the reception, in my embarrassment at being
watched by the entire crew of the Saxonia, plus the disembarking
passengers, I swept them into the nearest warehouse. We then proceeded
to their suite in the Adelphi, where we had lunch, mostly consisting of
bottles as far as I can remember.

Later on that afternoon I was anxious to get to London. Gerry had
passed out cold by that time, so I dashed round the hotel, armed with
his money, and got them to reserve a private compartment on the train.
Later, having explained that my friend was 'indisposed', two porters
wheeled out an unconscious Gerry on a luggage trolley.

The whole motley party, myself being well-watered by that time, arrived at the station where the process was repeated. I managed to find the reserved compartment, which was in the name of Gordon Hotels, the company which then owned the Adelphi, except that the labels got mixed up and the notice on the door was marked 'Reserved for Mrs Gordon'. I tipped everyone generously, drew the blinds swiftly, and explained to the conductor that we did not want to be disturbed as Mrs Gordon was not quite herself. The sobered-up party reached London, where we delivered 'Mrs Gordon' to 4 Harriet Walk, and I went on to Iver to Mama and Papa, who found me rather well, except that Mama said that my breath smelled like a brewer's bung.

On my return from the States I had hoped to find a job with Columbus O'Donnell's new supermarket venture, but it never got off the ground. In order not to have wasted my vast experience chopping meat, stacking baked bean tins, wrapping cheese and banging cash tills, I applied for a job as assistant marketing manager at the colourful and famous advertising agency of Coleman Prentice and Varley (CPV). The managing director of the agency, John Pearce, used to be my brother Alex's boss at Picture Post, thus I managed to shoehorn my way into the job. As the advertising business in those days was very freewheeling there did not seem to be a great problem. Either you pleased the client and sold his dodgy products in which case you were 'in' (with unchallenged expenses), or you were straight out into Grosvenor Street, back to public transport and 'ex- advertising' (which was not the greatest reference).

I soon realised that I had landed on a distinctly different business planet – one that very closely resembled the recent TV series of Mad Men. After a problem with one of my clients, I reported back to John, who had clearly had his first early morning refreshment – which equally clearly was not tea. He leant across the desk and looking straight at me with his steely eyes said, "Remember Vincent that you can't play chess with people who can't play chess." End of interview: useful advice absorbed and successfully put into immediate action.

At first I spent time learning the ropes in various departments, and at one point found myself sitting next to Jane, the account executive in charge of some of the main fashion accounts. I helped to look after the telephone and the main fashion client, Jaeger. At that stage

I knew nothing of the mechanics of the advertising business apart from sucking-up to the clients and trying to sober-up the creative departments to meet deadlines. I knew nothing of how blocks were made, layouts, or even the correct names for female garments.

Jane was in her late twenties and was having an affair with one of the copywriters: they were particularly randy and random. Mind you, the entire staff was engaged in a fair amount of sexual activity when they weren't drinking – it was amazing that there was enough time left over for the clients. Anyway the said copywriter swapped partners and ceased to assuage my colleague's appetite, with the result that she went missing with a temporary breakdown and then shoved off altogether.

As a result, I was sent for by Colonel Varley, the boss and owner of CPV, who told me to take over the Jaeger account. I gagged and told him that I was taken on for marketing and knew nothing about advertising, but he just waved a not quite steady hand (alcohol, not Parkinsons) and told me that neither did he when he started; that apparently for some reason the clients liked me and that the client was *always* right. I shrugged my shoulders and took the chance.

Initially all went well, and despite my ignorance I found myself as executive group head of the main fashion accounts. The plusses were compulsory attendance of fashion shows in London and Paris, increased salary and expenses, and access to the Executives' Bar which was free and very well attended from 5pm onwards – by which time most of us had sobered-up after client lunches. The fashion shows bored me – having no knowledge of actually dressing women, which I regarded as against nature – but the compensation was that the models were actually very attractive, and mostly with normal bodies (not the poor skeletons of today). Some were great fun, but I learned not to try anything funny, or serious for that matter. The client remember, always came first.

My advertising career accidentally lasted three fun years, before my lack of professional skills caught up with me and I was fired. This was done in a gentlemanly fashion: I was asked to transfer to the Rio de Janeiro office and to get there in three days. I got the message, and left, rather like applying for the Chiltern Hundreds seat in Parliament. This was the traditional CPV method of being 'let go'.

In the meantime, a few triumphs, the principal one being the Jaeger Christmas full colour back page in *Vogue* and *Harpers*. Colour blocks of that size took ages to make and it was not until late August that I realised that we had not commissioned it yet, and none of my useless staff had reminded me. At that stage Jaeger exclusively used the famous photographer Norman Parkinson, who cost a packet and was, like most great artists, somewhat tricky. It was to be a silver evening dress, as I remember, and I asked him if he could do the shot immediately, as we could just make the copy date by bribing the block-makers. To this he replied that it was out of the question as he was going to Haverford West, a tiny place on the western edge of Wales for his holiday and nothing would persuade him to change his plans. I told him that I would lose my job and CPV might lose the account after thirty odd years. He then said that it was really my problem – with a tremendous shrug that I could feel, even through the telephone. Desperate, I said that I would bring the whole crew right over there for the weekend if only he would click his finger and achieve the (unspoken) goddamn shot. All very well he said but there was only a beach there, and no other location. Desperately I said that that would do, and I would see him on Saturday morning.

I set off for Haverford West with the dress, the model, her dresser, my assistant, an umbrella-type Christmas tree and yards of reflecting silver paper in case of weak light. Saturday morning saw us standing by a silver Christmas tree planted in a sand castle on the beach. It was cold. There was no sun. No electricity or lights of course, and the shivering model was swathed in blankets. Parks was poised under a black awning with his camera. Hours later there was still no sun and the vodka flask was dry, but I had to admit that Parks was a real professional even if dead tricky. Finally after some interminable time had passed, the Welsh sun peeped out of the clouds for a few seconds. There were shrieks all round. I tore the blankets off the model while my assistants held the silver paper up. Two clicks later and the sun was gone. Parks shrugged and away he went to continue his holiday with a "Good Luck!" shouted over his departing shoulder. Well as luck would have it, the one pose was a wonderful picture and won the Leyton annual photography competition for a colour fashion shot. The result was a very satisfied client, endless trade presentations and yours truly for the first – and last – time an advertising hero. Needless to say, I did not dwell on the accidental issues involved. What a game it really was.

My Jaeger client was always demanding and looking for a new and exotic angle. The whole creative department were once put in a complete sweat when the client demanded something sensational for the launch of a new Jaeger cashmere sweater. I suppose today one would drape it on a sensational naked model, but that was before lap-dancing days and we had to think of something else. We also had to satisfy the professional vanity of Norman Parkinson. Then, after the fourth drink in the Executives' Bar – Eureka! What about 'Cashmere in Kashmir'? Brilliant, thought the client. Parks was ambivalent until he was tempted to fly to Kashmir with his wife as the model; all expenses paid of course. I will always remember the expenses bill by the item: 7 rupees for two packs of cigarettes, given as a tip to the goatherd... The whole shot consisting of a sunny hill, two goats, and a model wearing a cashmere sweater, could equally have been taken on the Sussex downs, or even a studio. As one of the layout fellows said, "So what's about Kashmir then?" to which I replied in a judicious undertone, "So what's about advertising then?"

My downhill path in the advertising business started when one of my clients, a national brand of stockings and underwear, insisted on a top review of the account, due partly to a few 'slips' such as a half page in *The Evening Standard* featuring last year's ad instead of this years. Oh, my efficient staff! Anyway the meeting was set up consisting of the directors responsible, heads of departments, head client executive (in the shape of a very nervous me), and of course the head of all: owner and genius Colonel Varley.

The client team all came down from the Midlands and proceeded up the broad steps of 34 Grosvenor Street to the boardroom on the first floor. The clients had been told that Varley had had a minor motoring accident but still hoped to make the meeting. In mid-staircase, the highly disappointed and unsatisfied clients were passed by Varley's chauffeur and the concierge, carrying a large rolled-up carpet. Out of one end peeped a pair of shoes and from the other end, the leonine head of the noble Colonel issuing sound alcoholic snores. The clients stared in amazement. "That can't be Colonel Varley surely?" they gasped. I replied, as if it were a common occurrence at 4.30pm, "I'm sorry to say, I didn't notice." There followed one of the more difficult meetings that I can remember, followed eventually by the loss of the account. This was not regarded as totally my fault, but the wrong half page in *The Evening*

Standard had already put me on the 'ready to move to South America' list.

One of the last unfortunate errors in my CPV career was when there was a panic for a colour drawing to be made overnight by the famous French artist Gruau, who had designed the original Jaeger typeface using three lines for each letter. Gruau lived in Paris, and I decided to sacrifice myself to go there personally to get the drawing executed. I cannot say that my sacrifice was entirely unconnected to the fact that my destination was neither Nottingham nor Manchester, where I had to occasionally go to view undergarments or children's shoes.

So off I set, having had the brilliant idea of inviting a girlfriend to accompany me and model the dress. The drawing was duly done, with me helping to pin the garment on the model, with slight shakes acquired as a result of a jolly nightlong exploration of the latest Parisian nightclubs and watering holes. We return to London in triumph, rushed it round to Jaeger, who agreed that it was indeed a sensational drawing, with perfect lines and colours. The only thing wrong with it was that the dress was on back to front. After a few four letter words, no more said. Not quite the last chapter, but definitely closer.

Another part of the closing chapter was with our clients Norvic Shoes, who made a vast series of less than glamorous, but highly practical, shoes for solid ladies and gentlemen, not to mention children, with a market mostly in the north of England. They had asked for an exciting promotion (for a change) but one that would not cost too much. After much thought and Scotch, I decided that we might have a better chance keeping the bloody shoes out of it. I decided on a competition to be run along very simple lines for all their shoe shop distributors, with glamorous prizes. I had thousands of leaflets printed and mailed out to the shops, but had overlooked my lack of knowledge of northern English argot. My headline ran, "The first prize in the Norvic competition is a fabulous weekend for two in Paris, the most romantic city in Europe. Your first night will start off with a sensational bang!" Etc. etc. I did not know the significance of what a 'bang' meant in the north, until I was advised that it meant what we southerners would describe as a 'fuck'. Hundredweights of leaflets were withdrawn at great expense, and another black mark in my book.

My final undoing was when I was given the 'Spirella' account. This company made corsets and bras for women who were much too well endowed both above and below, to wear the normal range of lingerie. They were sold through a vast army of part-time 'Spirella Corsetieres' by home calls, rather like Tupperware. The advertising problems were very prohibitive even for my fevered imagination and energy. Sadly the account – and my career – came to an abrupt halt after my assistant and I attended the annual Spirella fashion show in Welwyn Garden city.

There were about two hundred corsetieres there, no men of course, just us two unfortunates. We survived the first bra fitting, as an enormous lady thundered down the catwalk and the head corsetiere showed the audience how to tell a 'soft bosom' apart from a 'hard bosom'. The test was made by the corsetiere pressing her spread fingers on the bosom in question through a see-through length of muslin, which made it even more immodest. The fitter pressed hard, and the bosom started flowing between her fingers. She shouted, "Corsetieres! Is this hard or soft?" "Soft!" shouted the corsetieres in unison. This was followed by another giant corseted lady with bosoms reminiscent of a well-endowed Roman marble statue, on which the fitter nearly broke a finger, and to which there was no question of the answer: "Hard!"

The next scenario was my undoing. This time it was bras for women who had no chance of fitting into the largest sizes on normal sale. Out strode a lady named Brenda with the biggest tits I had ever seen, to some Wagnerian music on the loudspeaker, with a bra which must have been designed by the engineers who built the Forth Bridge. She twirled around at the end of the catwalk – at which for my luck I was in the front row – and the fitter shouted out, "Now bend over Brenda and show the corsetieres how safe your Spirella bra is." She did this right over me while I prayed that nothing would fall out and give me a black eye. She was then instructed to turn round and repeat the exercise, thus presenting me with the biggest corseted bottom I had yet had the privilege of seeing in my sheltered young life. The only thing I could do was to hope that she had not had baked beans for tea. At that moment my assistant George sitting behind me burst out with a serious explosion of church giggles. This was too much for me. In spite of sitting in the middle of the Executive's row, I started shaking uncontrollably, with tears pouring down my face. On the way out the advertising director just said to me that it was highly unfortunate and totally out of place that I found it so amusing. It was then that I sensed that it was goodbye to the client, and my three-year career of skating on thin ice. So, when Colonel Varley sent for me on Monday and told me to report to the Rio office by Thursday, I bowed out gracefully, my pride and self esteem intact.

I did miss the job, in spite of the client pressure and constant struggles with the creative department and so on. The people I worked with were mostly fun – if a trifle bitchy – not to say ruthless. One of the main things I missed was the free bar (run for the department heads), which was open until very late in the afternoon. There must have been a canteen of sorts but I can't remember it, probably due to the free bar. As far as alcohol consumption was concerned it must have been a photofinish between advertising agencies and Fleet Street, CPV being the undoubted leader in the consumption stakes.

From East Bronx to El Morroco

CHAPTER SIX
Wolfskin Coats and Crocodile Shoes

ONE OF MY closest companions, ever since meeting him at Downside, is Gerry Albertini. Although he is younger than me, he left Downside at the same time after a disagreement with the school authorities over a bookmaking venture. Not being obliged to work due to his ancestor's success in rail transport in southern America, he was able to indulge in all the natural pleasures of life somewhat earlier than his academic or working friends. While most of his contemporaries were confining themselves to tennis and ping-pong during the hols, Gerry managed to indulge in more absorbing pleasures.

When challenged about any element of his eccentric behaviour Gerry would always retort, "What would you expect? I was on a train to Nice at the age of three months with my mother and nanny. When they got off the train they found me missing. Nanny, no doubt suffering from the contents of one of the bottles in the baby's bag – not milk certainly – had overlooked to unload me from the luggage net above the window. So I had continued my journey, asleep, to Monte Carlo, where I was removed from the train by the station master."

Gerry's mother, Nora Reynolds Veitch, lived in White Lodge
in Richmond Park, now the National Ballet school HQ. She had
remarried after the death of Gerry's father to the splendid one-legged
survivor of World War One, Jim Veitch. During the Second World
War he was commander of the Ascot Racecourse Internment Camp
for enemy civilians, spies, cranks etc. I knew one of the inmates quite
well, who called it Ascot Concentration Camp, so I had two sides
of the story. My prisoner friend, the owner of important estates,
having fought bravely as a British officer in the First World War, had
become rather eccentric in worshipping the Nazi Party and Hitler,
pictures of whom decorated his country seat. He had to be put away
for the duration as he would have been quite capable of hanging a
swastika from one of the chimneys. I told Jim, the commander of the
'concentration camp' that he must have been quite a tricky prisoner, to
which he replied "You said it," with a sigh, sipping a large drink, which
in fact represented his main retirement occupation.

The rules at White Lodge were quite plain. No noise till 4pm,
when Nora woke: hence no vacuum cleaners, only silent brushes until
then. Those were the only restrictions: the rest consisted of wonderful
entertainment, oceans of drink and lots of animals including various
birds, and a wandering chimpanzee whose name escapes me.

On one occasion the imperturbable butler, Taylor, approached
Nora during a large dinner party. She turned round, surprised to be
interrupted in the middle of the main course. Taylor then declared,
"Madam, the ape has stabbed me," and fell down in a theatrical faint,
showing that the chimpanzee who was very playful had indeed stabbed
him in the back with a butter knife, but fortunately with more damage
to his tail coat than to him.

Some other memorable members of the staff were Albert the
footman who used to lend money to Gerry at 20% per week. He was
subsequently repaid by Gerry who used to pawn some of the family
silver that was not on display. John Cruden the chauffeur was also very
powerful in the whole ménage and always went to the south of France
to Cap D'Antibes with Taylor. We adored the dinners at White Lodge
and were always driven back to London full of booze.

Another eccentric resident of a wing of White Lodge was Nora's
sister Madge, who had a great weakness for strong drink and as a result

normally kept to her wing from whence one heard the continual clinking of empty gin bottles, which for some reason were kept in her bathroom. Why, I cannot think, as there was total acceptance of alcoholic beverages throughout the establishment, both by the owners and staff.

Not long after Gerry was born, Madge decided to marry, much to everyone's amazement. After the wedding celebrations in White Lodge, the happy couple were driven away by the chauffeur in the Rolls for the honeymoon. At 3am the next morning she rang her sister and asked Nora to send for her. On being questioned why, she moaned quietly, "I don't like it. I want to come home." Whether it was the fact that friends had loosened the screws of her marital bed – sending her sprawling – or something else equally traumatic, history does not relate. However, on return she settled down happily in the 'clinking' wing until she was finally gathered to the 'heavenly Gordons'.

Nora rented a fabulous villa by the sea at Cap D'Antibes in the south of France, where she repaired for the summer season and where Gerry used to invite my brother Alex and I out for our holidays. The first time I flew there, I was asked to bring out a spare false leg for our host Jim, as he'd had a gin-assisted trip, and had broken the other one. I arrived at Nice airport with the leg in a large croquet set box, and was stopped and inspected by Customs. They tried to charge me a vast sum of duty on it, as it was very elaborate, with knee breaks and so on. I said that it was not a present as I already had a box of chocolates, but it was for my host who, poor man, was missing a leg and anxiously waiting for this one. Answer, big French shrug and further demands for money. I said that I did not have the money anyway and could hardly arrive without the leg. A long confrontation ensued, during which I asked them, why, if they were charging duty on his legs, weren't they charging duty on my legs? After this logical but unanswerable question they finally gave in, and I was able to present my legless host with his other leg.

When I went down to the sea to swim the next morning, I had a fit seeing a leg sticking out of the rocks in stocking, garters and smart shoe, but no body, until I remembered my trip of the evening before and realised that Jim was having a swim.

Alex and I shared a room there and one night, after a rather unsuccessful session at the casino, Gerry and I decided to go home. I remember we had to leave our watches with the doorman to enable us to borrow the taxi fare (it was still early days, and 'Golden Boy Albertini' had not as yet established his world-wide casino credits). We had met up with Nada Milford Haven there and she and Alex, having spent more time at the bar than the roulette table, decided to conclude the night at the infamous Blue Bar. Upon being woken the next morning by the famous Taylor, with the breakfast tray, I realised that Alex had not made it home the night before. This still being my early days with that splendid family, I rather nervously said to Taylor that he had better not mention to Madam that Master Alex had slept out, as I was not quite sure what the reaction would be. Taylor's response, dressed in a morning suit, regardless of climate, drew himself up and with an impenetrable expression, said "I assure you sir, Madam would not mind if Master Alex had slept with a dead policeman." Then he glided silently out of the room.

On another visit, when I was met at the airport by John the chauffeur, I asked him how things were up at the villa. He replied that I might find things a little quiet for the next couple of days, as the night before the house party had been rudely disturbed by the sound of Gerry stark naked, chasing a large and very attractive girl, also naked, round the lawn in the pouring rain. Apparently she was shouting "It's too wet Gerry – too wet." Whatever may or may not have happened during the precipitation, she became a good friend of ours and made a very happy and grand marriage in the years to come.

Talking about the South of France, I am reminded of a splendid incident recounted to me by Nora. After the war, she was taken to see an ageing Frenchman living in a magnificent villa in Cannes, overlooking the sea. On entering the drawing room she noticed a highly polished piece of ebony, more or less in the shape of a banana, mounted on a silver stand on the mantelpiece. Noticing her glance, the old boy stroked it lovingly and said, "Madame, do you know that this object paid for the whole of this villa?" Apparently in his prime he was what was known as a 'taxi dancer'. This meant that he was in a group of handsome men ('gigolos') who attended one of the cafés where ladies – usually rich, bored ones, of various ages – came for *thé dansants* where these gentlemen would dance with the ladies – two steps, waltzes and tangos – to the accompaniment of a string orchestra, in return for a discreet tip at the conclusion, when the faintly elated ladies would return to their tea and cakes. The old boy in question added to his appeal by carrying the said piece of ebony in his pocket, thus increasing the 'elation', leading to a more generous tip, and possibly a *paso doble* later in the evening, thus adding the odd brick or two to his villa.

SO, IT WAS with Gerry I stayed while I was working in the advertising game at CPV. We lived a colourful life at his mews house in Harriet Walk. I paid towards the rent and ran the housekeeping, which mainly consisted of ringing the wine merchants. I shall never forget a joke Gerry played on me there. Leaving for work one day, while Gerry was sleeping-off the previous night, assisted by one or other of his bevy of female acquaintances, I woke him to say that he was running out of champagne and that I was catching a train, and he had better get off his arse and ring Berry Bros for some more. This he grumblingly did, but must have confused his speech, a usual hazard at that time of day. The result was that the man at Berry Bros mistook what was meant to be six dozen, for sixty dozen. I was away for the night, and in my absence a lorry arrived with sixty cases of champagne. The house was tiny, with nowhere to store that quantity of champagne, but Gerry, instead of sending it back, had the amusing (to him) idea of storing it in my tiny bedroom. When I returned, all I could find was an Egyptian-style Sarcophagus with a tiny tunnel leading to my bed and Gerry and his merry followers wetting themselves with laughter. I took my revenge by ringing up all our chums in London to come round and help me by drinking our way through to my dressing table and wardrobe. Some party, I must say, but after a thousand swallows, I finally got through to my shirts.

Apart from stumbling on the odd champagne cork, what passed for normality at 4 Harriet Walk was resumed. The usual visitors came to help Gerry fill his bath, give him shaky tips and put on his bets. Two regulars spring to mind, 'The Colonel' and 'The Vicar', neither of whom I believe had actually been connected with either the army or the church, but somehow the soubriquets suited them and stuck. The Vicar was the most original and marginally more sober of the two. He was a great betting man, and originally connected with the early *Chemin de Fer* parties of which eventually John Aspinall was the tsar. One day Gerry and the Vicar were in one of their favourite morning watering holes, namely the bar of the Sloane Court Hotel. They were duly lowering powerful drinks and playing liar dice on the bar. Gerry then admired the Vicar's rather splendid – if a trifle flashy – crocodile skin shoes. "Yes," said the Vicar, "they are made of banana-fed baby crocodiles." The game continued with Gerry winning everything. The Vicar having lost all his ready cash challenged Gerry to a double or quits, naming his shoes as his stake. The dice were thrown and Gerry won, upon which the Vicar slowly took his shoes off, put them on the bar, and marched out in the pouring rain into Sloane Square, muttering ginny imprecations as he walked through the deep puddles. Gerry has the banana-fed crocodile shoes to this day.

When the Almighty was finally about to gather the Vicar, Gerry went to see him, and the dying Vicar motioned Gerry's ear close to his mouth. Gerry was expecting possibly a few sacred confessions before his demise, upon which the Vicar murmured in a hoarse, dying whisper, "Remember Gerry, life is just a fucking game – a game – but you've got to win the bugger." Perhaps not the most elegant dying words, but maybe not the most incorrect ones either.

Eventually Harriet Walk came to an end and has been rebuilt. I wonder what ghosts may wander there? I remember the house opposite had a rather gay butler who was heard clucking his tongue saying, "Quite disgusting... all them girls going in and out of there, and some of them naked and all." I hasten to add that much of this exotic traffic was due to my friend, as I was obliged to preserve most of my energies for my work – not an occupation that 'Dear G', as I called him, ever sullied himself with.

I remember when Gerry started collecting vintage cars before his cash flow was somewhat reduced by London's gambling fraternity. One day I went with him to collect a Hispano-Suiza, which had been specially built for André Dubonnet for the Targa Florio race in 1924. It was a splendid car, the enormous carriage of which was made entirely of tulipwood planking, like a yacht. It was an open two-seater with gears and brake outside the chassis. Having bought it off some country gent, for at that time an immense amount of money, we cranked it up and stopped at a remote village petrol station with those old see-through glass tanks, and a hand-operated pump. An ancient man commenced pumping, and went on and on. Having got to forty gallons he gave up with a puzzled look, and got on hands and knees to look for the leak, but we discovered that it held 65 gallons! Gerry had great fun with it, and one year had it driven to the South of France where it proved to have greater bird-pulling power than any open Bentley two-seater.

The good times suddenly ended for dear Gerry when he was called up for temporary conscription in the American Airforce (he is a US citizen). I was not able to follow his Air Force career too closely from that distance, but gathered that due to his faintly eccentric attitude to life, and polished English accent, it was somewhat chequered. I believe he was in the intelligence section (a choice I had to question) and made Corporal twice, with an interval in the Air Force 'cooler' of three months where the poor chap had a very rough time, and as a result has not been in jail since. From memory his rest behind bars was due to a fracas over a girl in a nightclub that ended in Gerry taking a swing at a military policeman – not a very wise move.

After all this, when he was stationed in Germany, I joined him in Frankfurt on a weekend leave. After twenty-four hours of combing through the less salubrious establishments of Frankfurt-am-Main, Gerry took it into his head to show me one of his favourite bars that he used to frequent in Bremen. I happily agreed – not knowing then where Bremen might be – but we got into a taxi and said 'Bremen'. As Bremen happened to be about 330 kilometres away, the driver retorted, "Are you drunk?" to which Gerry replied, "Of course, naturally" and waved a giant roll of notes. After some hours and a miraculous kip in the back of the taxi, we got out at a very drab and dodgy dockside bar, which held many happy, and I imagine somewhat sordid memories for my friend when he was stationed in Bremen.

I was desperate for something to eat, but Gerry was only interested in liquids. Fortunately while drinking at the bar, I managed to buy a giant German wurst and commenced wolfing it down in its cardboard holder, and enjoyed it immensely until I realized that I was crammed up to a sailor who was enjoying, in the full sense of the word, a girl leaning up against the bar. I am told that that particular position is known in Liverpool as a 'knee trembler'. I imagine it must be a port speciality of some kind. Anyway it was enough to put me off my sausage and I dragged Gerry off to a more salubrious establishment, which to say the least was not too difficult to find.

Then continued our usual thorough research into what Bremen had to offer in the way of nightlife. Short answer – plenty. Finally, towards dawn I said that I had had enough of everything except proper sleep for the last 48 hours, and insisted on checking into some half-star hotel that was not too fussy about accepting two totally luggageless drunks into their hallowed premises at 7am. Eventually I woke up, and found to my amazement that I was sharing a bed with an Air Force corporal – who I finally realized was Gerry in his regulation underwear and socks. As I paid the bill, which was very modest, the proprietor said, "That will be ten marks (or whatever it was), but as this man," he continued, eyeing up Gerry, "slept with you, that will be ten percent more."

We then headed for the airport buying a case of 'Steinhager' – a particularly strong schnapps – which we had rather taken to during the night's festivities. We checked it in instead of luggage (of which we had none), and flew to renew acquaintance with our toothbrushes in Frankfurt. When finally leaving that city and having a farewell sip with my friend in a bar near the station at 7am, I clearly remember a girl sitting opposite with green hair, green nails, a short green skirt (showing not too much evidence of underwear), sipping a glass of green Crème de Menthe, trying to attract our attention. Genug! Enough! I cried and dashed off to England to spend a few days at a Lyons Tea House. The Priory had not yet opened in those days.

Travel with Gerry was always eventful, but fun for the most part. I accompanied him to New York once to help him with some legal problem. He had just bought an amazing long wolfskin overcoat at the 'Way In' (which had just opened on the top floor of Harrods, retailing the couture version of Carnaby Street's 'with it' clothes). I told him that there was no way I was going to travel with him wearing that ridiculous outfit. Fortunately, although it was late October, it turned out to be a very hot day and he was forced to carry it on his arm. Duly seated on British Airways first class, Gerry put the coat on the seat beside him, got the backgammon board out and we started to play. Along came one of the camp flight stewards to take our order. He glanced at the amazing coat rolled up in an empty seat across the aisle and lisped, "And shall I get it a saucer of milk sir?" I had a fit of the giggles, but my friend was not amused, and commenced losing at backgammon, which did not improve his mood.

IN THE FIFTIES London was finally getting over the gloom and shortages of the war. While not forgetting the horror, the bombing, the missing and wounded family and friends, people were finally able to get on with life. This was the time leading up to the swinging sixties, Carnaby Street and so on. Casual sex under war conditions was replaced by reasonably well set-up establishments offering a mouth-watering selection of ladies who in turn offered comfort, discretion and enthusiastic pleasure. There was an establishment called 'Buntys' where I was compelled (naturally) to accompany friends from time to time. Bunty, a splendid lady who lived in a mansion-flat would receive us in a velour housecoat (not always totally closed) and a cup of tea in hand, closely followed by a ginger tabby cat.

After a warm welcome over tea or a shaky sherry, financial arrangements would be made. Oh, those were the days! The joy people got for the cost of a dry martini. The girls were introduced, and most of them were amateurs, just trying to make some money on the side, which made the whole thing seem somehow more pleasant and civilized. Bunty herself took great pleasure and interest in the activities, and tended, cup of tea in hand and pussy behind, to 'accidentally' open the door of a bedroom a crack, "tut tut" rather loudly, murmur, "Oh dear, what fun, pardon me" and pass on, smacking her lips.

The most popular girl there was Renee – a great goer – and in discussing her with Bunty she said, "Really, Renee does enjoy it so. It seems a crime that she charges, and you will be interested to hear, my dear, that she is a Brigadier's daughter." The information about Renee's social standing did not particularly arouse me, but it slightly amazed me that English snobbery extended to sex. "Mais toût le monde à son choix," I thought with a continental shrug of the shoulders.

There was also a very well-known and classy establishment run by Mrs Featherstone-Hoare – known as 'Feathers' – much patronised by my friends, which also employed some amateurs. There was one famous occasion where a friend of mine met his sister on the stairs, much to his amazement.

At one time I was sharing a flat with some chums, one of whom, a trifle pompous, was a young Guard's officer who used to go off to Feathers every Tuesday evening. When I queried him as to why he was so regular about his sex life, he replied that he was regular about everything. He continued by saying that the great thing about Feathers was, "that one is received in a proper drawing room and given a glass of sherry – which is included in the fiver – and some of the girls are actually ladies." I silently thought to myself how lucky for him that they weren't men.

Apart from these sorts of establishments, there were a number of nightclubs with hostesses whose favours extended beyond a handshake and discussion about the weather. Two of the best known were the Bag of Nails behind Regent Street, and the Stork Club in Swallow Street. The Bag was a bit rough and ready, but much favoured by my army friends, especially for bachelor parties. The Stork was owned and run by Al Burnett, who had some kind of entertainment background. It was packed with girls and very jolly. When things got a bit quiet, and the cabaret girls on the stage were getting a bit too tired to switch their ostrich feather fans the full ninety degrees demanded by the law, Al Burnett would take to the stage to encourage the company to partake of the questionable products of the establishment's cuisine, shouting, "Order your food now, Ladies and Gents, from our renowned kitchen! The food here is untouched by human hands, we only employ gorillas."

The headwaiter was called Pip and was mainly occupied as the procurer. He would approach a well-oiled patron and say, "Good evening 'Mr X' or 'Lord Y', we have a new girl tonight, barely seventeen and never been touched." Most likely the patron would wake up in the morning (the girls were all outpatients) and realise that without makeup the 'girl' was well past seventeen and clearly already possessed a PhD in sex.

Many jolly evenings at this club came to a temporary end for us when we were banned for a year. It all started when Gerry Albertini, brother Alex and I popped in for a gentle mouthwash late one night after the Star Pub, one of Gerry's favourite watering holes had closed. While standing, waiting to be seated, a small man started shouting at

Gerry, who told him to shut up, upon which his even smaller companion took a swing at Gerry saying quite correctly that Gerry was standing on his companion's foot – a fact that Gerry was clearly at that stage unaware of. Gerry's answer was to pick the small man up and hurl him across the room towards a table for six, which caused glasses, bottles and ashtrays to shower the neighbouring tables. The net result was a general affray with people throwing things at other tables, which they thought had been thrown at them. The tired fan-dancers on stage fled screaming, and I, the innocent one, was carried out by four waiters with my feet not touching the ground. Pausing by the entrance I saw one of the original short men and, in an alcoholic stupor, seized his hand to shake it and apologise for my friend's misunderstanding. Whilst doing so, his colleague behind me grabbed a gin bottle and tried to break it on my head. I passed out and woke up lying on the pavement of Swallow Street with Gerry shouting for an ambulance. The Stork, having thrown us out, and it being a tough establishment, sent a waiter out with a hastily scrawled bill for damages demanding for 'Mr. A.' to settle up. Upon which Gerry picked up the waiter and threw him through the swing door, bill and all, and he went crashing into the cloakroom partition. I later recollected being stitched-up in Charing Cross Hospital.

For the record, and despite all this palaver, Gerry became one of London's more famous playboys, described as 'Golden Boy Albertini' in the gossip columns.

The next day I had an unbelievably sore head and was unable to open my mouth. However youth will out and I joined Gerry's party at the greyhound stadium in White City where I drank through a straw. Another nightclub ban followed which, after about a year, was duly annulled with cash and we were welcomed back with a jolly evening.

The two most chic and respectable nightclubs were the Four Hundred in Leicester Square, and the Milroy in Park Lane. The Four Hundred was the more sedate of the two with good after-theatre food and the band 'Tim Clayton' who would play certain important and frequent patron's signature tunes on their entry. As a French friend of mine said, "Je trouve tout ça très Anglais," referring to certain husbands and wives sitting at separate tables in the company of a lover, quite ignoring each other, and continuing a happy marriage in daylight hours.

I remember a hilarious incident when Aileen Plunkett who was much prone to practical jokes, replaced a young man's smoked salmon with a Dutch cap. The poor fellow, on returning from the dance floor, tried unsuccessfully to cut it up in the dark. The Milroy was a bit more 'nightclubby' but still patronised by royalty, and dark enough to be mistaken as quite proper. The band was led by a very smooth character called Paul Adam, who was away from his podium half the time, chatting up the lady patrons. In a famous case taken against him for dereliction of duty, he described his behaviour with the ladies as 'projecting his personality' whereas it was obvious he was just trying to get into their knickers.

Another famous establishment was the Casanova Club occupying a house in Grosvenor Street, and owned by one Rico Dajou. He was a small, fat Romanian with licked-over strands of hair on a bald pate. His usual greeting line was, "Pity, you should have-a been here last night. It was-a Princess Margaret here, and the Duke of ... Tonight it's only Chews." This spoken loudly, offended the said 'Chews' and the other patrons who did not want to be taken for Hampstead residents.

One night I shall never forget, I went there with brother Alex, very much the worse for wear by that time, and King Michael of Romania. Alex just about made it to the top of the stairs, clinging to the bannisters, followed by an embarrassed King Michael, and a young me behind. A new waiter who did not know Alex stopped him at the top of the stairs, asking him whether he was a member. Alex, unable to reply due to his intake, paused, clinging on to the banisters with both hands, with King Michael by now even more embarrassed standing to attention behind him. Suddenly Rico Dajou standing in the middle of the restaurant spied *his* king amongst our small group whom the waiter was holding up. He kicked the waiter very hard on the shin and shouted, "Get out you cunt, ees Keengs comeeng!" much to the embarrassment and amazement of the diners.

The last incident I remember about Rico was when I was in the ground floor bar at the Casanova at midday with a friend, the bar being empty apart from a rather middle-aged American couple who had probably strolled round from Claridges. In rushed Rico, who had clearly already had his mid-morning mouthwash. He had another, and then launched into a very loud description of a woman he had met in the bar the day before. "It vas-a dis woman, I tell you Vincent," he panted as his tongue slid out left and right, liberally dispensing spittle. "She had a mouth like a ripe mango, a neck like a zvan, I tell you." The bar was silent except for his ranting, and the American couple's eyes were on stalks. In a final crescendo of spit Rico waved his cupped hands and shouted, "It vas breasts standing like roksh," at which point the couple quietly slid out, as the wife seized her no longer somnolent husband by his sleeve, with a murmured, "Come along dear."

AT THAT TIME, as well as working at CPV during the day, I also took it upon myself by night to run a restaurant come nightclub, called 'Chez Sophie', or 'The Green Street Club'. As I remember, we were not too fussy about the membership qualifications, and I cannot remember anyone being blackballed at the door so long as they had cash on them (this was before credit cards came into their own). It was a Polish establishment run by Sophie Terne, a diminutive cabaret singer from pre-war Warsaw with considerable voice and humour, not to mention not-inconsiderable age. Her partner both financial and carnal was an immense Pole called Stas Mikula with tremendous alcoholic and sexual appetites.

I frequented it with pleasure, but it was only doing well at weekends, as the Polish community at that time consisted mostly of Poles who were not very well off and lived in the suburbs. On being informed by them that they were thinking of closing, I told them they were mad, as it was such a fun place. They then made me a 33% partner for nothing on the spot in the hope of me filling it, and boy did I fill it!

We installed a wonderful Canadian pianist who played non-stop for the dancers and for Sophie's cabaret also. He must have had immense energy for all that, but was a tricky bastard. He would stop in mid-dance, or song, on the stroke of midnight, extend his hand and demand cash to continue for a couple of hours. Needless to say he got it, and probably deserved it, but this public demand for money I felt lowered the tone of the establishment – although by that time of night, together with the endless vodkas, I doubt if any of our patrons would have noticed or cared, especially if Harry Hambleden was executing his Cossack dancing on the table with glasses flying. My brother Alex would often come, and occasionally had to be carried out. It was the sort of place you took your girlfriend, rather than your fiancée.

The atmosphere was always tremendous; it was in the basement with two rooms consisting of a bar, restaurant and a small intimate dance floor. There would have been no room for modern dancing, but only for old-fashioned body hugging two steps (or no step). Sadly the takings were not too good, as most of my friends signed their bills and failed to pay, claiming they could not remember their presence, or recognize their signature – both quite reasonable I thought, as unfortunately I was usually in the same state.

The food was atrocious, produced by a drunk Polish chef, who used to steal raw fillet steaks by strapping them to his leg, under his trousers, and then flogging them at half price the next day to some other establishment. The headwaiter was a wonderful character called Alphonse, a Frenchman of North Algerian extraction – a great wit, who managed to keep the tables so dark that people could not see what they were eating.

My grandmother, on her only excursion for dinner there (her idea, not mine), said staring at her dark plate, "I cannot see anything," upon which Alphonse replied, "In that case you are lucky Madame." I remember going to the pantry once before dinner, looking for Alphonse, and found him sitting on a chair clad only in vest and shoes, balancing the chef's daughter, wearing even less, on his lap. When I asked him what the hell he thought he was doing, even though I must admit it was pretty obvious, he replied, "Don't worry Monsieur Vincent, it won't take long." (Ça se fait très vite).

Among other memorable, but disturbing events, was when we were raided by the police, and had up for 'serving drinks after hours'. It turned out that my partners had thoughtfully put the licence in my name, but equally thoughtfully had forgotten to mention it to me. I had to duly turn up at the Marlborough Street Magistrates Court. Great discussion went on as to what I should wear. Not too toff-like, nor quite resembling a tzigane bartender. I forget what the final choice was, but I duly attended with apprehension, and totally unnecessarily accompanied by a number of noisy friends, who came for the show. Due to my powers of persuasion (or was it my bullshit?) we did not lose our licence, and the fine was light. However, to this day I imagine I must be on police records, but mercifully not for theft, or paedophilia.

Eventually I resigned, as in spite of youth and strength, the lack of sleep was beginning to show, both in the takings at the club, and the satisfaction of the daytime clients at CPV. I left with regrets on both sides, but continued to patronise it as if it still belonged to me, but was careful never to eat anything else other than fried eggs and bacon, knowing that even a tipsy Polish chef could not muck that up, and the contents being of no great value would have been unlikely to have been strapped to his legs.

The main reason for my lateness leaving that splendid establishment, apart from the company of a very attractive fellow Polish lady who ran the bar, was the leftovers. By that I mean the girlfriend, or wife, of a patron who had had a row and departed leaving her in tears. Being of a kind nature, I tended to join the damsel in distress, put my arm round her sobbing shoulders, order a bottle of champagne (which in common with many of the other patrons I tended to forget to pay for) and duly console her into the early hours.

ONE OF THE most amusing incidents in my brother's colourful, but faintly debauched life (hence the poor, divine man paying a severe penalty by dying at the age of forty-one, having overtaxed his liver with a final bottle of champagne), took place at a party in his flat in Lennox Gardens. He and his pretty and very colourful Polish wife Basia, were concluding a 'trzy dniuwka' party, which translates into a 'three dayer'. They had been all over the place, God knows where, and were concluding at about 9.30am, just after I had called in on some errand. There was still a hell of a party going on, and the place was full of people – some of whom they knew – in various states of sobriety, happily opening bottles. As my brother used to say, the good thing about a hangover is that it can always be postponed by having another drink. There was a Hungarian band in colourful jackets, pissed as newts, who had been picked up in a Knightsbridge club at closing time. They were leaning over a reclining Basia who had a champagne glass in hand, raised over her partially open white silk blouse (to let in the air, she said), sawing away on their violins with Hungarian gusto. I stopped to take in the amazing scene, but could not see Alex. I finally found him in the hall, lying on the floor, completely passed out. At that point the front door bell rang, and Basia passed me, blouse flying, to turn away what she must have thought was a gatecrasher. Instead there stood a uniformed collector from the London Electricity Board, holding his bike, and clipboard. Slightly taken aback, the poor man asked whether Mr Poklewski Koziell lived here, because the electricity bill had not been paid for months, and he had come to cut it off. Basia replied, "Yes, he does the bastard – I am housekeeper and he does not pay me either." "Sorry," said he, "But I have a job to do."

She swept him in, both of them stepping over the prone body of the electricity board's debtor, into the drawing room where the Hungarian band were entertaining the Bacchanalian orgy. Too shaken to open his mouth, he was sat down by Basia, who called for the band to serenade him while opening a bottle of the dreaded strong Hungarian 'Bulls Blood'. He refused her drink, saying "No thank you, I only take a little beer at weekends, and in any case it's a bit early for me." Basia replied, "Nonsense!" as she tipped a tumbler down his throat to the sound of a *chardash* echoing round his head. Several tumblers later, he became somewhat maudlin, and held her hand telling her that he was so sorry about her working conditions. He went on to say that he'd had this unpleasant job – of cutting people off – for some years and no one had ever offered so much as a cup of tea, until today. He then concluded by thanking her profusely for his amazing treatment, and told her not to worry as he would remove the file altogether and that they would never get a bill again. He was then kissed and embraced warmly in thanks by Basia, and escorted to the front door, followed by the violins in full flood, stepping over 'the bastard's' body on the way. He was last seen wheeling his bike, which he was quite incapable of riding, weaving his way down Lennox Gardens.

One of Alex's last memorable gestures was when he waved down a taxi on the opposite side of Oxford Street to the main entrance of Selfridges and asked to be driven to Selfridges. The cab driver said, "You're here already Guv," pointing across the road. Alex then explained that he felt unable at that hour of the morning to negotiate the Oxford Street traffic, and would he take him there all the same, which the driver duly did, no doubt murmuring, "You do get some queer types in this job…"

GERRY'S BACHELOR PARTY, before he married Laurel Heath, had to be the bachelor party of all bachelor parties. In retrospect it was not unlike some of today's footballers' parties, which are much frowned on, but possibly better planned as none of us were actually arrested. Now I come to think of it we were exactly eleven, a full football team, all close friends of Gerry's, including myself as best man, brother Alex, our mutual friend Casimir Stamirski, Paddy Kennedy (the landlord of the Star pub) and other colourful characters.

We set off from Heathrow to stay in a most luxurious hotel in Barcelona. Everyone was rooting for Paris, but I banned that, as knowing the explosive possibilities of that crowd, I refused to go to a city which I visited frequently and where I might be recognised. On arrival, we booked the best brothel in Barcelona – the Villa Montse – for our sole use, and in case the information might have been incorrect, it was decided to send a scout in the afternoon to test the goods. Casimir, who was the only fluent Spanish speaker among us, and who adored organising, volunteered to go, but as his speciality and tendencies were not women, it was decided that he could not be entirely relied upon for this particular task. After a well-lubricated team meeting, the task was entrusted to my well-experienced ruè brother Alex. He duly went off to do his reconnaissance, and returned in the early evening looking like a spent salmon, informing us that the establishment was indeed excellent and capable of dealing with the entire team, to its entire satisfaction.

An immense, especially-ordered dinner followed accompanied by the continual popping of corks like a Dom Pérignon machine gun. We duly piled into cabs and headed for the brothel. On arrival we were ushered into a waiting room full of stout Spanish gentlemen patiently waiting, legs crossed, reading the newspapers. It was quite clear to me, and some of the others, that the 'Madame' had lied about the exclusivity of the booking. The thought and look of the queue put our more choosy group off, and we parted full of indignation and Dom Pérignon burps for the bars and nightclubs of the city. The remainder – less fastidious or less anaesthetised – stayed and apparently much enjoyed a night of sexual flamenco. I remember returning to the room I was sharing with one of the latter at about 5am to find him perched on the bidet with a worried face pouring a bottle of Fundador brandy into it. I said surely it was intended for a different part of the body, i.e. the mouth, but he said that he was taking precautions against Spanish crabs. I was rather grateful that I had confined myself to the dressed variety at dinner.

When the festivities finally wound-up in a flurry of tickets mislaid and monumental hangovers, the working class, which included me, headed back to London by plane, but the bridegroom, accompanied by Alex and possibly one other decided to continue the party by rail, God knows or remembers where, while we had to report to the waiting bride-to-be that her beloved had given us the slip. She was highly displeased to say the least, and when they finally appeared in London three days later, there were some unpleasant scenes, which I had wisely decided to absent myself from, until the forthcoming marriage got them glued together again.

MY OWN FIRST marriage was to Natalie Potocka, a descendant of one of the leading Polish families. It was 1958 and I was twenty-six at the time, head-over-heels in love, and totally possessed by her. It was the sort of thing that happens to lads of eighteen these days, and perhaps it's a case of the longer you wait the further you fall – who knows?

Natalie was my age and the greatest of fun. She was very attractive, sexy and amusing, plus being Polish and multi-lingual. We married against everybody's advice: family and friends. They all loved her company but made it quite clear that, "the lady was not for marrying." I stubbornly went against the tide, and subsequently paid for it. When everyone says the same thing without exception, they are usually right.

Let's just say that after one year of turmoil, madness and troubles, as well as my wife's tendency to be unable to confine herself to the marital bed, I decided to end it. In retrospect, I have nothing against her, and in fact felt sorry for her as she really had no chance in life. She since died some years ago and may she rest in peace.

As happens in life, moments of tragedy and drama are sometimes accompanied by hilarity: such was our divorce. In those days, gentlemen, of whom I counted myself one – even on marginally shaky grounds – were always expected to be the guilty party. Although I was certainly not the guilty party, I had to agree to give evidence of adultery. Through the services of her lawyer – I suspect a member of her club of admirers – I was provided with a lady whose profession was to participate in these divorce charades.

Thus, on a particularly hot August night, I had arranged to meet the lady in the Ritz bar. I chose a Saturday, knowing it would be pretty empty and I was unlikely to meet any acquaintances. We had not met each other so she told me that she would be wearing a red carnation. I waited at the appointed hour, watched with interest by Edward the barman, when in came a lady holding a carnation on a long stem with a distinct droop to it, waving it in front of her like a semaphore signal. I bought us both drinks, very strong ones I remember, and being a gent I swept her off to dinner at the small Wheelers restaurant, off Jermyn Street.

We had quite a normal conversation: she was not a tart, not particularly attractive, but reasonably dressed. She explained that she was a teacher, without disclosing exactly what she taught, but that she topped-up her income with this particular service. We finished dinner and the dreaded moment arrived. We had to be witnessed entering an apartment at number three Green Street, over the club 'Chez Sophie', by two detectives who had to take pictures. I had arranged to have two bedrooms so as not to increase the agony, and after some final large slurps, I ushered her into one room and escaped into the other. In the middle of the night I was awoken by the sound of a foot being dragged across the floor (the woman was unfortunately handicapped with a club foot). She entered my room and I sat bolt upright and asked her what she wanted, to which she replied, "As you have paid for it, do you want it?" Impressed as I was by her honesty, I declined her services pleading the heat of the night and the amount of drink consumed. She did not appear to mind, and may well have been relieved. The next morning, at the appointed hour, we were photographed hand-in-hand leaving the apartment by the private detectives. End of story, and a divorce certificate marked 'adultery with a woman unknown'.

1 ▲ 3 ▼   2 ▲ 4 ▼

104

5 ▲ 7 ▼   6 ▲

1. Vincent's father Alfons (Alik) and Maniuta Poklewski Koziell, circa 1895
2. Alik Poklewski Koziell, his sister Maniuta and youngest brother Stas
3. Vincent's grandmother, Baroness Agnes de Stoeckl in court dress
4. Vincent's grandfather, Baron Sasha de Stoeckl in court uniform
5. Vincent's mother, Zoia de Stoeckl, as maid-of-honour to the last Empress of Russia, Alexandra Feodorovna - on the occasion of the 300th anniversary of the Romanov dynasty, 1911. This court dress has recently been donated by Vincent to the Alexander Palace Museum, Tsarskoe Selo, near St. Petersburg.
6. Zoia Poklewski Koziell, in The Ladies Field magazine, 1919
7. Poklewski Koziell family in Japan during their escape from Russia

105

1. Fancy dress ball in Poklewski Koziell family house in St. Petersburg, circa 1910
2. Alex and Zoia, Poland, 1938
3. Alex and Vincent
4. Some of the beaters at Lançut, Poland
5. After a wild boar shoot, Poland

4 ▲ 5 ▼

1 ▲ 2 ▼

1. Shooting scene, Lançut: Count Alfred Potocki, Vincent, Zoia, Colonel Witold Morawski, and Alex
2. Prince 'Kiki' Radziwill
3. Count Alfred Potocki with two of his Lançut arabs
4. Duke and Duchess of Kent arriving at Lançut with Count Alfred Potocki
5. Main entrance to Lançut showing the doorway through which Count Alfred drove his coach and four

3 ▲ 4 ▼

5 ▼

2 ▲ 3 ▼

1 ▲ 4 ▼

5 ▼

6 ▲ 7 ▼

1. Alik Poklewski Koziell
2. Coppins cottage
3. Zoia and Alik Poklewski Koziell
4. Agnes de Stoeckl
5. Vincent, aged 12
6. Vincent, Zoia, Alik and Alex
7. Christmas at Coppins

1 ▲ 3 ▼

2 ▲ 4 ▼

5 ▼

6 ▲   7 ▲ 8 ▼

1. The Duchess of Kent, photographed by Cecil Beaton
2. The Duchess of Kent and Prince Michael
3. The Duke of Kent and Zoia
4. Left to Right: Princess Alexandra, King George VI, Princess Elizabeth, Princess Margaret, Duchess of Kent, Queen Elizabeth, Duke of Kent
5. Princess Elizabeth (present Queen), Princess Margaret
6. Duchess of Kent and Winston Churchill, Coppins
7. Mrs Roosevelt, Prince Michael (godson of President Roosevelt), Duchess of Kent
8. Zoia with friends including: Nada Milford Haven, Gina Philips, David Milford Haven, Prince Philip, Duchess of Kent and Harold Wernher

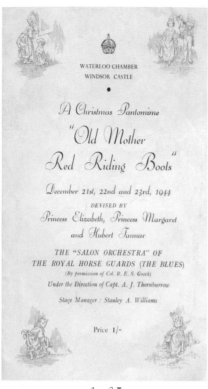

1 ▲ 3 ▼   2 ▲ 4 ▼

1. Pantomime programme
2. Prince Philip (present Duke of Edinburgh)
3. Zoia and the Duchess of Kent by the air-raid shelter
4. Bomb crater near Coppins

1 ▲ 2 ▼

3 ▼

4 ▼

1. Downside school
2. Vincent scoring for a cricket match
3. The Abbott
4. Vincent doing the high jump

HE'S teaching them how to do their SMALLS

IT'S a far cry from hunting hares on the Mendip Hills to showing London housewives how to wash their "smalls."

But debonair, 25-year-old ex-public schoolboy Vincent Poklewski-Koziell, is enjoying this job.

Peter, secretary of the Downside Beagles Hunt Ball Committee, Bath, is known as Mr. Peter Vincent to the housewives of the county council flats in Stockwell-gardens West, South London.

He works as salesman and demonstrator for a firm of washing-machine manufacturers.

And the 250 housewives in the flats know him as "The Count."

"It must be because I speak with a slight foreign accent," says Peter. His parents came from Poland. He was born in London, and went to Downside School, Stratton-on-the-Fosse, Bath.

Peter's no washout when it comes to doing the "smalls." But it can be embarrassing. . . .

Immaculately dressed, with umbrella and briefcase, Peter arrives each day by car at the wash-house.

"This job gets a bit embarrassing at times," gulped Peter as some undies were whipped past him.

Then, mopping his brow after hours over a hot tub, he added :

"It would be nice to go hunting now—to get some of the soap suds out of my hair."

1 ▲ 2 ▼

116

3 ▲

1. Newspaper cutting about 'Mr Peter Vincent'
2. Vincent demonstrating laundry equipment to Wandsworth council housewives
3. Vincent greeting the Duchess of Kent on his stand at The Ideal Home Exhibition

CHAPTER SEVEN
Gay Sardinia

AFTER CONCLUDING MY advertising career at Coleman Prentice and Varley, I looked around for my next job. It wasn't long before I was offered a job in a private bank that a Romanian friend of mine had recently started. So, yet again, I entered another career that I knew absolutely nothing about. Again, a colourful career, although perhaps I should have heeded my fathers' dictum that the Poles always claimed you could never catch a Romanian because he always has soap on his balls.

I had some time before the job started, and I remember reading a 'Do It Yourself' tome entitled *Teach Yourself Banking*. I cannot claim to have learned much from it, although I dare say it might have come in useful to the board of Northern Rock. I never quite discovered what 'Private' banking meant, but soon realised that my Romanian bank was extremely private, and I suspect confined itself entirely to financial operations using the well-worn acronym 'OPM' (other people's money).

I found myself installed in a very grand office in Cockspur Street, Trafalgar Square, with an accountant and secretary, plus my friend the chairman. I realised that apart from those two, I was the sole employee – probably a good thing in view of the fact that my first monthly pay cheque bounced.

My banking career started on a rather unstable footing, when my incurable sense of humour lost us a client, and nearly cost me my job. We went to a curious and very odd office of an Indonesian mining company, which no longer mined copper, but still had a quotation on the stock exchange, and which the boss wanted to buy as a 'shell' company. The chairman was of a totally Dickensian appearance: extremely old, with white whiskers and a pince-nez. He had obviously overlooked that the mine had not produced anything for some years, and launched into a lengthy diatribe about mining, and the significant deposits he firmly believed were still there. It was very hot in his office and the word 'karang' – clearly a local mining word – was endlessly repeated. I was nodding-off during this lecture and was only kept awake by the ticking of at least fifteen antique striking clocks, which he collected. Midday struck very loudly, as the office was just next to Big Ben. Then one of the clocks in the office struck, and I realised that they were all slightly unsynchronised, and that they would all chime in turn, and twelve times at that. By the time the eighth one commenced (after we had had eighty-four chimes already), I started shaking with suppressed laughter, followed by tears and sneezes, while the old boy droned on and my boss gave me dagger looks. I had to leave the room, and signalled that I had to get back to the office, and escaped, followed by the fading sound of chime after chime. Needless to say, the mine remained unsold and may still be there with its *karang* undisturbed.

I continued my banking career with luck and a following wind, and soldiered on. All in all I had quite an interesting time, with a few trips to Hong Kong, Jakarta and Bali thrown in. I don't think we made much money in these places, but it certainly beat visiting the North Welsh Valleys and Newcastle on Tyne. My boss who had a distinct penchant for the high life, especially when away from his wife, introduced me to some very exotic locations and establishments where I was able to fill in the gaps in my education that were not catered for by the monks at Downside. Then things appeared to go into overdrive and I found myself in great danger of doing some really hard work as, for nearly a year, I spent each week divided between Ireland, London and Sardinia.

After five years of what felt like riding a shaky financial surfboard on top of a high wave, I parted on very good terms. Meanwhile my

Romanian friend moved to Belgium where his financial career came to a rather sticky end. During those five years I had learned quite a lot of financial know-how. I doubt if it had too much to do with investment banking, but more to do with plain making money, which is presumably the main purpose of work. In retrospect, if I knew then what I do now, I would have made 'serious' money, and be now sipping superior vintages.

THE SARDINIAN ADVENTURE started in the early 1960s when my boss's friend, Rafael Neville, discovered a particularly beautiful corner of Sardinia. Rafael sought our help in financing the creation of a small resort to be called 'Porto Raphael', to be located along a few sandy coves adjoining the village of Palau, opposite the island of Madalena, an Italian naval base.

Rafael was a very special sort of Spaniard. Well-born, in fact from the noble family of Conde de Berlanga, he had spent a rather unconventional youth chiefly due to his pronounced homosexual predilections. As a consequence of this he had been expelled from school early, for appearing for his first communion dressed as a girl. Having thus clearly stated his sexual orientation, he went on to lead a very gay life in the south of Spain before moving to Sardinia.

Rafael was an extremely vivid character in every way and extremely lovable and popular with everyone. Camp he most certainly was – he made Sebastian Flyte from *Brideshead* seem like a Foreign Legion sergeant by comparison. I remember meeting him for the first time and being slightly taken aback by his appearance and gestures, but was soon won over by his immense charm. We were spending the night in a hotel, prior to his driving me to Palau and the then unbuilt Porto Rafael. After dinner we were enjoying our n'th glass of Sardinian brandy – marginally rougher than methylated spirits – on the balcony of the hotel suite overlooking the moonlit bay. Suddenly he put his arm round me and said, "Why don't you marry me daahling?" I riposted, "I'm afraid not. I like you very much, but I am not that way inclined. Why don't you marry Casimir [our mutual gay friend]." He replied sharply, "Not that old Duchess!" although he was in fact a great friend of his.

People forget how large Sardinia really is – the second largest island in the Mediterranean with one and a half million inhabitants. The reason for its 'discovery' after the war was that huge as it is, no self-respecting Italian would visit or develop it due to the endemic malaria. Thanks to an enormous grant from the Rockerfeller Foundation after the war, the malaria was eradicated. The result of years of neglect by the mainland, and endemic malaria, meant that the inhabitants were not particularly physically attractive, being of small stature with the women sporting moustaches from an early age.

Being rocky, dry and mountainous, it was poor agricultural land largely owned by a very small number of absentee landlords all of whom had vast estates producing goats, pigs and a small amount of olive oil. Fishing and banditry, in the form of kidnapping, were just about the only rewarding occupations. Then, in the latter part of the 1950s, the island was 'discovered' by the Aga Khan who created the Costa Esmeralda and Porto Cervo amongst others. Then developers (like us) created leisure complexes around the beautiful shorelines, much to the amazement of the locals.

Our first steps as 'developers' started in Rome, where we had to get permission to import the currency. In those days – as in these – the most difficult Italian permission had to be obtained in some slightly bent fashion. That was where we made the error. We got an appointment through our provincial Sardinian solicitor, who was a friend of the Prime Minister at the time, Antonio Segni (who was also Sardinian and therefore a member of the fraternity).

My boss and I were led down an immense marble hallway in the treasury palazzo by two flunkeys and two assistants to the Secretary of the Treasury, who received us very formally and offered tea. My boss made his long presentation about the development in his perfect Italian, while I danced around unfolding maps, and unrolling the figures and calculations. Most of them were, if truth be told, mostly figures of our fertile imagination, but impressive for all that. At the end of about forty-five minutes, during which Signor Ministro remained silent, we all stood up and the Minister said, "No." We walked back down the marble halls in a state of shock, when one of the group took me by the shoulder and said in a kindly voice, "Excuse me signor, but if you don't mind me saying so, the Minister makes the rules and cannot break them, but I

being his deputy can. Pity you aimed so high and did not come to me."
That was our first lesson in Italian affairs, but we learnt, and eventually
got the permission through a convoluted process, the exact details of
which escape me.

As Porto Rafael was as yet a totally untouched beach, rocks and
wild scrub, we stayed in the village of Palau. It was the little port for the
tragetto, or ferry, from La Madalena. We stayed at the only so-called
'hotel' namely the Albergo Serra, owned and run by Nicolino Serra. The
'hotel' consisted of maybe eight or ten rooms, reached by a staircase open
to the dust road before Signor Serra chose to build the front wall of
the hotel a few years later. As a result, there was always a menagerie of
stray cats and dogs, plus the odd drunk competing for accommodation. I
never discovered whether the missing wall was due to lack of money, or
simply lack of energy.

I got on very well with Nicolino. He was a small, stout figure, slightly
hirsute, who wore a stained vest that just covered his well-rounded tum.
He always had appalling garlic breath, which one hardly noticed in the
end, as we all reeked of garlic after the first day. Sardinian food was
dreadful in those days and garlic was the only thing that made it edible
(whether pasta, goat, fish bones, or some other unknown animal).

So the financing of the development went on in slow and eccentric
stages. In the beginning there was insufficient water, so Rafael sent for
a water diviner called Doctor Moronga. He arrived and, fortified with
liberal litres of powerful local plonk, he staggered round for several
days with his divining fork and showed us where he shook most. He
then went away with a belch and a fat fee. Rafael had the hole drilled
for several days, but no water appeared. Rafael then threw a wobbly in
the square and shouted, "I will put the drill up Moronga's arse if I ever
see him again!"

Eventually water arrived, but the building and the plumbing was
not quite up to British standards. I remember showing my friend
Charlie Judd his room after his long hot journey from Dublin; he had
a thorough wash in the hand basin after which he pulled out the plug,
whereupon the entire contents emptied out on to his new white trousers
and poncey suede shoes. The builder in his helpful way shrugged his
shoulders and announced the obvious – that the pipe was missing.

The learning curve proceeded with notorious builders and mayors, all with their hands out, followed by lots of drinks and absolutely no hurry at all. Having sweetened endless palms, one would discover that they were the wrong ones, and had to start all over again. Some years into our development, Maureen, Marchioness of Dufferin and Ava, decided to build a villa at Porto Rafael, subsequently referred to by Maureen as 'Villa Costalotta' due to its building expense. I will always remember the plumber (he of the missing pipe) who was also the mayor, proudly strolling down the main street with one of Maureen Dufferin's chic mahogany loo seats framing his head and neck. Maureen was one of the three famous 'Golden Guinness Girls' who were daughters of Ernest Guinness. They frequently changed their husbands and names, but were always known as the Marchioness of Dufferin and Ava, Aileen Plunkett and Oonagh Oranmore and Brown.

I found learning the local languages – a mixture of Italian and Sardinian argot – rather difficult, so I sought the help of a young lawyer. Paolo Riccardi was very tall, twice the height of the locals, fat, jolly and with an insatiable appetite for skirt. When I introduced him to any English women Paolo would always ask me in his appalling French if they were available – ignoring the fact that they usually understood.

He once got me into terrible trouble. We were all at a big exhibition and conference of building and tourist development in the local county town of Sassari, where I was fêted as, "Il grande banquiere Inglese" and much sucked up to by the regional chairman, a very fat, pompous man surrounded by a coterie of obsequious assistants and supplicants. The next morning I spied the chairman and his allies walking down the opposite side of the street and I quickly asked Paolo Riccardi how I should greet the chairman. He said that I should say, "Bon giorno il Presidente de mei coglione." I repeated the phrase twice to learn it by heart, crossed the street, bowed and the cortege stopped. I shook the chairman's hand and repeated my phrase. He went deadly pale, leant back against the wall and I thought that he was going to have a heart attack. The cortege looked totally shocked and shaken beyond belief and I realised that something unspeakably awful had happened, so I quickly bowed and ran. Paolo was nowhere to be seen, and I only heard a roar of laughter from a neighbouring street. What I had in fact said was "Good morning President of my balls."

Needless to say I was never allowed near the town authorities again, and much money had to be spent repairing the damage. The other time Paolo dropped me in it was when on my way to the vegetable stall in the village, he advised me to ask the old lady for some special figs, and said they were called 'Ficca di donna' whereupon the old girl fainted, and I subsequently learned the difference between figgi (figs), and ficca which is part of the female anatomy.

A YEAR INTO the Sardinian development I met and married Annabel de las Casas. We were married at St. Mary's Cadogan in the pouring rain, and left that night for our honeymoon in Sardinia, thus combining pleasure, duty and economy.

The wedding reception was at Londonderry House, followed by a splendid supper and hooley with band. We left in our host's Bentley at 2am and caught a plane to Rome in the middle of the night, arriving in the Grand Hotel in Rome early in the morning, and so fell into bed for an extremely platonic wedding night/morning. We caught the overnight ferry to Olbia, Sardinia that evening (there were no flights to Sardinia in those days). There we were joined in our tiny half-built hotel of ten rooms in Palau by Peter and Clare Ward, and Johnny and Mary Manners.

I had not invited them exactly, as I thought it might make the honeymoon somewhat crowded, but it happened like this. In early June, Johnny Manners bearded me in the old St. James Club, and said, "Vincent, old boy, Wardie and I and our old girls [they weren't!] want to go to Sardinia next time you go." I told him that I was going in July, but it would be on my honeymoon, and it would not exactly be in Annabel's mind to be joined by that crowd, love them as we did. However Johnny, never one to take no for an answer, said that I had no idea how boring honeymoons can be, and that of course we needed some jolly company. Never having refused the offer of jolly company, I nervously agreed to broach the subject with Annabel. To my surprise she somewhat apprehensively agreed and the die was cast.

The Albergo Serra was one of the more primitive hotels this side of the Khyber Pass. My great chum Casimir Stamirski had done his best by tying together two rather spartan army issue metal beds, called *retté* in Italian, on which rattling platform we were expected to consummate our honeymoon. There was a washbasin that emptied into a bucket underneath – that is unless it had been moved, in which case one was treated to an unexpected foot wash. No bath – that came later – but a shower that was directed straight on to an electric heater for the water. Nicolino Serra the proud proprietor, in his usual uniform of stained singlet, waved his pudgy arms assuring us that we would not be electrocuted. I took a chance, or rather a shower, because otherwise I knew I would not be accepted onto the marital wire-mesh bed after a day in 100 degrees heat. I must confess that I found it bracing, but whether it was the electricity or the water, I could not tell.

The honeymoon proceeded, and grew like topsy with other friends in the village, until poor Annabel was under the distinct impression that she was at a permanent cocktail party, but enjoying herself nonetheless, until an unfortunate incident took place. There were by that time about sixteen of us dining at a long table in the middle of a small street, with copious drafts of the local Sardinian red, called *Jerzu*. (I remember in later years our Irish friends calling for more bottles of "Jaysus"). It was I suppose in those days a bit rough, but with the alcoholic content of port. I remember sitting next to the late Lady Knollys, who was there with her husband, and her being faintly amazed that I was there on my honeymoon.

At last, seeing how the Jaysus was getting slightly out of hand, Clare Ward, Mary Manners and Annabel decided to retire to their rooms at the hotel. By that time Johnny had procured a bottle of Sardinian brandy, which would have doubled as a great firelighter. The result is, I am ashamed to say, that what with the drink and the company, I completely forgot I was on my honeymoon and just thought I was having a jolly evening with the boys. So when Wardie and Johnny decided to get a cab to Capo D'Orso, where he heard there was a German camp with several hundred under twenty-five, well-built German girls panting under canvas, I willingly agreed to accompany them.

About two miles up a rocky road I suddenly recalled my honeymoon and told the boys that I had to go back. The selfish bastards said no, there was no question of them turning back, and as I could not walk back in total darkness on a twisty, rocky mountain road, I had to proceed. Fortunately the said panting maidens were being guarded by a sinister bearded Sardinian with a two barrelled shotgun pointing at us, shouting in Sardinian dialect, which we did not understand, but which clearly meant 'Fuck off!'

By the time we got back to the hotel, Clare and Mary gathered what we had been up to and the interfering wenches went and woke up Annabel, saying, "How could he? It's all right for us being married to those two old drunks, but you! And on your honeymoon!" Having duly worked her up they told her to lock the room, and waited, looking over the banisters for the denuement. In due course we arrived and I found my door locked. I rattled the handle. A loud pretend snore issued from behind the door. Humiliated, with the gang watching, I had to get down on my knees and whistle through the keyhole, then demand that the door be opened. "If not," I pronounced, "I shall sleep in my club!" I really must have been *sou comme un Polonais*.

The next day began on an icy note, not to mention a thundering headache, and I was treated to a large portion of cold tongue. However, with the combination of sunshine and masses of humble pie, an ideal honeymoon was resumed in spite of the absence of florists.

Another amusing incident in the early Sardinian days was when our friend Edward, Duke of Kent, was staying with us and wanted to cash some travellers cheques. I immediately realised that a problem was looming. The only bank in the village was the Banco de Sardengna, hastily opened when the yachts and *beau-monde* started to arrive in Palau. The bank consisted of a very small empty shop, with little light, only one window and no air conditioning, and it was run by an ill-tempered, well-moustached old bag with bad breath.

That day was extremely hot and I told my friend that I would gladly advance him the small sum required and we could settle up in London. However, the royal determination was not to be denied, so we set off to *al banco*. There was a queue of yachtsmen and villa owners sweating profusely in a hundred degrees, while the lady took her time suspiciously inspecting travellers cheques and different coloured passports, all comparatively new to her.

Our turn finally came and we bent over her tiny cage in saturated T-shirts. I tried to keep my mental cool and forgive my friend for his determination, but then the fun started. He did not have the ordinary American Express cheques, but some which were of a different design; moreover, ones which had to be signed on the back and not on the front. "No e un travellers cheque," shouted the lady as she shoved them back at His Royal Highness, who was understandably less than pleased, but stood his ground holding the sweat-soaked cheques. Finally in my halting Italian, and with the help of the growing queue standing behind us in the tiny oven of a room, we managed to persuade her to proceed. He duly signed the cheques 'Edward', as royalty are wont to do, upon which she said that it was not a name but a Christian name, and insisted that his surname was the one on his passport which was headed HIS ROYAL HIGHNESS, and said that he would have to sign that on the back.

He naturally remonstrated that his bank, Coutts, would think he was drunk or had gone mad if he did that. So, a complete stand-off ensued, with madam's arms akimbo over damp hirsuite armpits, staring malevolently at HRH. I finally stepped in and said that there was no other way, and that he would just have to do as he was told, and explain to the morning-coated gentlemen at Coutts the result of the 'International Incident'. This he duly did with very bad grace and accompanied with many a sigh.

WE SPENT MANY happy years in Sardinia, and built a rather ugly house next to the Ward's house, in a wonderful position on giant rocks, overlooking a fabulous sandy cove. Eventually, the place got developed, but it never lost its character, with Porto Rafael itself consisting of a tiny piazza with little connected houses all round, and Rafael's house and bar with a permanent day and night party. Rafael would appear in constantly changing outfits, with a handbag to match, and his arm round a good-looking sailor from La Madalena. Needless to say his presence and personality drew the gay crowd with the result that one benefited from the company of all the pretty girls, according to the saying that "In the kingdom of the blind, the one-eyed man is king."

Part of my job at Porto Rafael was to help and supervise Rafael, the latter being quite impossible, because as soon as the question of money came up, he got the vapours, and fished a bottle of vodka out of his bag (a lady's one naturally) saying, "Daahling Vincent, daunt upset me about sheety money. Let's drink and go and look for lovely sailors." I accepted the drink and declined the sailors, having convinced him that I was what he regarded as 'queer' by preferring girls. Being like most Spaniards unable to pronounce a 'y' he called his small wooden boat his 'djat'. We once had a ceremony of unveiling a picture of the djat, which he had painted as a present to 'her' (the boat) accompanied by music and an immense amount of alcohol, which he consumed all day long. He would keep a small vodka bottle in his handbag for the intervals between bars. This of course eventually caused his premature demise.

Some years later there was a memorable occasion when I persuaded a great friend of mine, a Dane called Michael Raben, to join me for a few days in Porto Rafael. Michael, very macho and father of several boys agreed, but having heard rumours said, "I hope there'll be no queers there." I said, "Forget it, it's full of them, but also full of unrequited dollies." He acquiesced with, "Okay, but if any man touches me, I will belt him." So we duly arrived in Porto Rafael, having left our wives in London, and entered Rafael's bar, me in great trepidation by that point thinking that the whole idea could have been a great error. Rafael approached us from behind the bar, in pink shorts and a lacy t-shirt, carrying a handbag. He hurled himself at me with a smacking kiss and a, "Hello Daahling." I could feel Michael tensing dangerously beside me as Rafael asked, "And who is your good-looking mans friend?" I replied, "A Danish friend who has come for a few days, Rafael." "Hurrah," Rafael replied, "I have just bought a big four-poster bed and we will all have a party in it tonight: mens and womens with your Danish friend in the middle." To my horror I saw Michael's bare arms tensing their muscles beside me, and the veins in his forehead beginning to swell. He barked out, "I'm afraid I would not be much use to you, I would only snore." Rafael clapped his hands together and chirped, "Then we will all kiss your snore." It was simply too much for Michael and I, and we collapsed with laughter – thank God. Later that night, after a million drinks, we were seen dancing across the piazza dressed as women.

CHAPTER EIGHT
Taken to the (Dry) Cleaners

THE FIRST TIME I went to Aileen Plunkett's castle, Luttrelstown, near Phoenix Park in Dublin, was when staying with my old school friend John McGuire. He took me there to a dinner party, having probably promised her someone who, if not exactly fresh meat, would certainly be able to keep up with the chat, flirting and certainly drinking. All that happened in spades. We wisely decided that even by Irish standards it would be unwise to drive back, and were escorted by the butler to the 'Bachelors' Tower' where rooms were always kept ready for spare guests, who had either been invited or were simply unable to leave. I suppose John and I were in the latter category.

I was woken by a knock on the door by the footman named Gerry who grew to be a great friend and ally in years to come. I was lying in bed feeling decidedly foolish in my evening shirt and loose black tie, nursing a cracking hangover. He was holding a silver salver, with what I took to be a frozen tomato juice on it. I said, "Oh, a tomato juice, how wonderful!" He replied, "No sir, it's something stronger, sir." "Don't tell me it's a Bloody Mary?" said I. "No sir, its known here as a 'pink special', but very similar to what you mentioned, sir. Madam gave special orders that you should have one." From that moment on I became a devoted member of the Luttrelstown set, and a firm friend of the eccentric Aileen until the end of her long life of ninety odd years.

To illustrate some of her style and wonderful eccentricities, at the height of Aileen's reign at Luttrelstown I counted eighteen indoor staff: kitchen, butler, pantry staff, footmen, chauffeurs, six housemaids and a tiny bent figure whose job it was to go up the various tower staircases all night to top up the wood fires in the bedrooms and bathrooms. So if one tottered to bed at 4am, if not later, there would be a fire still blazing, and the fires were in addition to an extensive central heating system!

In those days Ireland was not really too well supplied with flowers, apart from large private gardens, and the Luttrelstown garden did not produce many for some reason. Perhaps the gardeners were too busy mowing the lawns, walking the dogs or drinking. Thus, for really big and smart weekends, the Duchess of Windsor's secretary, who also helped Aileen on international matters, was flown over from Paris smothered in bouquets for the house. Another person that helped with the finer points was her friend the decorator, Felix Harbord, who was permanently changing the curtains. The problem however was that the Irish Customs were very strict on any imported goods, due to severe protectionism. As a result, poor Felix was obliged to wrap them round his body under a vast Astrakan collared overcoat, and as a result this tall figure, by that time looking like Atlas and Joe Louis combined, could be seen mincing his way through Dublin airport pouring with sweat on the coldest day.

The happiest memory I have of that extraordinary place, Luttrelstown, is meeting my Annabel – wife to be. It was during a big New Year's Eve 1960 houseparty, when the castle was probably at its full-blown and drunken best. Endless guests from England, France and elsewhere had been invited, accompanied by their children, nannies, hairdressers and maids.

At lunch on New Year's Eve, I noticed a very pretty girl pushing a pram in the park outside the window, and thought that nannies were certainly improving and getting younger. It was, in fact, Annabel with Rupert, her son of ten months, who had been born after his father, Basil de las Casas had died. Basil had been married to Neelia, Aileen's elder daughter, hence the Luttrelstown connection, and his sons Mikey and

Kevin, were spending most of their time with Annabel. At the time, I did not know this, as she had lunched in the nursery.

That night in the crowded ballroom, the 'dark stranger' disguised as a chimney sweep (an old Irish custom) arrived pretending to have come down the chimney, and announced somewhat the worse for wear, that the New Year had arrived. I suddenly spied the very pretty 'nanny' from lunchtime, across the room, looking resplendent in a white satin evening dress. I secured an introduction from Aileen, and we were left together. I raised my glass to her to wish her a happy New Year, and asked her whether she had had a happy last year, to which she replied, "No, my husband died" – poor thing, she was then only twenty-five years old. She then asked me whether I had had a happy one, to which I replied, "No, my wife left me."

She always swore that from that moment she knew for certain that we would marry. I can't say that I was as far-sighted as her, but I definitely made sure that I would be visiting the nursery for the remainder of my stay. The rest is history, as they say: I fell in love with them both. Meanwhile the party continued at an increasing pace, and Annabel having retired to the nursing quarters to check on Rupert, went to bed sober, while I accompanied Aileen downstairs to the nightclub before returning upstairs for a serious breakfast, then bed and oblivion.

A typical Luttrelstown occurrence took place that night. Nora Fitzgerald, a middle-aged spinster of immense fun (who owned an established wine merchants and supplied us with any stock that she had not consumed herself), made a rather dramatic exit. She decided to leave the party and got into her car which was parked in front of the castle. This was pre-breathalyser days, and I am sure the whole apparatus would have melted had she given it the slightest puff. Anyway, she put the car into reverse, put her foot down, and the car descended sideways down the area between the drive and the kitchen windows. As one of the staff who was washing up at one of the wooden sinks put it, "Jaysus, there was the most terrible crash, I looked out at Miss Fitzgerald's car jammed sideways in the ditch, but before anyone could do anything, there she was emerging out of the car with the door opening upwards like a boat's hatch. Not a bother on her either!"

She was taken safely home to Dublin by one of the more sober drivers, and I can remember being woken at lunchtime the next day by the sound of a mobile crane hauling the car out. I remember Aileen holding court that afternoon holding a cocktail in a bed covered with dogs, saying she had the car taken away as soon as possible, as "wasn't it terrible" and, "what would people think" while obviously enjoying the whole episode immensely.

There was another wonderful occasion at one of her parties, which was full of the smart bejewelled international set. In those days they did not arrive in private jets but with private lady's maids and hairdressers. As the party gathered steam and the Irish got down to some serious drinking, a young friend of ours, Edward McGuire, a rather bohemian painter with a tremendous weakness for Guinness (reasonable I suppose as Guinness was paying for the whole party), went totally over the top. He picked a fight with me, among others, and started lashing out. The stronger ones among us were attempting to throw him out; not very easy, as it was a long way out. Aileen appeared with an agitated face in front of the grande society of Europe exclaiming, "Oh how terrible, and in my house too!" and then in a low voice to me, "Quick Vincent, go and fetch my camera." By the time I returned the affair had turned into a proper scrum and Edward was underneath a pile of people, with a footman holding him by one leg, and a burly man neither in a black tie or livery holding the other. Aileen shouted to the footman, "Who is this man?" to which the unfortunate footman replied from the floor, "He's the detective Modom, here to keep an eye on the jewels." Another jewel of a party at Aileen's.

Just after Kennedy was elected as US President, he appointed a well-heeled and party-fund-generous pal called Grant Stockdale to be Ambassador to Ireland. Aileen decided to give a ball for his reception at Luttrelstown and asked all the usual suspects, plus the grand and the diplomatic corps. First of all His Excellency, not having been trained in diplomatic protocol or manners, turned up about an hour late (clearly already well lubricated), wearing black knotted boot laces instead of a black tie over his dinner jacket, and a questionable white lace shirt. His wife who was less vulgar but a trifle nervous sat next to me at the table, and looked with alarm at all the silver cutlery laid in front of her. "Oh dear," she said as she turned to me, "how do we start?" I then told her to relax and use the cutlery on each side together but in turn, and if she avoided a course not to forget to put the allotted instruments aside. I felt proud that my lesson in dining etiquette was successful, but wondered all the same why the Washington authorities had not thought to have given the poor woman a short induction course – or a book at least. In any case Mrs Stockdale was charming and very grateful.

After dinner, the dancing in the ballroom commenced, whereupon His Excellency spied the lovely Annabel, to whom he had not been introduced. He grabbed her with his well-intoxicated arms and propelled her onto the dance floor. About three minutes later I heard a shriek and Annabel rushed towards me shouting, "The bastard has bitten my neck! What are you going to do about it?" The result, I am ashamed to say was nothing, as I could not face making a scene under the social and political circumstances. Instead I said that in less sophisticated American society, it was probably regarded as a form of sexual compliment. "Coward!" she shouted and avoided me for the rest of the night.

A rather grand American lady near me, witnessing the shenanigans and general behaviour, turned round and in a shocked voice asked me, "Where on earth does our Ambassador come from?" I replied that I understood he was a real estate developer from Miami, to which she drew herself up and replied, "One might just about go there, but one certainly can't come from there." Next time we were happily rewarded with Raymond Guest as Ambassador, a sort of chalk and cheese contrast, not to mention Raymond's excellent private cellar at his residence, and his attractive French wife.

Another famous – although less extensive – establishment belonged to Aileen's sister, Oonagh Oranmore and Brown (whose name depended on which husband she currently enjoyed). Luggala was a Victorian Gothic folly, tucked away in the Wicklow mountains at the bottom of a long hill on a loch. The house was always filled with actors, singers, writers as well as Oonagh's own gang of adherents. Parties were monumental and the quantities of drink served, in original Waterford glasses, made Luttrelstown seem like The Priory.

I remember once searching for a loo and wandered through the bedrooms that went eccentrically into each other without a corridor. I suddenly came across the Rolling Stones in two rooms, rolling joints and girls simultaneously. I tiptoed away, unable to partake in either. On another occasion there was a party at which Mr and Mrs Brendan Behan were absorbing alcohol in truly poetic portions. At one moment

Mr Behan spied Annabel, whom he did not know, but gathered from her voice that she was English, and pinned her against the wall while howling a rebel song at her, inches from her face, until I succeeded in removing him. She was very shaken, not by the song, but by his vile brewery breath, loaded with alcoholic moisture, being pumped out over rows of brown uneven and certainly unwashed teeth.

We then witnessed the most amazing thing. Mrs Behan, who was hardly behind her husband in alcoholic intake, reached her glass forward to a slightly inebriated domestic, had it refilled and emptied it in one. She then leant back from a standing position and slowly sank, until she was prone and quite unconscious on the carpet. No one looked surprised or took much notice. Oonagh nodded to a couple of staff who seized her arms and legs and carted her out of the room. This was clearly a normal occurrence at Luggala, by the male guests anyway, as Oonagh kept a ground floor dormitory with a line of school beds for gentlemen who had passed out. They would then awake in the morning, as once happened to my brother Alex, with their shoes neatly arranged on the floor at the end of their bed. I remember that my friend Edward Maguire stayed there once for a fortnight – having only come to dinner.

AFTER A YEAR of marriage working three days in Ireland, two in London and weekends in Sardinia, my wife gently reminded me that I was wedded to her, not to Ireland and Sardinia as well. All this was before the era of the yuppie, jet flight and globalisation, when that sort of work schedule is regarded as normal for executives with consequent damages to health – particularly the liver – and needless to say, marriages. So, a more normal pace of life was arrived at with our decision to settle in Ireland.

We started by renting a furnished house with four bedrooms and garden in a genteel suburb of Dublin called Blackrock: very few crooks, apart from some of the whitecollar residents, but plenty of crooked little fingers around dainty tea cups. I remember my first encounter with middle class Irish discrimination. When the owner of our rented house ('Ard na Loy') was showing us around, I started chatting to his dog. The owner, an Irish language teacher, politely informed me that there was no point, as the dog only understood Irish. Another more public example of that kind of discrimination was an advertisement in the personal columns of the *The Irish Times* for members of the longstanding Dublin Badminton Club, the headline of which ran, 'DUBLIN BADMINTON CLUB – Memberships now available (Protestants) for this season.'

Although I had frequently been to Ireland to stay with my school chum, John McGuire, at his magnificent house in Blackrock, I had not entirely taken in the total difference of the Irish atmosphere and life there. The Irish are of course renowned for their wonderful sense of humour, general attitude to life, and their capacity not to be disturbed by anything like clocks or timekeeping.

On the subject of humour, I am reminded of John's father, Senator McGuire, quite an establishment figure and owner of Brown Thomas, the smartest department store in Dublin, chairman of the National Employers Union, and bank director amongst other things. He was a fervent Catholic and had installed a magnificent altar in the parish church. One day he was ruminating on the news that coincided with the launch of one of the first space rockets and the day of the bodily assumption of Our Lady into Heaven (which had come out as a Papal edict in the latter half of the nineteenth century). Leaning back in his splendid drawing room with an amazing collection of old master pictures, he quietly announced that, "If we had known about these things when the edict came, we would have wondered if she was still going."

Another example of Irish self-deprecating humour was one of Tony O'Reilly's favourite sayings, "The definition of an Irish queer is someone who prefers women to drink." Tony himself, who was at that time an Irish rugby hero, had just (or rather his unfortunate wife had) produced triplets. He was in a taxi in Dublin when the driver, who had read the news in the evening paper and recognised his passenger, lent back and said, "Jaysus Tony, you must have fallen asleep and left the engine running."

The last bit of Dublin humour – and one of my favourites – was told to me by Joe McMenamin when he was at Dublin University some years ago. He was visiting a notorious dance hall, come pick-up joint, with fellow students. His friend, after many tiring efforts, managed to pick up a young girl, probably like him living on three pounds a week, or thereabouts. After a few dances, which gradually became increasingly intimate, the place closed and he hopefully suggested that he could escort her home and then would she offer him a cup of tea perhaps? She replied, "Have you a car?" Whereupon the penniless lad, who had come by bike, reposted, "Jaysus, the nearest I have to a car would be the horn."

The chat at dinner parties was fabulous and continuous: horses – both racing and hunting – land, politics and jokes, and it all often ended in song. The weather was not discussed much: after all how long can one keep up a conversation on rain? And sex, not too often. It was, after all, a fairly small country and therefore discretion was much appreciated, although it did obviously exist as the number of christenings accompanied by wetting the wee one's head with Jameson's whiskey testified.

At one of the earlier dinner parties I attended, I remember sitting next to the wife of a famous pianist. A very jolly and pretty lady, but my conversation on music being confined to but few notes, I proceeded to the usual, and asked her if she had an occupation apart from turning the pages of her husband's music. To my utter amazement, she said that she was a sex counsellor. I did not even know that they existed in Ireland, and I was – unusually for me – rather lost for an answer. However I merely raised an eyebrow and said, "How interesting" and changed the subject. At the end of dinner however, while getting up, I could not resist saying to her that it had been a great pleasure to talk to her, and had she, by any chance, a piece of advice to give me *a propos* her profession, to which she replied in a hoarse whisper, "Remember to use it," as she slid away.

While the vast majority of Irish dinner parties were the greatest of fun, there was the odd Dublin one given by a 'grand' Foxrock denizen, which tended to be a pretty tedious performance. One that stands out in shaky, overdiddled food, overdressed and oversized wives and not quite enough drink, was given by one of the professionals connected to a deal that I was involved in.

There were about sixty people present, of whom I vaguely knew four. I was greeted by an over-corseted hostess with a mountainous well-powdered bosom, supporting a large corsage of flowers, together with a posse of similar friends oohing and aahing over each other's frocks, and all solidly overweight from over-visiting Bewley's café in Grafton Street. They all tucked into 'the meal' with a chorus of, "reeley, how loverely" with little fingers crooked like worms on a fishing line. They returned with plates piled high with cold salmon decorated with twisted ribbons of Brylcreem, cold turkey, stuffed (the Lord knew what with) all well garnished with sugared lemon and orange slices, and bristling with a mini-maginot line of toothpicks with cherries on the end, followed by endless sticky puds. All 'reeley' elegant, and I finally reeled away having over indulged in Bristol Cream sherry and mulled wine.

I STARTED OUT as a director of Brown Thomas, the chicest department store in Ireland, which belonged to the family of my chum John McGuire whom I had known from Downside days. I settled in as a sort of (I have always been a 'sort of' in all my many careers) financial director, and I still am a director to this day. It has been owned by another close friend, Galen Weston, for many years now and has a number of branches in Ireland. I am still there for sentimental reasons, God knows why, as I am over eighty, but at least Galen has the good sense not to consult me anymore, and I have the wisdom and grace to agree with him at board meetings when they take place.

In 1965 we moved from Blackrock closer to the centre of Dublin. I bought a roomy Georgian town house in Oakley Road, Ranelagh. It had plenty of rooms, a nursery with separate stairs (thank God), and a large garden. Life was pleasant and great fun; one was young enough to both work and play hard. Moreover there was still time to be close to the children who were at local day schools, although they now seem to suffer from loss of memory and claim to have hardly ever seen me.

To prove the opposite a number of nursery occurrences stand out in my memory. On one occasion after Sunday lunch in the nursery dining room, Eliza, aged four, had a tantrum and being consigned to the bathroom by her mother, lay down on the floor and hammered on the unlocked door with her feet. Finally she ran out of steam, walked into the nursery and announced that she was going to run away. Annabel retorted, "Why don't you?" upon which Eliza took a book under her arm and proceeded up the nursery staircase saying, "I will, after my rest!" On another occasion – a guest having fallen out of a lunch party – Eliza was commandeered for the dining room, and sitting with head barely above the table, felt obliged to fill a general silence, and announced to everyone's astonishment that, "Last Tuesday was Mrs. Kat's birthday." This world-breaking news was lost on most, as they did not know, and I had forgotten, that Mrs Kat was her nursery school headmistress. From then on it has become a much-used family classic. Whenever someone announces something totally unimportant, obscure or unintelligible, it's known as a "Mrs Kat".

Another nursery school story of my son Sasha, was when he came home and proudly announced that he was appearing in the Christmas play as one of the Three Kings. When asked how he would know when to come on to the stage, he said, "Someone gives me a push." Sure enough as we sat longing for a drink, his moment arrived, the side curtain parted, and a great hand shoved the fat little king forward, stumbling in his anxiety to hold onto the gold. With pride in their hearts his parents departed home with the chubby little king, for a well-deserved drink, and the poor child for some watery nursery cocoa.

This recalls to me a comic, if rather pathetic experience of some friends whose child was due to appear in a school play, and who made her parents promise to attend. Unfortunately the play occurred in the middle of their first long-planned luxury holiday in the Caribbean, but in spite of a modest income, they dutifully broke 'the package' in the middle in order to attend. When the day arrived they discovered that their child appeared on stage as a tree. Such can be parenthood…

On the whole, I very wisely left the upbringing of the children to their mother Annabel, and a motley collection of *au pairs* and nannies. I did however train my youngest daughter Sophie from the day she learned to speak, to react to any unsociable noise I might happen to accidentally make (i.e. loud tummy rumble, frontal or rear escape of wind), to immediately respond with her sweet lisp, "Excuse me, Daddy." This duly deceived a number of people, and also caused great hilarity. One day the joke slightly backfired as I was deputed to collect Sophie from her nursery school down the road. We were returning on the bus with a full crowd of worthy genteel Dublin ladies. They were all staring at a gross, fat and malodorous drunk snoring in a corner seat. Suddenly the said gent let out a thunderous fart, which must have been heard by both decks. Up pipes little Sophie, "Excuse me, Daddy" at the top of her voice. There were looks of horror all round, accompanied by amazement that something so small and neat could produce such an explosion. I was so embarrassed that I had to snatch up the poor child, and jump off the bus to walk home.

Meanwhile, back in Dublin, life went merrily on. I joined the old established Kildare Street Club for boozy lunches (we did not have 'units' in those days, and I would in any case have had to add the odd zero to the stated allowance). I remember going to a medical for a life assurance policy, and was advised by an Irish friend, that when asked how much I drank, just to say that I only drank 'socially'. It worked perfectly. I suspect that the doctor was pretty social, and I have been extremely social ever since.

I eventually joined the committee of the club, and was involved in its merger with the University Club. When I was made chairman of the joint clubs, and was asked how someone called Poklewski Koziell could occupy that august position, I replied as follows: "While the Kildare Street Club originally was formed by officers of the Imperial army, and the University Club by members of Trinity College Dublin (or Oxford and Cambridge only), the only person on the joint committee they trusted was me. The reason being is that I have not been in the Life Guards or the Indian Cavalry, and I have never been to any kind of University at all."

Two family events at Oakley Road, stand out in my memory. We had Tim and Antonia Wardell staying, and they were enjoying a particularly active post-breakfast marital moment, when Nanny McManus, old, slightly dotty, and very old-fashioned, burst into their room shouting loudly in her deaf voice, "Anything for the coloured wash?" I had a lock installed.

The other occasion was when we were informed that due to rebuilding of the water mains, our road would be cut off for twenty-four hours, and we were advised not to run baths or washing machines and to conserve every drop. Annabel informed the entire household, and we all took serious note. Unfortunately we went out to dinner that night, which turned into what the Irish call, "A class of a party". The next morning, Annabel having left to take the children to school and then go shopping returned at 10.30 am. I, in the meantime, having totally forgotten the water emergency, decide to nurse my hangover with an extra deep hot bath awash with Floris essence. On entering the house she could not believe her nostrils, and she stiffened like a pointer at the smell of verbena drifting down the stairs. She rushed up, opened our bathroom door, saw her husband playing scented waves over his ample tummy, and shouted, "You selfish bastard!" I spent the rest of the day, having emptied the tank, buying wet wipes and bottled water, trying to save our marriage.

One of my more successful enterprises was to invest in a delicatessen store in Dublin with two close friends and a splendid old boy who knew his business backwards, and needed finance for a new location. It was a great success, and I well remember calling in on Friday evenings with the children who were handed out free sweeties, while I received my cash dividends in the form of oily fivers which reeked of smoked salmon (plastic gloves were only used by doctors in those times). To this day I cannot eat smoked salmon without calling to mind an Irish fiver.

Among my many enterprises 'on-the-side' was an investment in a mushroom business, possibly an unfortunate description. I had a friend and neighbour called John Wilson Wright who had a thriving mushroom nursery and who said that he could sell more than he could grow. I heard that all you have to do is to hurl mushroom spore into a dark cellar and cover it with shit (strictly speaking, horse manure) and wait for the results. I decided that even with my limited horticultural knowledge I could master that. So I set about forming a company called Midland Growers, with John, Tony O'Reilly and Conor Crowley.

It was decided that the most useful part I could play would be to secure a few tons of horse manure a week for the facility. I knew that my family had been in coal and steel, not to mention gold, but manure? I could feel my ancestors stirring in their graves, but decided that in these democratic times, needs must. I thus found myself accepting every invitation to dinner with the racing, breeding, and horse-selling crowd. They were slightly amazed at my sudden equine interest until I explained that it was not turned-on by the front of the horse passing the winning post, but by what it passed at its rear end. I eventually got out of the manure business when Tony O'Reilly sold Midland Growers to Guinness at a reasonable profit, and I no longer had to read the profit and loss accounts while holding smelling drops under my nose.

Taken to the (Dry) Cleaners

BROWN THOMAS BECAME a public company and we started to extend its 'empire' and diversify its business. One move was to take over a company called IMCO, which was the largest dry cleaning company in Ireland, with fifty-five branches throughout the country. My first move as a chairman was to try and learn something about the business. This entailed spending a couple of weeks in a shop stinking of dry-cleaning fumes, inspecting peoples frocks to detect damage and pontificate on the removability of various spots and stains. In between, when my eyes weren't dancing with the spots – and the fumes – I would take a turn on one of the steam presses, as the cleaning machinery was quite beyond me. (To this day I feel a dishwasher is a total scientific mystery, a fact that I jealously guard and maintain.) The press was bad enough, as the most dreaded and easy thing to do was to put a double crease in trousers, only curable by putting them through the whole process again. Duly having become an 'experienced' cleaner, I took up my job as chairman at the head office over the central Dublin factory in Blackrock, right on the sea, and reasonably safe from the fumes.

It had always struck me that experienced surgeons and dentists never discuss their professions at dinner parties, in order to avoid the inevitability of the lady sitting next to them showing either a scar on their stomach, or their back teeth – neither of which turns one on. I quickly learned not to mention that I was the chairman of IMCO cleaners as, soon after assuming that prestigious position, the lady next to me at dinner lifted her armpit to show me a stain that we had failed to remove. Having 'drink-taken' as they say in Ireland, I somehow managed to resist taking up a soda water siphon immediately to remove the offending stain, and asked her to send the revolting frock to the chairman's office immediately.

The final straw was once, when leaving church in a crush on a Sunday, a pompous, but important, businessman tapped me on the shoulder as I was making the sign of the cross at the holy water font. He proceeded to instruct his wife to bend over and asked me to inspect a stain on the generous posterior of her Sunday best, which we had apparently failed to remove. The body of the church, anxious to get out for their Sunday 'jar' were pressing behind me, so resisting the temptation to advise them to try holy water, I concluded a negotiation in the graveyard outside. Talking of God, thank God we sold the business soon after.

Another of Brown Thomas' take-over bids was more successful. It involved buying an old established department store called Revingtons in Tralee, in West Cork. I was sent to Tralee to negotiate the purchase of this remarkable icon of an old fashioned and totally unaltered Irish provincial department store. The ladies dress department still carried a great notice reading 'Mantles', the hat department 'Bonnets', another 'Manchester Department' and so on. The pine floors were so worn by many years of footsteps (no 7-inch heels, but sensible shoes and boots) that the shiny knots in the floorboards stood out as clearly as the surrounding hills. The staff, who were all around my grandparents' age, shuffled round slowly bent not out of politeness, but from age.

The owner, Mrs Revington, was an imposing widow of amazing character and great fun, but not one to be toyed with – as I subsequently learned. My friend, John McGuire, the boss and owner of our group had also brought Don Callaghan, the managing director, with us. His job, I imagine, was to check the stock, which was roughly the same age as he was, and also to check me in case my natural exuberance, well-fuelled by the local alcohols, prompted me to offer a higher figure than necessary to the indomitable lady; who as it turned out insisted on conducting the entire negotiations in her favourite pub. This was known as 'Nick's', who was the owner of that splendid establishment. The décor was wonderfully traditional and minimalist. Minimalist not in the sense of today's fashionable decorators, but in the Irish country pub sense, of being untouched by paint, mortar, or replacement light bulbs since the day it was built many years ago. The only colours being black and white, to match the pints of Guinness draught stout, lined up on the wet counter. Mrs Revington immediately explained to me that she was 'on the dry'. This was a statement which at first took me aback, in view of the meeting taking place in a pub in which it was evident that she was extremely well known. However it turned out that her being 'on the dry' meant that she only drank large vodka and whites (lemonade) of which she managed to get through an immense amount, without turning a hair, while making us Dubliners blind drunk and therefore pliable.

The pub closed at 10.30pm – doors, shutters and all – but the regulars stayed on and we finally left much the worse for wear. During the protracted negotiations, all the tricky financial questions were fielded by John to me, being the group's financial (so-called) expert. Realising that I had a foreign name Mrs Revington kept on referring to me as 'Gonzales'. For the sake of the deal, I swallowed my pride (and one of the innumerable pints), until near the end of the negotiations, by which time poor Don Callaghan was asleep in the corner. Finally Mrs Revington said to John, "What about it then?" to which John replied with a pronounced slur, "You better ask our financial director." To this she replied, "You mean yer man Gonzalez?" at which point my Polish pride and gallons of stout overcame my commercial cunning, and I said loudly, "My dear Mrs Revington, my name is not Gonzalez." To which she replied, "Then what the hell is it?" All this was conducted in front of an attentive, if highly inebriated audience – it being 1.30am. I drew myself up, and swaying gently said, "My name is quite simple – it is Poklewski Koziell." She replied, "Jaysus, that's not a name, that's filthy talk!" There were roars of laughter all round, including me, and a figure was agreed on. Of course we celebrated by a few, quite unnecessary rounds, and off we rolled to the hotel.

The next bleary morning we met Mrs Revington in the store, whose freshness was getting on my whiskey-sodden nerves. I was determined to get my own back on her somehow, and having spotted a pretty girl behind a counter at least forty years younger than the rest of the staff, I asked Mrs Revington what the girl did. She put her hand up in front of her mouth and whispered, "That's our unmarried mother." I noticed that on the girl's finely sculptured left bosom dangled a Pioneer Pin. This was a widely worn symbol in those days, and indicated that the wearer had forsworn alcohol, and meant that one should not offer them a drink. I replied tartly, "At least she doesn't drink", to which Mrs Revington replied, "No my dear, she prefers the horizontal stuff."

Another amusing incident from Tralee stands out. A good deal later than the Gonzales night, I was trying to buy a shop in Tralee, in order to open a branch of IMCO Dry Cleaners, of which I was chairman. I had many dealings and meetings with our solicitor, as one did with any real estate deal in the country. While I was there he, being Clerk of the Course, invited me to join him and his wife at the big day of Tralee races. I was taken there by a lady friend of his wife's who insisted on visiting a couple of pubs on the way, the main result was that I lost three times to the three-card-trick man (the first and last time I was exposed to that form of gambling). With a shrug of my shoulders, drunkenly muttering, "There's one born every minute" I was swept off to a local lady's grand town house for 'tea'.

There was no tea, but gallons of whiskey. I can just remember two things. I was introduced to a gentleman called Barney, slumped in a corner chair, who due to his day's intake was unable to reply, but managed to open one eye in greeting. "Barney is a man of very few words, don't mind him," said the hostess. Then we were asked to commence tea, which consisted of consuming more dark brown liquids which did not resemble tea too much, in taste anyway. At that stage the hostess produced a large piece of roast meat resting on china platter, which she placed on the sideboard. She then fetched an electric carving knife to demonstrate it to us, as they had just appeared on the market. She switched the frightening weapon on, and leaning over the sideboard at a dangerous angle, pressed it down at full speed on to the meat. At that stage she lost her balance, falling forward. The knife went clean through the meat, after which we heard the china platter shattering, followed by sawdust as the knife pressed on into the sideboard with the owner trying to balance herself on it, until she was lifted off by the onlookers. At that stage the 'tea' broke off, and the assembled company all left, with the exception of Barney who was unable to rise from his chair.

Taken to the (Dry) Cleaners

CHAPTER NINE
The Troubles

WHEN THE TROUBLES between the north and south of Ireland began in the late 1960s the population of the south took a basically anti-British view, and pro-IRA, although in the circles one moved in, that view was not really mentioned aloud. However one sensed a certain tension on the matter between one's English and Irish friends. This, I suppose, was only natural on the part of the Irish after such a long, on the whole unpleasant, and at times vicious, occupation. The British, on the other hand, regarded it as normal that the Protestant planters should rule the north and run most of the judicial, police and army functions. This left the lower layer of the so-called working classes in an inferior position, branded by their origins and religion. The British really had the same attitude to the matter as they did to the rest of the British Empire, conveniently overlooking that *de facto* it no longer existed, and were somewhat surprised as to what the fuss was all about.

Having said that, living and working in Dublin, Polish as I was, with an English wife, and hampered by what my friend Tony O'Reilly called "Vincent's plummy English accent", I kept my counsel. I felt a bit sorry for myself having spent so many years honing my Polish gutturals into English plums, and then finding myself in Ireland, too late to assimilate an Irish lilt. Talking about Irish accents, in my thirty-two years of living there, I never heard anyone say "begorrah," and came to the conclusion that it must have been a music hall invention to typify an Irishman.

During this beginning period of the troubles we gave quite a large dinner party, I think for Harry and Camilla Erne who were staying with us from Northern Ireland. There was a mixture of our Anglo-Irish and Irish friends, and before dinner Annabel and I decided that on no account would we raise the subject of 'the troubles', as that would simply pour cold water on the whole evening. However, after dinner by which time a serious dint had been made on the wine cellar, Tony O'Reilly raised the subject while making some point. I saw Annabel making a signal at me with alarmed eyes and I realised that something dramatic had to be done. Therefore I plunged in saying very loudly to Tony, so that everyone could hear, "Did you know that Captain Boycott was Harry's family's agent?" (Captain Boycott was the British land agent whose ostracism by his local community in Ireland gave the English language the verb 'to boycott'.) There was a total gasp of disbelief, both of the fact – and the fact that I mentioned it. Total silence followed. I prayed that I was correct in my assumption that Harry would not let me down. All eyes turned to him for his reaction. He looked up and said, "Quite true, he was, and a damned efficient chap at that!" Hysterical laughter broke out, further corks were popped, the party went on through the night and the only troubles were the ones the guests had in driving home.

One of the more amusing incidents I was involved in at this time was when on my way home from work I got overtaken by an overpowering thirst (as one does) and entered the nearest pub for a pint of stout. It was not a very high-class pub, very dark with a row of dark-clothed men in cloth caps silently pulling at their cigarettes and pints alternately. I went up to the bar and asked for a pint, upon which a clearly drunk man came forward and said loudly with very stale Guinness breath, "Git out of our country you fuckin' Brit." I summed up the situation quickly: whilst I did not want to retreat from my foaming pint which I had just paid for, neither did I want to start an altercation with him, as a fight is to be avoided at all costs. Nonetheless, I replied in my unfortunate accent that as a matter of fact I was not a Brit. He grunted back, "Fucking Brit." By this time the entire pub was on its toes beginning to enjoy an early cabaret. Seeing that he was a man of limited vocabulary, I challenged

him to speak to me in his native language and I would reply in mine.
I took a fairly safe bet that his sort of Dub (Dublinese for Dubliner)
would not "have the Irish" as they say. The room took a pull at their pints
and looked at me. I then broke into a short impassioned speech in Polish
calling him everything really filthy, of which I have a large vocabulary.
After finishing I said, "Over to you," whereupon there was no reply from
the Irishless one, who staggered out of the pub, muttering "Fuckin' Brit."
Then everyone roared with laughter while I swallowed my pint, took a
bow and left thinking that it might have been a close one.

THE TROUBLES GOT worse and sadly came to roost with us.
Harry Erne, owner of Crom Castle, had kindly granted us a life lease
on Dolly's Cottage in an area called Mullinacoe, on the Crom Estate
in County Fermanagh. It was a lovely Victorian vicarage which had
been lived in by Harry's mother during the war, and then abandoned.
The deal was that we restored it. It had no electricity or water, but as
it was on the shore of Loch Erne, we renewed the pump and bathed,
cooked and drank with the faintly peaty coloured water without any
problems. It tasted very good, and the colour went well with Scotch.
I installed cylinder gas lighting, candles, blowlamps and gas geysers.
We had a heavenly few years there, mostly at weekends, putt-putting
across the lake to the castle on a loch dinghy with a small 'Swallow'
outboard. The most romantic night I remember was the night of the
Apollo moon landing for which we dined at Crom and watched the
whole event on television (we naturally did not have one as they don't
work on bottled gas). When it was all over, we piled into the boat on the
moonlit loch and looked up at the perfectly lit moon, hardly believing
the achievement we had just witnessed.

In the end, the whole house was burnt down by the IRA. The mile-
long drive through the woods actually crossed the border, and as a result
neither north or south police, or fire brigade, came near it. In retrospect,
as we went there before The Troubles began, we might just as well have
restored a weekend house on the Golan Heights. We, thank God, were
not there. There was nothing personal in it, as I was Polish anyway,

and Catholic to boot, and we went on alternate Sundays either to my Catholic church or Annabel's Protestant one at Crom. They simply did it for the hell of it, knowing that it belonged to the Crom Estate and that the British government would have to pay for it. The same happened some weeks later when we were staying at the castle, and they blew up Harry's milking parlour. He fortunately was liked by all, in spite of being an English nabob, House of Lords, Lord Lieutenant and all, and as a result was not murdered, as many of the people of both religions that he knew (and I knew a few of them) in the district were.

We knew a sweet lady, a close neighbour, who was an ex-parlour maid from the castle. She lived with her husband Tommy Bullock, and cleaned the house for us after we had stayed at weekends. Her husband was a B. Special (a sort of police version of the Protestant territorial army), and was shot dead when the IRA knocked on his farmhouse door one night, and then for good measure put a bullet through his wife's neck behind him, and killed her. The next week the loyalist (Protestants) carried out a totally equally pointless killing of a Catholic in Derrylin nearby, in revenge. And so it went on. One had to admire Harry and his wife Camilla for sticking it out all those years bunkered in behind bullet-proof glass every night, as did his cousin and neighbour James Abercorn, Lord Lieutenant of Omagh.

Some other Trouble 'episodes' that I was involved in come to mind. I had an investment in a brand new carpet factory in Newry, which is a large town in the Republic, right near the border. One day I was in Belfast seeking a handout from the Ministry as usual, as the factory was new and we were bringing jobs to a difficult part of Ireland (we got it eventually, but to no avail sadly as politics forced us to close and pack up in the end). Anyway, I was in Belfast train station and decided to go into the buffet to seek refreshment and support for my meeting in the Ministry, and popped out to the gents in the middle. On emerging, I was amazed to be confronted by an emptying station, and went to the buffet to fetch my briefcase. The buffet which had been full was totally empty and closed by police tapes, while my abandoned briefcase stood by my chair in the middle. After much explaining that my briefcase was not a bomb I was finally allowed to go, but without my drink.

On another occasion I was visiting our spinning mill in Monaghan in the south, about twenty miles from the carpet factory in Newry (the

North). The road between was known as 'Bomb Alley' but the rumour was that our managing director, by chance, and a Catholic at that, had negotiated a *laissez passez* with the provisional IRA through their chaplain – such were those days! On entering the spinning mill, where our twenty-seven employees were busy at the long spinning machine, I suddenly saw a notice in bold spray paint letters on the big wall opposite, 'PROVOS RULE HERE!' I told the mill manager to remove it immediately, but he apologised and said that he dare not. I lost my cool, and told him to send for a ladder, sponge and turps as I intended to remove the paint myself. He then pointed out to me a young fellow of about eighteen years at the end of the spinning line, and said with a meaningful look, "Do you see that big bulge in his right jeans pocket? That's not his lunch, it's a gun."

I suddenly warmed up my 'cool' deciding that it was definitely a case of *force majeure* and that a Briggs umbrella was not the weapon one would use if ones opponent in a duel had a Colt revolver, and thinking of my wife and children – not to mention myself – hoofed it back to Dublin. We closed the mill the next week for good. Twenty-seven more to be added to the Monaghan unemployed. One asked oneself, who gained? Answer – no one.

During the time that I was a shareholder and director of Wright Carpets in our brand new factory in Newry we were, as most start-ups are, operating on a tight financial rein. The government in Belfast were eager to improve employment, especially in troubled border areas such as Newry. As a result they were very accommodating with grants, employment incentives and so on, but of course this meant meeting the government representatives for lunch each time. As they were usually the hosts, they insisted on lunching in the Europa Hotel, newly built in the centre. It was a very smart multi-storey hotel. The only disadvantage it suffered from was that it had been bombed by the IRA no less than thirty-three times by the time peace was declared in the North.

At the time I was attending these lunches, it had probably only been bombed around twenty times. However this did not exactly fill one with confidence, especially as the personal searches as one approached the hotel exceeded today's airport procedures. The fact was that it was probably the last hotel in the world one would have chosen to partake of luncheon in, although the food was good, and the staff were friendly (I'm sure they were especially chosen from races that did not know where Ireland was, barely spoke English, and were probably told to expect frequent fireworks from the supporters of Guy Fawkes). Unfortunately on top of all this our tough, brave hosts would insist on our eating at a table on the first floor, right in front of a big plate glass window. Greedy as I am, I found myself unable to distinguish between roast beef and plum pudding, while my nerves directed me to the gent's loo every ten minutes on the excuse of a bladder weakness. The loo, being in the middle of the hotel, was a statistically safer place to pass lunch, and in my calculations increased my chance of survival by fifty to one. Perhaps I am not made of military matter after all.

Another incident from the Newry connection stands out in my mind. Having exhausted the government vaults in the pursuit of our carpets, I persuaded a London merchant bank to send one of their loan officers over to Ireland to consider a long-term loan. I met the young ex-officer from a chic regiment at Dublin airport, where he arrived in a smart pin stripe suit, bowler hat, umbrella and small briefcase. His briefcase contained numerous boring questionnaires with rows of figures, which in due course I managed to fill up with the use of my fertile imagination, and maximum optimism, but for the following reasons was of no use.

I drove him up on the main Belfast road, talking incessantly in case he asked me too many awkward questions about looms, threads, and other obtuse and unexciting carpet-associated queries. We arrived at the borderpost on the southern side to be told that we could not proceed further as there was a "class of an incident" taking place up the road. I got out of the car and proceeded to walk forward, spurred on by the urgent loan weighing on my mind, to find a large articulated lorry jack-knifed in the middle of the road about fifty yards away. As I watched, the said lorry was pulverized in an immense explosion, which practically blew my spectacles off. I turned and ran back to the border post, to find the guards safely concealed inside, but no sign of my banker. He eventually emerged from a ditch, where clearly army training had instructed him to jump, in the event of enemy fire. He was as cool as a cucumber, but covered in mud from top to toe of his immaculate outfit. I did my best to brush him down, and insisted on continuing our journey to Newry on an 'unapproved' road. There, unfortunately, we were stopped by an alerted British army patrol and made to spread-eagle ourselves against an armoured car, prodded by rifles, and thoroughly searched, in spite of my protestations that we were in the carpet business, not munitions. As we drove on I tried to appeal to his patriotism and explained that we must not give in to these brigands; but I must admit that my optimism on the subject of a loan had started to wilt. Needless to say, following a long and polite inspection of the works and humming looms, we received an apologetic letter two weeks later. It seemed that the credit committee had 'carefully considered' the circumstances (which they were kind enough not to enumerate) and were unable to consider the loan.

YET ANOTHER INCIDENT that comes to mind was when we were staying with our great friends, Bill and Daphne Montgomery who live at Greyabbey in the north. Bill at that time was the chairman of the Belfast Opera Company, and we were at the opera in black ties when suddenly there was a tremendous explosion a block away in the middle of an aria. We had a fit, but the orchestra and cast – you can imagine which side they were on – did not even blink and steadfastly continued. The soprano dropped a note, the flautist misplaced his little finger for a moment but the show went on. The only person who appeared most disturbed by the explosion was the conductor, who I think was probably a visiting Italian, poor man. However, he pulled himself together and, baton shaking, continued – although I thought that he was likely to be facing a dry cleaning bill. It was the last time we went to the opera in Belfast, but bombs apart, we far preferred the entertainment offered by the numerous Montgomery family at Greyabbey: wonderful singing and acting – not just up, but professionally – and an unlocked wine cellar. They live on the edge of Strangford Lough with a beautiful view, which reminds me of a story Bill recounts.

In the nineteenth century the Marchioness of Londonderry, who lived nearby in the famous Mount Stewart, decided to be modern and venturesome, and to give the entire staff – some seventy souls – the day off (most unusual in those days), and hired a steamboat for their day's picnicking. The sea lough being huge and frequently very rough, duly sank the boat with all the occupants. Her friends were heard to say,

"Poor Marchioness, how dreadful to be without staff!" while her more practical friends remarked that if one really had to do those sort of things one should only send half the staff at a time.

THE 'NORTH' WAS not all doom and gloom. I remember Harry Erne in his ever-present entrepreneurial spirit had decided to organise a jazz festival in the grounds of the old ruined castle, near his present castle, Crom, on the shores of the beautiful Loch Erne in County Fermanagh. There was a whole ox roasting over a vast fire, bands, singers, swingers and all. The festival involved thousands of jazz- sex-and-drink-crazed youths from surrounding towns, villages and Belfast; plus, being Fermanagh, the pouring rain. Harry had encouraged John Maguire and I to bring up a jolly group of friends from Dublin to add a touch of gaiety and class (which class, I ask myself?)

We hired a bus for the two-hour journey, loaded it with thirty friends and fifteen cases of drink and set off. Rather unwisely, I started opening the drink and by the time we had reached O'Connell Street the party was in full swing. On we went through the pouring rain and then the dark. Two hours were up and I noticed that we were not there, and the bus was swaying along tiny roads and around hairpin bends. The driver was struggling to keep the bus on the road around the bends in the pitch black to the accompaniment of frenzied song, and the sound of empty bottles rolling around the floor. I went forward, and knowing the way well, asked the driver where the hell we were going. He replied that he was told by CIE (which was the national transport authority from whom we had hired the bus), to take us by the 'scenic route' as they assumed that we were overseas tourists. The fact that it was totally dark and pouring with rain, had not for a second caused him to consider a change in the normal route.

An hour overdue I managed to guide him to Crom where our happy, and totally inebriated party, joined the equally inebriated mobs, wading happily in a sea of mud mixed with myriad empty beer cans and discarded clothing. We duly tramped through the happy mob (the locals being quite unshaken by the bursting heavens) to the sound of mud-sucking wellies, clanking beer cans, well-planted – though rather wet – kisses, and of course jazz.

We reached the Song of Erne which was Harry's converted barge, where we settled down to have a few totally uncalled for drinks 'after the journey'. From that moment on, I must admit, the memory grows dimmer, but I do remember, in order to avoid the barge's loo, disembarking to decant into Lough Erne. The reason was that flushing the loo on the Song of Erne was more difficult than trying to start Stephenson's rocket, without steam. On the edge of the water I saw our friend Pat Crowley in her knickers, having persuaded someone to pull her water skiing on Harry's speedboat – without wearing skis. This is a difficult achievement even on skis, which incidentally she had never achieved either. The result was an immediate and immense splash, a vast mop of red hair coming to the surface, many very expressive Celtic imprecations, and Mrs Crowley, ex-model, striding proudly to the shore holding up the remains of her highly distressed knickers – the bra having escaped into the silent depths of Loch Erne.

The night and the water-skiing wore on, plus of course the drinking. At about 6am, with the sun rising, our host Harry decided to give a demonstration of water-skiing, I think to impress a young and very shy deb. I escorted the girl into the speedboat and sat beside her in the back to better see his Lordship 'do his thing'. The boat took off driven by a young blood, whose blood alcohol by that time must have been immense. The young virgin clung to me in the cold slipstream, and watched Harry rise from the waves in his boxer shorts, which then of course opened in the slipstream, like the curtains in a Punch and Judy show, upon which his manhood dropped out. There was of course nothing he could do about it, as he was holding on for dear life to the towbar and the water was very dark and freezing. I felt the girl stiffen with horror, fascination and embarrassment. I just put my arm round her shoulders in a very consoling and avuncular way, and told her that she was not to worry, she was just looking at life. As the Noel Coward song goes, "I wonder what happened to her?"

Nobody remembered the journey back to Dublin, which was reached at about 10am, by which time several relationships and marriages were on the rocks, but due to alcoholic amnesia, no one remembered what the problem had been, and life among the 'Dublin Gas Company', as Eileen Mount Charles later dubbed us, went on as usual.

CHAPTER TEN
Between The Wars

IN THE MID-SEVENTIES, we bought Stacumny House, near Celbridge in county Kildare. It was largish, old, typically Irish country house on about six acres of garden, with an orchard and stables. In those days it could be safely described as being in the country, with small roads leading to it, and fields surrounding it – even the occasional visit from the hounds. Now it is several European Union roundabouts and traffic lights away from the city, and the drive to Dublin feels more like 30 miles than 15.

It was not long after this that my darling wife Annabel developed cancer. After courageous struggles she finally succumbed in 1977, at the age of forty-two. After her death, I began to realise with some shock what wives really did in life. My struggles as a mere single man with a large house, organising the education and clothing of four children, as well as juggling various businesses and charity-work, sometimes proved too much and became difficult to manage. On reflection I don't suppose that either the education or clothing were brilliantly achieved, but any shortcomings do not appear to have marked them in an adverse way. Just as they depended more on me, I was kept going by them, their wonderful company and permanent, if sometimes eccentric, needs. Half terms in two countries – England and Ireland – sports days, clothes lists, and a permanent bad conscience about purposefully avoiding parents' matches and school plays. After all, what could I contribute to parents' matches apart from backgammon and mixing exotic cocktails?

In fact the additional activities that I was thrown into were salutary in that they shook me out of depression – if not memories – and made me get on with life. After all, children are not something that one can put off. However, as always, they were a wonderful, loving and comforting presence, although I could have done without some of their school affairs.

I remember especially the struggles with the girls' school list from St. Mary's Convent, Shaftesbury. Once after trying to decipher the underwear list, which was about as understandable as advanced Sudoku, I remember a conversation with the headmistress, who was a fairly stout nun, to the effect that I had sent several sets of brown knickers for Sophie (my youngest), where I had clearly confused her waist measurement with her inside leg measurement. She reproached me by saying, "Really, Mr Poklewski, the knickers you sent for Sophie would have fallen down to *my* ankles." As for the academic discussions, I managed to keep my end up without either betraying my ignorance, or nodding off.

When my stepson Rupert left his prep school, Headfort, in Ireland, I was advised by the headmaster that the most suitable school to send him to was Gordonstoun in Scotland. This I duly did, but I was faintly alarmed by the reports of his learning abilities. Eventually I realised that I needed to visit the school. This was easier said than done, as it involved an extremely uncomfortable and arduous two-day outing from Ireland and across Scotland to Elgin, with little drink or food.

I finally arrived shivering, as it is seldom above zero in that part of Scotland, and was given a filthy lunch in the canteen of stringy stew made out of retired laying hens. The sort of dish my father would have referred to as "Fricassée de poulet Tchaikovsky" (meaning a symphony in strings) accompanied by milk or orange squash – neither being on my normal wine list. His housemaster, Mr Scott, told me that he could not understand why I had not come to the parents' cricket match. I bit my tongue and avoided telling him that I disapproved of such unnatural practices. Upon me telling him that I was worried about Rupert's less than exciting academic reports, he twirled his handlebarred moustache and told me, "Rupert's a jolly sound chap and damn good at the long jump." After the tiresome journey, foul food and lack of drink, this remark proved too much for me; I told him that I was delighted about the long jump and that I was sure it would come in handy in Rupert's future life, when jealous husbands returned home, but that I could not accept that it was a sound preparation for adult life. Mr Scott practically twirled his horrible moustache off (with a faint spatter of chicken stew still visible) and told me that in a long career of education, he had never heard such an extraordinary remark from a parent before. There ended my first and last interview at Gordonston (but not the last bill).

The next term the school became co-educational and busloads of well-built girls in straining black knickers were imported to the school. That was when Rupert changed to the short jump. After all his uninspiring school reports, he eventually trained to be a pilot and became captain of three categories of passenger jet – a feat that requires considerably more than the five times table.

I came across a letter the other day from the headmaster in reply to mine which informed him that we were taking Rupert out of Gordonston to learn French in a job in Cannes.

Gordonstoun School
Elgin
Morayshire
IV30 2RF

From:
The Headmaster

2nd June, 1977

Dear Mr Poklewski Koziell

   Very many thanks for your letter about Rupert and
for confirmation that he will be leaving at the end
of the term.

   Sorry though we shall be to lose him, I'm sure that
your decision is a good one and that the practical
skill of speaking a foreign language fluently is best
taught and caught by staying in the country.

   I spent some time in Europe last holidays and was
more than ever impressed by the fact that there is an
interesting and good living to be had in Europe.

   J.W.R. Kempe

No comment.

ONE PARTICULARLY VEXING parental duty was my obligation to go to a parent/teachers conference at St. Mary's Shaftesbury for Eliza's sake, as she was then approaching the leaving stage. Having sweated my way to England and then to Shaftesbury, I found myself plonked down on a folding wooden chair in the gym, after a shaky lunch with the senior girls, and a mass of what I can only describe as 'professional' parents being addressed by a butch woman from the Ministry of Education. She started by telling the girls that they did not have to become air-hostesses, but could become engineers, planners, pathologists and so on. I glanced around the hot hall and could only see a mass of girls sitting dreamily thinking of the Rolling Stones. When the dreary lecture finally came to an end I started to stand up, ready to flee with Eliza to a place of refreshment. But to my horror a professional, navy-jacketed father stood up and asked some bloody stupid question like, "My daughter wants to become a theatrical director. How does she go about it?" After a ten-minute reply, which called to mind Noel Coward's "Don't put your daughter on the stage Mrs Worthington!" a flood of other mind-numbing questions came from the audience. I was beside myself, drinks time having come and gone, so I turned to Eliza and said that I was going to stand up and ask a question. Intrigued and excited she asked what I was going to ask. I replied, "My daughter wants to have a baby. How does she go about it?" However, the presence of the headmistress Sister Louise and a scarlet and frightened Eliza (who realised that her dysfunctional and faintly eccentric father was almost capable of carrying out his threat), made me desist.

Another school duty took place some years later, when Sophie was at St. Paul's Girl's School in London, which apart from its well-earned academic reputation was renowned for its music. I had to attend an evening school concert, and knowing that Sophie, like me, was for her sins one of the least musical creatures in existence, wondered what possible part she could participate in. I was late, and just had time to greet Sophie rushing into the hall. I asked her hastily what part she was due to play in the concert, to which she replied on the run, "The piano." This floored me completely as the nearest ivories she had ever been connected to were on the rosary. It was only when I saw the grand piano being moved across the stage, and I recognised Sophie's bum straining underneath, that I understood what she had meant.

THE YEAR AFTER Annabel's death I took the three younger children to France to visit Rupert for whom I had obtained the position of 'Commis Debutant' in the restaurant of Cannes' smartest hotel, the Carlton. We started off on the French ferryboat, known as 'The Vomiting Venus' together with the car from Cork. The children were very excited and rushing around the large and rather smart boat, stopped, electrified outside the restaurant, where a very colourful seafood buffet was displayed with every kind of shellfish imaginable. Aware of the cost, the fact that we were all sharing a cabin, and the reputation of the Bay of Biscay, I managed to restrain them from entering, telling them that it was much too early and that we should wait until we had left harbour and got round the headland. My strategy worked and within half an hour they were staggering around poor things, totally pea green, and even the mention of lobster or mussels would have been disastrous. I managed to manhandle them on to their bunks, where they lay unpeacefully all night.

We got to Paris, where we stayed in a reasonably humble hotel near the Arc de Triomphe. Humble it may have been but which five star hotel would have made such a gesture? Upon returning to Ireland we received a parcel from that hotel containing a half-eaten packet of potato crisps – who has ever received something like that from a hotel? Mind you, perhaps if we had left a string of pearls, watch or radio they might not have sent them. Who knows? Onwards we drove to spend a couple of days with Rupert the waiter. We had a drama however on the way down. I was bowling along the motorway at 140km per hour, when there was a scream from Sophie sitting in the back seat. She was playing with her Tiny Tears doll which did anything from crying to drinking to peeing. Sophie had just put her on her tiny purple potty and was emptying the contents out of the car window when it was torn from her fingers by the slipstream. "Stop!" she cried, "I've lost Tiny Tears' potty!" I was between two lorries and a Mercedes, all racing each other at 140km/hour. "To hell with Tiny Tears!" I shouted in panic to more screams from Sophie. "I'll buy you two new Tiny Tears if we live through this journey," I cried. I never actually did and I have never been forgiven.

We finally reached Cannes where the children were awed by seeing their brother in his white linen uniform with golden chevrons on his shoulders, kicking the kitchen door open while holding immense dishes aloft. Rupert afterwards went on to become a chef in Paris, and like his stepfather (me) followed a number of varying careers, before taking to flying. I am afraid to say that although it has often been said of me that "He's flying", I do not possess the intricate skills it takes to fly a jet, and could not tell the difference between a cumulus cloud and a hangover.

AT ONE STAGE of my widowhood, a friend who was involved in arranging Irish shooting trips for rich Americans persuaded me to let Stacumny to a group. Neither Annabel nor my future wife Vicky would have allowed it of course, but I agreed to do it fully-staffed for a week (an agreement forced out of me by the size of the rent). They all duly arrived, eight of them as far as I can remember. I'd meant to move the children into the gate lodge, but forgot that I had asked uncle Stas and his wife Lucy to come from Poland at the same time, so finally solved matters with the kind loan of a clapped out lorry-caravan that Kevin and Mary-Jane Wiley, our near neighbours, used for picnicking (i.e. drinking), at point-to-points.

The girls were crammed in and rather grumpily survived the experience having to both wash and pee in a bucket, in spite of my generosity in providing at least two. I moved into Sophie's room in the main house and crammed myself into a two-foot six-inch wide bed, with my feet hanging over the end. At that time, I was employing a cook called Rose, an excellent chef, whose only fault was that she drank at least twice as much as her employer. Another disadvantage the poor lady had was a ferocious squint, which meant that she always looked at the ceiling while addressing one.

On their last night the Americans had a large and vinous dinner party, and as a result the cook and the butler (me) got particularly plastered. They had asked to be called at 7am as their hired limos were arriving at 8am. Rose had strict instructions to wake me, the maid and guests in good time. Come the morning, I was woken out of a deep claret and port slumber by the continuous ringing of the front door bell. I rushed down in my pyjamas to find the limo drivers trying to get in for the luggage. In a blind panic I rushed to shake Rose awake –

not a pretty sight – and then galloped around the bedrooms, shouting that it was 8am. A series of very curt replies came back through the doors, "It can't be, we were to be woken at seven!" I apologised and explained that there was a slight complication and that breakfast was ready – which was a blatant lie.

The dining room had been laid, but nothing else prepared. There was no sign of Rose. I dashed around the kitchen in my pyjamas boiling kettles as the guests began to bark orders through the hatch, "Black coffee, hold the milk! China tea, two eggs sunny side up, toast light! Eggs over easy!" Rose staggered in looking like the wrath of God. I was holding two frying pans on the go when I saw, much to my annoyance, that she was staring at the corner of the ceiling with her drink-enraged, pink, squinty eye. Suddenly I realised that her eye was not focused on the ceiling but on the top of my pyjamas, which were gaping open. Holding two egg-filled frying pans there was little I could do to help my modesty, and I told her to concentrate on the other sausages instead. The guests ate and left, forgetting to tip me. I passed Rose on to Mikaela Irwin who knew she was a great cook, without dwelling on her 'weakness'. She eventually left the Irwins after cooking many good meals and drinking the cellar dry.

DURING THE SEVENTIES, I travelled quite a lot to Poland, which although still firmly in communist control, was no longer totally under the Russian yoke. The immediate members of the family who remained in Poland during and after the war were my paternal grandmother who survived until 1949 (whom I did not see after the war), my paternal aunt Maniuta, who looked after her, and uncle Stas, my father's brother. They all had a very tough war as well as post-war existence and were constantly in my parent's thoughts as we, through good luck, lived in comparative luxury and comfort in England.

Uncle Stas survived the war as a district food controller around the Warsaw area. Due to his command of languages he survived and kept the family going by cheating the Germans, helping the hungry, fiddling the books and playing the black market. After the war he was arrested in Katowice by the communist police, quite simply because of his background, and imprisoned for some weeks in jail, crowded with many others in a confined space. I remember him telling me that they could constantly hear the shots of the many executions taking place in the prison yard outside, without having any knowledge of who might be next. However, uncle Stas, being very canny, survived by talking himself out of execution and was finally released.

Stas's sister, aunt Maniuta, suffered a worse fate however. She had secured a post as translator in the press section of the British Embassy in Warsaw and through the influence of the Ambassador, Cavendish Bentinck (a friend of the family), she managed to organise a brief visit to us in England. However on her return to Warsaw she was arrested with a number of others, by the communist authorities, and endured a long, trumped-up 'traitor' trial. Their offence can only be compared to a search for democracy and a subsequent desire to vote the governing powers out. There was no terrorism, bombing or assassination involved as we are now accustomed to witness, in the world as we know it. However they were all condemned for 'treason', several to death, and the rest to long prison sentences. My poor father sat through long broadcasts of the trumped-up trial on the Polish radio. Maniuta was given a sentence of twelve years. She was 57 at the time. Her sentence was spent in a horrible prison the other side of Poland from Warsaw, and she was only released when the regime changed in 1956 to a slightly more humane one under Gierek. By that time she was sixty-seven and having survived ten difficult years without access to a priest or doctor, she emerged riddled with untreated cancer, only to die after three months – so we never saw her again. In later years I met some old Polish ladies of aristocratic origins (their crime!) who had at one time shared a cell with her, and told us what wonderful character she showed in prison, and what an inspiration both spiritual and practical she was to the other unfortunate prisoners.

Finally, after many years and the beginning of the political thaw, I was able to travel to Poland to stay with uncle Stas and his splendid wife, Lucy. She was a pillar of strength, and had led a group of co-operative ladies in the hard times (I imagine they must have been a communist version of the Women's Institute). She delighted in telling me of the occasional outings, with picnics, consisting of yards of saved-up garlic sausage, bread and an average of a bottle of vodka a head – talking of which, I had never come across a woman with such a strong one. Both Stas and I (who were not in the bottom league of drinkers, by any standards) were left at the starting gate by auntie when it came to vodka.

I eventually bought them a comfortable apartment on the ground floor in the centre of Warsaw, where I used to stay with them on a divan in the living room. I took Sophie with me for a visit to Poland, where aunt Lucy made us share the sleeping arrangements. After a particularly boozy and convivial scattered family evening, I woke up in the middle of the night with a shock, wondering where I was, and realising that I had a female bottom in my face. On remembering the party and the fact that I was in aunt Lucy's flat, I had a fit and broke out into a cold sweat. Then after careful exploration the bottom turned out to belong to a sleeping Sophie, who in her slumber had crawled into that position on the narrow divan. That reminds me that when she was older, and I would pinch her bottom, she would say with a lisp, that she has since conquered, "Don't do that, that's incense" being unable to pronounce 'incest' – not that she understood the full meaning of the word.

On that occasion, aunt Lucy was watching Sophie getting dressed one morning, and was bemused to see her putting a plastic bag over her sock. When asked, Sophie explained that she had a hole in the sole of her shoe, and the bag stopped her foot from getting wet. Aunt Lucy was horrified – even children in Poland during the Cold War were not wearing plastic bags over their socks! A shopping trip was immediately planned, much to my dismay as it was already drinks time, and the last thing I wanted to do was to be dragged round the Warsaw markets in search of shoes. Sophie was delighted with the attention, and spun the whole trip out, shaking her head each time a pair of shoes was suggested, just like the Queen. Meanwhile, I had to endure many of those 'How could you?' looks from Lucy that are sometimes the lot of a single parent.

On another occasion I left Warsaw with uncle Stas for my first visit to St. Petersburg to view (from the outside) two of the family properties, on the Fontanka canal (Fontanka 24) and Novoissakievskaia 4, where he had been brought up. The Fontanka property had belonged to my great uncle Stanislas, who had been a diplomat. The other property, near St Isaac's catherdral had belonged to my grandfather.

It was a fascinating visit and one learned a bit about the old Stalinist regime. First of all, although we were travelling as two private individuals on the St. Petersburg Express, and not in a group, when we got out of our sleeping car we were met by two men in Homburg hats. They greeted us by name, introduced themselves as from Intourist (the government travel agency), and explained that their job was to take us in a limousine to our hotel, free of charge.

They were of course from the NKVD government secret service, which I believe in those days employed over two million people in the USSR. They duly got a signed receipt from the hotel for us, and left bowing politely. The hotel had some fifteen or twenty storeys, with a concierge on each floor to hand over or receive one's room key, needless to say noting time and details each time. Our concierge was a jolly, young, and very fat lady who said, "You are Eengleesh, yes? Now, I order Eengleesh breakfast for you, egg and pig. You see, I spik perrfek Eengleesh." Stas pointed out to me that the police suspended in cabins above the traffic lights on intersections were for noting the coming and going of cars, and not for the controlling of lights, thus the whole population was well-supervised.

Another bit of communist behaviour we noted was upon entering the enormous dining room, which contained a dance orchestra in full swing, barely any dancers or diners, and a mass of waiters standing around and gossiping. After twenty minutes of sitting at a table and being ignored, I finally persuaded a reluctant Stas in his fluent Russian to wave to the Maitre D' who came over and said, "Don't worry we have noticed you." Ten minutes later a waiter came over with an enormous menu and waited with satisfaction for us to select our dishes, after which he told us they were all 'off' the menu, and informed us what we could eat. At the end of a very shaky meal, he came over with the change that I had left as a tip on the plate and simply said that we had left some money behind, while handing it back to us. So, back to our rooms in Warsaw to feast on the goodies I had brought with me.

My departures to Poland in those days were fraught with what I had to carry, such as loo paper, soap, plus varieties of food, and most important of all, raw meat. I always found it bizarre to have to visit the butcher's *before* my trips to Poland – a country that used to be famed for its red meat and pork. Lucy's main request was for lamb, as it was apparently difficult to find in the Warsaw queues. The result was that in those pre-Ryanair days – when weight did not matter so much – I carried huge loads. Unfortunately on occasion I was held up at the airport because blood was dripping from a suitcase or hand luggage (no vacuum packs then!) and questioned at length as they obviously suspected I was transporting a dismembered body out of the country.

The luggage on the return was equally bulky, as I could not resist buying all sorts of trash for the children and myself, simply because of the exchange rate on the black market. The children would watch me unpack with disbelief as my suitcase was always laden with strange and useless objects, like forty metal skewers or packets of nutcrackers 'only 18p each'. In fact, my daughter Sophie recently found a letter describing the contents of my suitcase on a return from one of these trips: "I watched him unpack and it was like a delicatessen. This is what came out of his suitcase (excluding normal clothes etc.): 1 pistol, 2 Persian helmets with nosepieces, 11 blackmarket tapes, 1 plastic cane with silver top, 1 potato-carrier's basket, 1 engraved coal ashtray, 1 box Polish chocolates, 1 embroidered tablecloth, 3 round printed tablecloths, sausages *ad infinitum*, 12 tins of black caviar, 4 bottles of Zubrowka vodka, 1 malt whiskey, 3 ½ litres of Scotch whiskey, 2 crystal vases, 5 packets of easy-cook kasha, 4 packets of soused herring, 1 ½ smoked eels, 2 metal vodka glasses, 1 gilded wooden monkey, 2 reproduction print posters and 1 plastic Russian summer hat."

On one visit to Poland, I can remember buying dinner for four, including beer and masses of vodka, for twenty-four shillings. But one had to be willing to queue for everything. Talking about queues, I am reminded of an occasion reported in the paper during the war in London when an old lady was seen at the end of a queue in The Haymarket for the film 'The Tales of Hoffman'. Not being able to reconcile the lady with the subject, the reporter asked her what she was queuing for, to which she replied, "I'm not quite sure, but me 'usband will eat anything."

Between The Wars

The Ape Has Stabbed Me

CHAPTER ELEVEN
Skellingtons in the Closet

THE NAME OF the previous chapter 'Between the Wars' comes from my wife Vicky's description of 'between marriages', a phrase that owes more to her sense of humour than reality, I might add. It's amusing, but caution is advised in whose presence one uses it. Vicky and I first met under the roof of a mutual friend of ours, Nigel Pemberton, in Montego Bay, Jamaica. He and Vicky were 'close' friends at that time, and I happened to be travelling in female company just in case the world took me for a fifty-year-old widower (which I was), turning grey (which I also was), and turning gay in desperation (which I wasn't). We met for such a short time that it could not be called a *coup de foudre*, but I just had enough time to arrange a meeting in London. Vicky was separated from her husband Ivor Wimborne, and lived outside Paris, which I persuaded her, was *en route* to Warsaw where I was going. Then Nigel and Vicky came to stay with me in Ireland for a party I was giving, and that was more or less that. Nigel and I are still friends, and Vicky and I have been happily married for the last thirty-two years. She recovered bravely at the change of name from Wimborne to Poklewski Koziell, and the only person who had the bad taste to refer to it, was our friend Tyrone Waterford who, leaning on the bar of White's Club reasonably satiated with port after lunch at about 3pm, saw me enter and in a loud voice announced, "Here comes the man who is reducing Lady Wimborne to the ranks!"

Vicky, or Victoria Vigors (her maiden name), is a true daughter of the Raj, having been born in Bangalore. Her main dowry on our marriage was her son Ivor, at that time aged twelve. He has been a splendid stepson, much loved by his 'glued-on' family, and a successful musical composer and producer. Vicky's father, who died many years ago, who I never met, had a distinguished career in the Indian army. He commanded his regiment, Hodson's Horse, 9th Indian Lancers, and was commandant of the Viceroy's Bodyguard. He was chief instructor at the cavalry school in Saugur and subsequently commandant. During the war he commanded the Mysore State Troops. He was a keen sportsman and a fine polo player (9 goal handicap). One can imagine that with a pedigree like that he apparently was not someone who would put up with much nonsense, a trait that Vicky has to some extent inherited – although both had, and have, great charm. As a small digression, I came across his game book of 1911.

" Viceregal Lodge: Delhi, Wednesday, 1 tiger (9 foot, 7 inches) and 5 partridges.
    Gwalior: crocodile (17 foot, 4 inches), 9 geese and 1 partridge."

A trifle different from the shooting charts one sees in Gloucestershire and the Borders!

So, newly married, Vicky returned to Ireland where she'd spent some of her childhood after India. She describes herself as an 'Anglo-Irish horse Protestant from County Carlow' – the 'horse' bit comes from having being Master of the Pytchley hunt, and Master of the West Meath hunt in subsequent years. Fortunately she happily fell back into Irish life, habits, and eccentricities without even leaving a ripple on the pond. I do not know whether it was Stacumny or us that attracted an eclectic range of staff, residents and guests – but we sure had them all. Among the more colourful ones was none other than my old friend and drinking companion Gerry Albertini. He had dangerously reduced his net assets after a series of unfortunate race meetings and many sessions at green, baize-covered tables in a number of posh casinos, and had wisely decided to decamp and live with me in Ireland. After all his years of generosity I welcomed him with open arms, and set him up in the rebuilt Old Piggery next to the house. He loved the name and immediately installed a weather vane in the shape of a copper pig on the roof. He was a good companion although he had for some time given up what he called 'the grog' – but did not forsake his other two lifetime interests, namely gambling and sex. However one disadvantage of having him on one's doorstep was his tendency to ring me early in the morning (9am), with totally inconsequential information, for instance, to inform me that it was raining. This information was both unnecessary as we lived a hundred yards apart, and because it was Ireland. Strangely in Ireland, a day of pouring rain would always be called, "a fine soft day."

While Annabel was alive we had two cars, one of which was a luxurious sinking Citroen – which was reserved for our use – and the other a workman-like Renault 4, for staff, children, shopping and other less important purposes. When Gerry installed himself with me he started off by using the Renault 4. This always seemed a little incongruous to me, as I remembered his previous cars – Bentleys, Aston Martins, a vintage Isotta-Franchini, and even the tulip-wooded Hispano-Suiza. However, the 'readies' (as Gerry always referred to cash in his racecourse parlance) being temporarily short, he seemed quite content with my clapped-out Renault 4. Very quickly it got to the point when the staff got used to asking him whether they could borrow the car.

It was not until I married Vicky, and a second car was needed, plus I had heard that the bankers were answering his calls again, that during one of his early morning weather reports I suggested to him that he might buy a car. The immediate reply was, "What do I need a fucking car for?" He got the point however and immediately bought a smarter one than ours.

For some unknown and eccentric reason Gerry had to have somebody to cook his breakfast. She was a splendid lady who drove over from Leixlip every morning to make him an enormous fry up. Her surname escapes me, but she was always known to one and all as "Breakfast Eileen."

There always seemed to be a turnover of faintly eccentric people living in the Gate Lodge: from two teachers, to two Polish carvers and restorers. The latter I had 'slipped' into Ireland from the Royal Castle in Warsaw where they were working in very break-even conditions. Somehow I had been persuaded to take them under my wing over multitudinal glasses of vodka. Official they could not be, but after much restoring and carving of gilt mirrors and frames for us, they both flourished with their work. It was of an outstanding standard and was soon well known and singled-out for private collections and museums.

On the whole we were less successful with the gardeners. The lady gardeners seemed to lack either the skill or energy to till our stony soil. I remember one of them, I recall being named Rita, was always having a battle of wills with Vicky which on the whole was not very successful. Vicky was a far more experienced gardener for a start, and when spade came to shovel equally iron-willed. The end came when, in spite of much urging, the potato crop failed to appear, and one morning the spare car and Rita seemed to be missing. We let things be for a couple of days before raising a national police alert. However two days later we received a very jolly postcard to say that our car could be found at the car park of a distant provincial railway station should we be interested in collecting it, and in the meanwhile "Good luck to Mrs P. and her bloody potatoes."

We then employed another gardener, Mike. Shortly after he began work I went to see him in the log-shed to check that he was properly registered for tax and so on. He said that he was not registered for those things, and on being asked how he kept his wife and five children, he said, as he swung a giant axe in the air to split a two-foot wide tree trunk, "I'm on a total disability pension." I shrugged my disabled drinking arm and wondered how I could join that club. Clearly whatever disabilities he claimed from the Ministry of Employment did not extend below the belt, as he'd taken a shine to Pauline, the cook and housekeeper. So not only was the cuisine disrupted, but the tool shed was doubling as a knocking shop at the same time. The final result was that he burnt out his car, the purchase of which I had underwritten, collected the insurance and shoved off to the USA with Pauline, leaving his wife and five children – and me with the bill for the car.

We ended our days in Ireland with a splendid couple, who answered our advertisement – from South Africa of all places. They were eager to leave the apartheid culture on a basis of conscience. He was a budding provincial museum director, and she was a very good painter. They had no idea what they were meant to do, poor things, while I, in my disguised ignorance simply said, "Everything." They stayed, became firm friends, and still are, until we went to England permanently and they back to South Africa where the political climate suited them better by then, accompanied by a bonny son they had produced in the bracing air of Ireland.

I have stayed in their charming house in Caledon, 70 miles east of Cape Town, where they are happy. He is a curator of an important museum, and she is a progressively successful artist. I think that they really enjoyed life together with us, although it must be admitted they probably carried out more of what I believe are described as 'chores' than me. They took to the Irish psyche perfectly, maybe because they were not totally dyed in the wool Africaner, being called Tizzie and Carol Mangiagalli.

A couple of years later I lost my driving licence having taken the odd glass of sherry before dinner at Castlemartin with the O'Reilly's. I had been stopped in Naas after midnight and made to blow up one of the early toy balloons, which promptly burst just like at a children's party. I was then humiliated by the burly station sergeant who made me walk through the police station holding a giant potty to the loos, murmuring in the meantime, "Take your time now", just like nanny used to.

The result was that I had to take on a driver, Pat McLaughlin, who was a splendid character and a man of many parts. We took him to Florida to the Windsor Club on a couple of winters, where he impressed the members greatly with his imitation of an English butler, being seen sitting on the outside stairs of the house cleaning my shoes. On another occasion after one of our more riotous parties, he put his head round the door of the library, still full of guests having one for the road at 3.30am before boarding their golf trolleys to go home. Wearing an army steel helmet (we collected hats), he said, "Shall I serve yous breakfast now? It will save you getting up in the morning." Eventually Pat moved on to Gerry when I got my licence back, and Gerry's finances improved.

Over the years we had an assortment of jolly Irish staff, which meant continual coffee parties went on in the kitchen, but not too much dusting, as one of our guests remarked, noting that Mrs Kelly our long-term daily cleared the dust from the drawing room chimneypiece with one tremendous blow from left to right. God bless her anyway, she kept us amused by never saying anything nice about anyone, and kept the shops going by the amount of plates broken. As Pat, the so-called butler would remark on hearing plates being fired round the kitchen in a good imitation of a Greek tavern, "Mrs Kelly is having a smashing time tonight." She did however manage to produce and bring up fourteen children in a two-room gate lodge nearby. Mrs Kelly always held the chair of the kitchen coffee mornings, which were usually thick with smoke and gossip. If I popped my head around the door, on my way out to a bicycle ride, I could tell what the local news broadcast contained. If she was smiling it was the announcement of a death, which always cheered her, and everyone else, up. This was nothing against her, as the two most popular bits of news one could announce in Ireland was that someone had achieved death or bankruptcy, although the latter word was beyond her, and instead informed one that they had gone "phoot." Other kitchen malapropisms were Mike the gardener's 'ulsters' (ulcers) and one of the gardening ladies was always complaining of her 'kidleys'.

Occasionally Mrs Kelly had a real juicer, and would arrive with a heaving bosom, one eye expressing horror and the other one intense pleasure, announcing that the new curate had upped stumps in the night, left everything behind, and had gone off with "that woman." "I thought all along that he had a funny look in his eye when he called on her," she proclaimed, quivering like a jelly. Not as funny as hers, I thought. Anyway this caused great pleasure all round, and even a satisfied nod from my Protestant wife, which I think signified that she did not find Catholics so unnatural after all. I kept quiet on the subject, but reflected that all the village confessions must have driven the poor man into a voracious sexual state.

The peculiar staff situations got sorted out after I married Vicky, and the parties began in earnest and continued unabated for all ages. Vicky soon got used to Irish timekeeping. One was usually invited to dinner at 7.15 for 8.00pm, but nobody in their right minds would turn up until 8.30pm or later, as dinner would never be served until 9pm at the earliest. It would last well into the night, probably until 3 or 4am, when the well-oiled guests would finally leave – that is, when they could find their cars. This was all really bad luck for well-brought-up Americans, who on an initial visit to Ireland would turn up at 7.20pm, only to find their hosts in the bath. One would see the wretched guests, when one arrived at 8.45pm, propping themselves up against the mantelpiece, having been plied with multiple 'jars' for one-and-a-half hours, just as the main party of guests arrived howling for drinks.

Shortly after we married, Vicky and I gave a fairly large dinner party. By ten o'clock, two of the more important guests had not arrived. Finally, Vicky fearing that the dinner would turn to ashes ushered everyone into the dining room. At this point a large brown Bentley screeched to a halt at the front door, and the couple came in, in a faintly dazed fashion. The wife turned around to Vicky and said, "Sorry my dear, but you see we had a lunch", an apology which the assembled company appreciated and understood perfectly.

To celebrate our marriage we gave a massive party at Stacumny. Among other excitements we hired the Maynooth Brass Band, well known in the district for attending religious, civil and political occasions. They arrived duly clad in their splendid uniforms, and marched up and down the drive at full blast as the guests arrived. By that time I was fired with drink and excitement and my (normally well concealed) weakness for exhibitionism came to the fore. I changed into a uniform from my collection, and crowned with an Indian army topee, led the band up and down the lawn. We had asked our staff to the party as well, and needless to say they arrived with various relatives. The Maynooth Brass Band realising this, saw no reason for leaving the party as the drink had not run out, and they were surrounded by friends. The net result was a madly successful, if a touch eccentric party, much enjoyed by one and all, including the overseas visitors, who did however remark the next day that we had made some quite interesting – if somewhat unusual – Irish friends. As for the Maynooth Brass Band, I have no recollection of when they actually left, but for the next few days the gardener kept on finding items of uniform and clothing in the shrubbery and herbaceous borders, which were duly delivered back in black sacks and received without comment.

At a later date our friends, Galen and Hilary Weston, asked if they could borrow Stacumny from us to give an informal dinner for their friend the Prime Minister of Canada, Brian Mulroney, who was coming to Ireland on a state visit. Unfortunately they had had to desert their heavenly home, Roundwood, in county Wicklow after a long and sinister attempt to kidnap them by the IRA. We were more than happy to lend our house, however what we did not anticipate was the security that had to take place beforehand. For three days, the house and grounds were combed by two security forces: Irish and Canadian.

For security reasons the local police force had not been informed at that point, as there were suspicions that there could have been some connection with the IRA. However, so as not to put the local nose out of joint, Sergeant Hughes, head of the police station at Celbridge, was given the task of seeing me with some important information on the morning of the dinner. We knew and liked each other well, and he duly came, cap under elbow and said in a low voice, "I believe you have a VIP for dinner tonight?" to which I agreed. He told me that he had come to warn me that the 'sniffer squad' from Dublin Castle, the police headquarters, were coming at three o'clock with their dogs. I said that considering all the security performance that had been taking place, I hardly considered it necessary, to which he replied that he imagined that the VIP would be using the toilet after dinner, and they'd better check it. I could not resist asking him whether the sniffer squad wanted to check it before or after the Prime Minister had used it. I fear that my sense of humour failed to raise a laugh with Sergeant Hughes, discussing such a solemn moment.

The evening started when the Prime Minister arrived with a motorcycle escort of at least fourteen police, and as a result, the gravel on our drive took days to recover. We had organised a local squeezebox man to receive the guests in the hall with Irish music and songs. Unfortunately the Canadian ambassador rather undiplomatically arrived forty-five minutes late, by which time the squeezebox man was well filled with Guinness, and in full flood with Brian Mulroney in equally full song. Catching the drinks, and the party spirit, as is my wont, I went upstairs and dressed up as a Canadian Mountie out of my large collection of caps and uniforms. Unfortunately I was unaware of the fact that there had been some scandal in Canada just recently when, I think it was the head of the force, had been obliged to resign in a blaze of publicity. As a result my appearance went down like a pork chop in a synagogue, with Mulroney shouting, "My God, that's all I need!" However the evening proceeded in a typical Irish way, with Stacumny overtones, and everybody satisfactorily fed and watered, including the motorcycle outriders who left in a spray of gravel and cheer.

Another memorable party was organised by Vicky and the children for my 60th birthday (long ago!) Supper and dancing took place down the road in Castletown House. Stacumny was not big enough and Castletown is the biggest Palladian house in Ireland, ex-Connolly family, and then owned by the Castletown Foundation. The usual 'great craic' took place, and was followed by a large hangover lunch at Stacumny, at which two memorable events took place. First, Jonathan Irwin leant back in his chair and not being a very capable rider, in spite of all his horsey connections, lost his balance and ended up in the fish pond, much to everyone's amusement and mutterings of, "Well, that's the nearest Jonathan's got to water in the last twenty four hours." The second event was that Vicky had hired a strip-o-gram girl clad in an itsy bitsy bra, miniskirt and what the Irish call a 'tong'. My son Sasha drove the mini-tractor with a large pretend birthday cake on a trailer behind it. Out popped the strip-o-gram from the cake brandishing a whip to wish me a happy birthday. Apparently she asked Vicky during the telephone interview, "Shall I jump out and give him a bit of a lashing – that will shake them." Vicky agreed, but it turned out even more dramatically than planned. By that stage of the afternoon, I was on my fourth change of outfit and was then wearing my cardinal's costume, complete with crimson hat. The sight of a cardinal, looking amazed, being jumped by a naked bird wielding a whip and kissing him a happy birthday caused a riot and the subsequent popping of further champagne corks.

The party then went on to Desmond Guinness's at Leixlip Castle, accompanied by Mick Jagger and Jerry Hall, who were also at the lunch. My last memory was singing arm in arm with Jerry, and her twin sister Terry, still featured in a memorable photo in our loo.

Leixlip, only a couple of miles away from us, figured quite a lot in our lives. It is an old and beautiful castle, with some very colourful people inhabiting it. When we first came to Stacumny, Mariga Guinness was the reigning wife there. A woman of highly eccentric personality and behaviour, but possessed with great intelligence and energy. She was a tremendous supporter of her husband, Desmond Guinness, in founding and developing the Irish Georgian Society and in saving Castletown House for the nation (before the whole estate was swallowed up by the Irish version of Candy and Candy). I was on the Foundation Board and remember many interesting and highly amusing meetings with 'the two Desmonds' the other being my friend the late Knight of Glin, who is sadly no longer with us, and whose company and witty sarcasm is sadly missed.

Leixlip was always great 'craic' to use the Irish phrase, and the visiting alcoholics could hardly be described as being anonymous, and would have never qualified for that worldwide organisation. Sadly the reign of Mariga ceased, but was replaced as wife and chatelaine by Penny Cuthbertson, and the out of the ordinary atmosphere happily continued, glass in hand.

During the rather painful and contentious Guinness divorce, both the ladies in Desmond's life continued to live in the castle in separate towers, proving awkward for some of us who were wondering which to visit first. However it was finally concluded, except that Mariga apparently owned, or claimed, a lot of the furniture and possessions of the castle, the result being that at one stage the majority of the grand reception rooms became empty, and even carpetless. Vicky will never forget visiting Leixlip for the first time, as Desmond and Penny led us round the echoing ground floor rooms, and Desmond remarked, "Isn't it lucky that Penny and I just adore dancing."

I also remember seeing Mariga in the arrivals hall at Heathrow Airport from Dublin, exotic clothes as usual, not to mention a large Edwardian hat decorated with what looked like a huge bouquet of flowers. She was clearly somewhat over-refreshed from the Aer Lingus cabin service, and had some difficulty in unlocking her handcase, which had a combination lock. I offered to help her, and asked for the combination, to which she replied very slowly, "Zero, Zero, Zero, Zero, Zero, Zero, of course, my dear."

Unfortunately I got involved in the tussle that continued for some time, as being a director of the Castletown Foundation I had to interfere occasionally on some of Mariga's unannounced raids on the house, where some of the contents did belong to her, but not all. I read in my diary during this time that while we were lunching at Leixlip, butler and all, Vicky and I were somewhat surprised to be eating with twisted old kitchen knives and forks. As Desmond and Penny noticed that we were slightly amazed by the cutlery, they remarked, "Unfortunately all the silver is locked up in case poor Mariga nicks it." When she died, she was given an amazing funeral, attended by all her friends and admirers, who all threw various fancy hats and umbrellas into the grave instead of the customary handfuls of earth. The grave had been given various permissions and it was underneath the arches of the giant folly tower on the Castletown Estate. RIP.

One extraordinary fact that popped up after we had sold Stacumny (to the late Cathal Ryan – son of Tony Ryan of Ryanair fame) was that when he had the stable yard dug up to install tubing for a swimming pool they found five human skeletons, or as the locals would call them 'skellingtons'. The suspicion of us having been mass murderers lurked over us momentarily, until the police and government pathologist authorities declared them to be twelfth century, and it was decided that the whole area of house, garden and orchard had been the site of an ancient cemetery. We were near to a number of early Christian ruins all right, and the fact that some further skeletons were found buried east to west, three deep incidentally, proved it. In some cases apparently the decapitated heads had been buried apart from the main skeleton, which meant that they had been executed. It was mentioned to me that it was reckoned there were about one thousand bodies around, but that is only speculation as no-one was keen to dig any further. We had no feeling, in retrospect, of having lived over a giant graveyard, although some of the children, on hearing the news, swore to having heard ghostly noises in the upper floors. I think one can happily ascribe that to imagination, or to the traditional corridor creeping of country house parties. The only comic result was that our Pat McLaughlin, remarked that he had noticed that Polly, our boxer, had appeared with some unusually large bones, after she had been assisting in the digging of the asparagus bed.

MY MAIN CHARITY occupation was the Irish Cancer Society, where I eventually became chairman for some years and managed to establish the home care service, which was the equivalent service to the Macmillan nurses in England. This was achieved by the board of the Society and St Joseph's Hospice in Dublin (which was the original hospice and preceded the famous St. Joseph's Hospice in London, run by the same order of nuns). They already had a small home care team, which we were able to enlarge from 3-4 homecare nurses operating only in Dublin, to now funding 30 nurses throughout southern Ireland. The initial funds were raised with the help of Jonathan Irwin, who organised that the entire profit of the first meeting of the newly rebuilt Phoenix Park racecourse should be dedicated to this purpose. These substantial sums, plus the first 'Daffodil Day' in Ireland did the trick. The Daffodil Day was thought up and organised by my late, close friend Charlie Cully who copied it from Canada. It was then subsequently copied by Britain. The idea was that our teams looked after the dying in their homes for the last three to seven days, on a round-the-clock basis. This enabled those who wished to do so, to die at home, rather than in a hospice or hospital.

Initially I spent a week with one of the teams (pretending to be a trainee doctor) and only then realised what these people do and achieve. When we were called in the patients had only around four days to live; they were stabilised and pumped full of morphine on a regular basis. Some were reasonably lucid, pain-free, if intoxicated, and indulged in optimistic chit-chat, but the real problem was the family. Quite often the husband, wife, son or daughter would not accept or take in that they would be dead by the end of the week, and for their sake one had to get the news over to them in a way that they might understand and accept. It was only then that I realised what sensational characters these nurses were, and that they had to occasionally change their duties in order to save their mental stability. In any case, it is only a certain type of person who is suitable or able for this kind of work. All I know is that it isn't me. For a week I went home all pumped-up by what I had done dealing with four or five dying people and their families. However, the following week I fell into a deep melancholy and knew that I would not be of much use to anyone.

At one stage, I remember being involved with an organisation for the promotion and help of battered women. I remember visiting one of their 'safe homes' where Vicky and I were let in, and then had the door locked behind and in front of us, in case a manic lover or husband was still trying to get any of the women. My friend Olive, who ran the place, suggested that I joined her on Inis Mór, the main Aran island, off Galway, where she was taking four out-of-control teenage girls for a weekend.

I agreed, and set off on the trip with extra provisions – namely a huge bag of sausages – on the back of my bike. After a long trip by train, ferry and bicycle I arrived and met Olive and the girls. Olive said that they were still under reasonable control, and enjoying the coast and the wild sea. Then I made my great mistake. Olive, their keeper, went off for a rest, and I took the girls to the one and only pub, as I was dying for a drink after pedalling all those sausages across the island. Forgetting their ages, the youngest being about fourteen, and the oldest I suppose seventeen, I told them to order themselves a drink. To my surprise the drinks turned out to be not cokes, but large vodkas. Before I could control the situation, they had two more, and then said they were going out for a walk while I paid the bill. I then realised that they were not dressed as schoolgirls, but more like hookers, which was clearly an occupation that they spent more time thinking about than school. Olive came back, and I suddenly found to my shame that I was alone with my sausages and no girls. Without doubt they had gone walkies around the island, offering services that were usually unavailable to the simple fishing and farming folk of the remote island. We could not find them, and the only policeman on the island had taken the last ferry home to Galway. We managed to alert the Galway police who said that they would come out the next morning to collect the girls (as they were all under official care). In the meantime there was nothing to be done.

In the morning Olive and I were waiting for the reinforcements from Galway when we spotted the four girls strolling down the main street arm in arm, singing merrily, stating that they had a terrific night with new 'friends' they had met, and that they loved the island and had no intention of returning to Dublin. At that stage I decided to beat a strategic retreat, and caught the return ferry that was just arriving with the police to collect my new friends, and so I waved them goodbye, with relief, but no sausages. I never heard what happened to the girls, but I thought at least some of the young islanders got some early sex lessons, which in those days they were deprived of at school.

Through our charity work, we got mixed up with some gypsy problems at one stage. In Ireland they are called 'travellers' and on the whole they are more tolerated than in the UK. There were two relatively unsolvable problems however. The first was their funerals, which had to be as grand and ostentatious as possible, regardless of the family's means. I encountered difficulty there in the Cancer Society, where despite assisting financially with those suffering the final throes of illness, it went against the grain in paying for the plumed horses of those who had sadly lost the battle for life. The other problem was the widely practised decision to burn down the caravan of the late lamented owner, and in my less generous thoughts, I imagined that the custom must have been invented by the caravan makers as a lucrative form of revenue. As a result of these practices, which were difficult for the charity to swallow, we were obliged to reduce our help.

Talking about travellers, I cannot forget an amusing incident (though not for some!) which occurred as a result of the heaviest snowfall that I can recollect in my thirty years in Ireland. Something like three feet of snow suddenly fell in one night accompanied by strong winds. As a result, every road was blocked and communities were unreachable. At the time there was only one dual carriageway in the country known as the Naas dual carriageway, on the Cork road extending some 15 miles from Dublin. The majority of cars that were on this section of road as the snow fell had to be abandoned – but the following morning the unfortunate owners walked to recover their vehicles, only to discover that anything that could be unscrewed, including all the tyres and wheels, was missing. As far as I can remember, in view of the weather conditions – which continued for some days – no one could actually be accused although it was said that the tread on many caravan wheels had improved miraculously overnight.

A more relaxing, amusing and fun charity that Vicky and I got involved in was the international organisation called ARCH which, with a totally volunteer work force, organised a weekly outing for mentally handicapped children, teenagers and young adults. These young people were normally kept at home and on the whole were lonely and bored, as their families couldn't manage to look after them the whole time. They were sweet, lovable, if sometimes difficult youngsters, who adored their weekly outings. We were not able, due to our constant moves and travel, to help on a weekly basis, but we used to organise a really super annual or bi-annual event at Stacumny, or a friend's house. The events always held surprises.

On one occasion at Christmas I was sitting disguised as Santa Claus, giving presents one-by-one to a very restless and rebellious queue. Finally the time came for the last boy in the queue, who ran at me, kicked me very hard on the shin, and shouted "Fuckin' Santa," as he snatched the present from my hands.

Our friends and neighbours, Denis and Jenny Harvey Kelly offered to give the next party in their house and garden, when poor Jenny was presented with a strange sight as she rounded the house towards the garage. There stood a clearly well-developed youth of indeterminate age, with his trousers round his ankles, measuring his manhood along the tow bar of their horse box. I remember her being somewhat taken aback both by the occasion and the length. History does not relate how she coped with the repackaging, but as I explained to her, there are always some strange things one has to accomplish in the name of charity.

CHAPTER TWELVE
A Siberian Summer

ON MY FATHER'S side I am totally Polish. Going back some centuries we were a family of 'szlachta' or landed gentry, which was in somewhat reduced circumstances by the beginning of the nineteenth century. What caused the reduction was never discussed, but not having heard or read of any scandals, I imagine that it was caused by the usual overspending which was common among that class, plus bad luck, either in the running of the estate or with gambling – both of which were common to the aristocracy. On the whole they loved every kind of field sport, not to mention their neighbours' and friends' wives, which did not help family budgets. Trade was abhorred and thus happily avoided, leaving marriage, gambling and war as the main means of enrichment.

Thus the Poklewski family lived near Połock in what is now Belarus, in comfort if not excessive ostentation. Then in 1830 my great grandfather Alfons Poklewski Koziell, born with great intelligence, ambition and *joie de vivre*, having done well at St. Petersburg University, set out at the age of twenty to seek pleasure and financial promotion. Poland, for the greater part of the nineteenth century was occupied under a tripartite partition between Russia, Germany and the Austro-Hungarian empire. Our estate was in the Russian sector meaning that

Alfons, owing to family connections, threw himself into the top society of St. Petersburg and commenced having fun. Alas, I suspect too much fun, which led to an incident that altered his life. He was attending one of the smart balls of the season and having taken his turn at directing one of the dances, as was the custom in those days, he fell into a tremendous argument with a young and important prince who was very drunk and unpleasant at the time, and made my great-grandfather lose his temper. Alfons being big and strong picked up the wretched princeling and hurled him out of the ballroom balcony into the bushes below. Fortunately, it being the ground floor and the snow thick outside, no physical harm ensued.

The result was a great scandal, and my ancestor, who was I believe in the right, was duly ordered by the court powers to get the hell out of St. Petersburg and report to the Chief of Police in Cherny Yar, a remote town in Astrakhan, until further notice. In those days it was a long and arduous journey, but before Alfons reached his destination, our family connections and high-placed friends obtained a court pardon for him, and secured his return to the capital. The said group of saviours then wisely decided that further balls should be avoided, and secured him a post as secretary to the newly appointed governor of Western Siberia, Prince Gorchakov.

The governor resided in Tobolsk, almost two thousand safe kilometres from St. Petersburg. There Alfons stayed, and due to there being no Trans-Siberian railway in those days to commute for pleasure, he got down to serious and successful work. After some five years of hard graft and promotion it was apparent that he had dug up some really strong entrepreneurial and commercial skills – until this time apparently concealed in the Poklewski blood. As a result Alfons resigned in very good reputation from the Imperial Service and set about developing a number of commercial services in what was then a frozen wasteland. At that time it was occupied by impoverished peasantry, exiled prisoners (both criminal and political) and the army, which had to defend the vast stretch between St. Petersburg and America, right through Alaska which at that time belonged to Russia.

In that part of Siberia one can imagine the numbers of horses employed by the army linking St. Petersburg and Alaska, and Alfons' first commercial activities were to undertake supplying the army with fodder for the horses. Unlike the other merchants and suppliers, being both honest and efficient, he secured the contract if not the monopoly, for the business. The fodder travelled by barges as there were no roads of a size or condition to manage heavy transport. These barges were pulled by horses – a slow and complicated business – so he decided to import the first steam boat on the river Irytysz and other Siberian rivers. The boat, called the 'Robotnik' meaning 'Worker', was carted over thousands of kilometres in segments, and finally assembled locally. The result was that the boat could tow up to twelve barges with fodder and also horses for return journeys. Thus the big family fortune began, and he ended up with a fleet of steamboats and several trading centres (a bit like the East India Company and others) in Omsk, Tobolsk, Ekatrinbourg and Tiumen.

Alfons eventually sold the fleet and bought out the state monopoly of vodka, established several distilleries, and became the largest supplier of vodka in Siberia, which considering that it was the population's principal drink, was a good deal. He financed part of the Trans-Siberian railway, being careful to guide it round his large country house at Talica (where the station was called 'Poklewskaya'), and he also acquired hundreds of peasant 'shebeens', or drinking dives.

Alfons ended up possessing 2,500 square kilometres of land and a series of gold, sapphire and asbestos mines in the Ural region, where he established a large glass factory and a metallurgic plant. This was in addition to the distilleries and breweries, other large estates and forests in Perm, Orenburg and Ousk. He prospered greatly in all these trades as he was trusted by the Russians from his reputation in the provincial government, and unlike the local merchants, did not cheat the authorities. Alfons thus became the merchant king of Siberia and he was reputed to be one of the richest men in that vast country. He established Catholic schools, hospitals and churches for the mostly Polish exiles who had survived their sentences as political prisoners in the Siberian gulags, but who were required to remain living in Siberia after completing their sentences. He thus employed thousands of Poles and presumably kept them – as well as the innumerable peasants, miners and so on – content in that vast and unfriendly near Arctic region, by producing 35% of the vodka drunk there.

Alfons lived until the age of eighty-one in Siberia, St. Petersburg,

Poland and Monte Carlo, enjoying a much-enlarged cash flow. His son, my grandfather, Vincent and his brothers were known as 'The Siberian Rockerfellers'. One of my great uncles, Stanislaw (at the time Secretary to the Russian Embassy in London), was one of Fabergé's best customers. Once, after a game of baccarat with King Edward he found himself owing £1 to the King, but was short of change. "Remember Poklewski, you owe me a pound," the King joked as he left. Shortly afterwards the King received a beautiful silver Fabergé cigarette box with a gold sovereign mounted on the lid. Easy come, easy go, as they say. His great grandson - yours truly - after a revolution, and two world wars had to start again selling vacuum cleaners.

So, in July 1986 I decided to visit some of the places and possessions that are technically mine. However, unlike some refugees, being well aware that history is difficult to reverse, I set out with Vicky not expecting to return with anything much beyond sausage and gherkin indigestion and a vodka hangover. Thus we set off from St. Petersburg into the world of "might have been". We boarded Tiumen airlines, the sight of our aeroplane giving us the dawn heebie-jeebies. During take-off, we were certain that the plane would disintegrate as it seemed to be undergoing a severe fit of mechanical Parkinsons. The flight did not reassure us, as the lavatory door came off in Vicky's hands, and we only hoped that the engines were better maintained. However, having breakfasted on a rather misshapen apple and a glass of vodka, we duly landed at the end of the runway, before the brakes gave up. Having decided to go home by rail on the Trans-Siberian Express, rather than risk a return flight, we entered the Siberian summer. The heat was intense, and we were told that it was usually either plus or minus 30 degrees centigrade there, and we were lucky we came in summer. However, both of us, having endured extreme climates in our day, accepted the lack of air conditioning, and the mosquitoes, with due resignation.

One of the reasons for the trip was that I had been having a lengthy correspondence with a slightly eccentric Polish teacher – Professor Fiel – who was a resident in Tiumen, Siberia. He was the son of a Pole who had been deported to Siberia during the war and who found he had to remain there. His passion, curiously, was to collect 'Poklewski' memorabilia and establish two small museums devoted to my great grandfather, Alfons Poklewski Koziell. Sergiush Fiel treated us like royalty, being chairman of the Siberian Russian-Polish Society, and whisked us off to what would be regarded in the West as a 'minus three star' hotel, where we were given a room on the top floor – needless to say the hottest one. The great luxury consisted of a very large and very old fridge, standing rather curiously in the centre of the room, cold but quite empty. I went down to the rather unreceptive reception, and complained that there was no hot water upstairs. The answer was a Russian shrug and the news that the lack of hot water was not confined to our room, and in fact there was none in the centre of the town, as the district heating plant was closed down for two weeks for maintenance, and that it was summer anyway.

I departed with a Polish shrug and raided the shop next door for vodka, soda water, tinned tuna fish and black bread, with which I returned to our mosquito-ridden oven of a room, for dinner. At that stage, my dear wife informed me that she was quite happy to view the Poklewski possessions in Siberia on condition that I did not repossess them. I reassured her that there was, alas, no fear of that. I had a cigar to cheer me up, presuming that a non-smoking room in Russia would be as likely as a non-sex room in a Heathrow hotel.

We were then taken to Professor Fiel's flat situated in a concrete Stalinist block, up some undusted but well-urinated stairs. Here we met a great welcome in their cosy flat full of Poklewski memorabilia. We had a copious dinner of garlic sausage, hard-boiled eggs and gherkins, washed down with generous glasses of vodka. We did not realise it at the time, but our Siberian menu did not change wherever we were for the next ten days.

The next day we then strolled through Tiumen, which is now one of the centres of the Russian oil industry with giant transcontinental oil pipes criss-crossing the place, between concrete blocks and tiny old Russian wooden houses as beautiful as the blocks were ugly. We arrived at an old church whose use had been changed to the city library. It was unlocked for us through three doors, giving one the impression that in spite of the presence of books, no one was actually encouraged to read, or in reality they were probably forbidden. An old 'babushka' then showed me about three hundred books in Polish and French from the library of our summer home 'Talica' – all with the family crest inside the covers. Having been checked by two suspicious women that I was not trying to smuggle one of my own books out, we were led out through the locked doors thinking how cheerful the Wandsworth prison library must be in comparison.

We then visited one of the old Poklewski trading houses and warehouse, now a psychiatric outpatients' clinic; a sort of communist version of The Priory one imagines, but marginally less luxurious to say the least. We considered putting the children down on the waiting list but decided to leave them at their English boarding schools where the comforts were probably very similar anyway.

We had lunch at the local version of Macdonalds with the young mafia and their birds. There were big dumplings instead of Big Macs, containing what looked like minced mice in brown water, served as usual with beer and vodka. Sergiush wanted to open a 'Poles in Siberia' museum in some rooms in the clinic with all our old family artefacts in it – I suspect that he wanted me to pay for it. We then were ushered to a local museum where we were proudly shown "The greatest mammoth skeleton in the world." By that time, what with the heat, dumplings and vodka, I felt that we could equally be looking at the greatest aspidistra in the world, for all I knew. In the museum, in Russian tradition, we were made to wear woollen slippers, in spite of the floors being raw concrete. We finished by seeing the Catholic church, built by my great grandfather, previously converted into the communist party leaders' meeting rooms, but now partially in use again as a church.

The next day we were fetched by Sergiush in what he claimed was a brand new taxi, which appeared to be older than me. The young driver in dark specs proudly produced a large pistol from a shoulder holster, and waving it in our direction shouted "Gaz! Gaz!" to reassure us, although Vicky saw him take out a clip of bullets before he handed it to us. Thus reassured, we drove for three and a half hours across vast plains and forests to Tobolsk, the original capital of Western Siberia where my great grandfather, Alfons, originally started as one of the governor's (Prince Gorchakow) secretaries. The town now consists of refineries of crude oil, (which travels 2,500 kilometres from the north of the province by pipeline), and rows of enormous concrete broiler houses, where workers live.

After more minced mouse dumplings we saw the lovely old 'Kremlin' on the hill, and the governor's palace where my ancestor started his career. Dear Serguish took me round in the great heat recounting all the family possessions in Siberia. They now all belong to the 'people', although judging by the way they live it does not appear to have done them much good. Never having possessed it all myself, I strangely did not feel bitter, but only proud that the family had played such a vital part in Siberian history. Sergiush introduced us to the locals as if we were an ancient Maharajal dynasty. They all seemed delighted to meet us, but in view of my age, uselessness and high cost of upkeep, seemed unlikely to want to nationalise me.

We viewed the grim old prison for travelling convicts, largely Poles from the 1863 insurrection, who arrived on foot, chained, in convict kaftans, having travelled for around two months, overnighting in similar penal prisons. After finishing their sentences, those that survived had to remain living in Siberia – two or three thousand miles from home. We wandered through the empty echoing corridors with their tiny barred cells, with two steel bunks and a hole in the floor, thinking of all the pitiful humanity that had passed through there, or died in misery, their only transgression: being Polish and fighting for their freedom. It would take over a hundred years (apart from a short interval between 1919 and 1939) to achieve it. Among other places and from here, Alfons was finally able to negotiate the release and employment of many thousands of Polish deportees in his various enterprises.

I remember my grandmother, who was born in 1858, telling me that it took her eight weeks to get to Talica after her wedding in St. Petersburg, travelling by boat and carriage and staying with friends *en route*. I imagine that the pampered folk of Moscow and St. Petersburg did not venture much here, as the landscape is not exactly dotted with chateaux. It now takes nearly three days by the Trans-Siberian Express.

The next morning we were received in Padun, a 'company village' of some 2,800 inhabitants, mostly employed at the distillery. The distillery, on a hill overlooking a lovely lake, was one of the original ones owned by Alfons. We were again received like royalty by a lady in local costume who was bearing a large ornate cake and a plate of salt, the latter being, I presumed, for the purpose of increasing our thirst. She was followed by 'the Management', consisting of several very stout ladies and a slightly frightening man, who was the chief engineer. The whole place gave one the impression that nothing either outside or inside had been touched, painted or repaired for 77 years, and looked like a vast steaming, clanking and leaking Heath Robinson erection, reeking of alcohol.

We were given a terrifying tour up and down ancient and highly dangerous ladders and platforms, with rusting gaps through which one saw a tangle of pipes and cylinders four storeys below. As we had to stop and taste the different vodkas along the way, including the 'Poklewskaya' with great grandfather Alfons' picture on the bottle label, we were soon seriously inebriated, and lost our fear of the rusting assault course.

The tour finished in the works manager's office, where, to our amazement, further undiluted spirits and toasts ensued, accompanied by caviar, sausages and cheese. All this before 11am, and as we consumed all this surrounded by ever-broadening smiles all round, I thought, thank God I am married to an Irish woman, as any other member of the fairer sex would have fallen headlong into the nearest still. Instead 'Pani Victoria' as she was addressed, said with a smile, swallowing her sixth noggin of the morning, with a contented and elegant flourish, that she really adored Russian offices.

Back in Tiumen again, we got up early and, clutching our two breakfast coupons, came down to a gloomy dining room that echoed with loud reggae music. We asked for two breakfasts (one with a fried egg), and got four fried eggs and no tea. I felt like throwing my phrase book at the sulky waitress. There were some Russian gentlemen eating in their singlets with purple noses, bursting eyeballs and hangovers of such intensity that they were almost catching. After a tour of the town we invited the Fiels to dinner in a restaurant they had suggested, but on finding a large room with a big band playing at a thousand decibels to the solitary occupants, who were a group of alcohol-damaged worthies with thirty-six empty beer bottles already on the table, we left and ended up in another equally empty and user-unfriendly restaurant.

A few days later we set out in the same decrepit 'brand new taxi' but with a new driver who appeared unarmed. I noticed the same photo of a pretty girl pinned to the dashboard, and wondered whether they shared her too. After one and a half hours, we reached Talica, our original Siberian home, and first visited the station which used to be called Poklewskaya, but curiously enough had not been renamed 'Talica' until 1963, which I suppose was because of the local respect that my predecessor had been accorded for some forty years after the revolution.

I stood and thought of all the streams of relations and friends who must have been ushered through by the stationmaster over the years, and was reminded of a bit of family history. My great uncle Jan (one of Alfons' sons) was a roué and faintly disgraceful – although very popular. He led a dissipated life and gambled at very high stakes all over Russia – managing to get through about $3 million in ten years until he went bankrupt in 1903. In his heyday he used to make his annual visits to the family home in Talica, where his brother Vincent, head of the family, reigned there with my grandmother who was a rather Victorian example of Polish gentry. Whilst she lived in great comfort in a number of houses in Russia and Poland, she professed to dislike excess. Thus great uncle Jan, who represented excess on an international scale, did not exactly see eye to eye with his sister-in-law. However, he reduced his exposure to boredom on his annual visits with his brother and sister-in-law by spending his time in a private railway carriage in which he arrived at Poklewskaya station, attached to the Trans-Siberian Express. The carriage – containing a gipsy orchestra, a good chef, masses of drink, chosen merry companions and pretty ladies of the night – was shunted onto a siding in the station where it remained for a few days as the party continued until the champagne, livers and guitar strings gave out. In the meantime, Jan dutifully went every afternoon by carriage to join the family for tea before returning to the more animated siding.

Jan eventually gambled everything away in Monte Carlo in a couple of very decadent years spent either in the casino, or with the finest kind of female company in a double bed. The rest of the family being rather embarrassed by his antics eventually paid his vast debts and pensioned him off on condition that he kept out of Poland and Russia. His 'pension' was something like fifteen thousand pounds a year which was hardly regarded as poverty at the end of the nineteenth century, but he was always referred to as 'poor' uncle Jan from then on.

There is a famous story about Jan's brother, Alfons, who had unfortunately suffered from meningitis at an early age and never fully developed mentally. Despite this handicap, he was astute enough to comprehend his brother's lifestyle. One day he was sharing a first class compartment of a train with a grand lady of good looks, who asked him his name. Upon discovering who he was, she mentioned that she knew his brothers Stas and Jan, to which Alfons pronounced, "If you know my brothers you are obviously a whore." History does not relate how the incident concluded, although I imagine a change of compartments must somehow have been involved.

In Talica, we were accorded official transport consisting of the school bus, the children being on holiday. It still worked, just, but Vicky nearly put her foot through a hole in the floor. The Poklewski house at Talica was a big, daunting Victorian red brick construction built in good old mill-owner tradition, more solid than beautiful, on the brow of a hill overlooking the town, works and railway. It is what the Russians call a 'Palac' or palace, which is a faintly exaggerated Russian and Polish word for 'Manor house', or 'chateau'.

The house is now a school for orphans and disabled children. We had to admit that the house's aesthetic appearance had not been improved by the fact that all the walls, halls and reception rooms were painted shoulder height sick green, with sick yellow above. Even the ballroom parquet was painted over with a brown shiny oil paint. We were shown round most of it, and returned to the ballroom, crowded with all the civic officials and local worthies who had greeted us on the front steps. We met a splendid old lady whose father was my grandfather's head chef and who travelled with him everywhere. She proudly told us that he was so important that he had his own sitting room near the kitchens. At this point Vicky pointed out that *she* cooked for me *and* she travelled with me, but did not have the luxury of having her own sitting room. There was much laughter all around.

By this time our 'Charles and Di' impression was increasing steadily as the crowd thickened and the video and TV cameras whirred. We tried to look intelligent and fascinated as we stared at totally blank corridors and walls. We then gave one of our two TV and radio interviews. During one of these interviews, I was asked, "What is the purpose of your grand visit?" to which I replied with a straight face, "To repossess it all naturally." This was greeted with such prolonged roars of laughter, from which I gathered that I was wasting my time.

We went on to visit the small museum by the station, full of Poklewski memorabilia and photographs. The eight museum committee ladies gave us an enormous tea, all clad in their best white lace. They included the chefs' daughter and the rest were mostly granddaughters of our servants, gardeners and grooms. They were touchingly full of my predecessor's public spiritedness and generosity in building churches, schools and so on. This certainly led one to the conclusion that they were not the ones that caused the revolution.

After a further tour of the town and a vile meal in a concrete restaurant, we were left in a guesthouse as the town hotel had burnt down. We were received by a Rosa Klebs look alike on the first floor concrete bunker, who forbade us to open the windows, locked us in and left. When she had gone we took off the sellotape sealing the windows and opened them. We then realised why she had not opened the windows, as we were assaulted by the stench of drains, followed by mosquitos the size of sparrows. A quick resealing of windows ensued and a generous use of our fly spray, after which the drains smelt like Floris essence. The night was spent on a metal bed that would have been banned in Dartmoor jail as being a cruel and unnatural punishment. In the morning, we happily left our stinking bunker. We continued our wandering and saw a heavenly old street of wooden houses and two big wooden barns, still standing after more than a hundred years. We met old locals, who informed us that the town's inhabitants had tipped-off our family, who left in a hurry through the back door in the middle of the night, just as a commissar arrived to arrest them. My family left Russia and their riches with only their clothes and jewels with them, escaping eventually via Japan. I suppose they were lucky to save their lives, unlike many of their friends. Needless to say, in the way of human nature, it seems the locals looted the whole establishment in due course. Apparently there are still bits of our furniture in the district, but I was not sure how keen I was to buy my own stuff back.

The next day, back in Tiumen, the Fiels took me to meet a 'beeznessman' (as they are known in Russia), who was a property developer as well as a big importer of office and domestic furniture and kitchens. He wanted to talk 'beezness' with me, which of course I could not resist. 'Mr Big' was around forty or so, with a small moustache and hard intelligent eyes. He did not at first sight appear to be a mafia type, but his young lawyer, who was by his side – bulging out of his torn mechanics shirt – certainly did. 'Tiumen grunge' I presumed, although I was told that he employed twelve other lawyers. Mr Big also had a very pretty, young interpreter who put me off my spiel rather by frequently crossing and uncrossing her admirable legs. After all that, I heard him talking perfectly normal English on the phone. He whisked me off – Mercedes, driver, bodyguard and all that – to one of his impressive showrooms, where I saw a vast Stalinesque desk for sale at $10,000 – an immense price for such a piece. We were then taken to a strange, very luxurious candlelit basement restaurant for lunch which one could only get into via a special doorbell, and which was totally empty bar two young ladies who gave the impression that they were not confined to serving food. Seeing my surprise at the empty restaurant he announced, "I like privacy" as the door was locked behind us. After a very exotic lunch starting with amazing caviar and special vodka, we said farewell and I decided to desist on 'beezness' just in case I ended being locked-up in less luxurious premises with less attractive jailers.

The day we left Tiumen, the Fiels failed to meet up with us, so we set off at 10pm in a taxi for the station, to catch the Trans-Siberian Express to St. Petersburg. As I am not a Russian-speaker I acted out being a train with puffing and whistling noises. The young driver did not get it, not being aware of steam trains, and obviously thought I was drunk. Just as I was wondering how one imitated a diesel train, the concierge came to our rescue, and having obviously seen more impressionists in his life, directed us to the station. We encountered a scene straight out of Charles Dickens – or more latterly Calcutta station in the rush hour. There were marauding drunks, crooks, beggars, gypsies and blind men hitting out with white sticks in an alcoholic frenzy. Mixed among this motley collection was a quiet collection of Asiatic tribes squatting on top of piles of stitched-up sacks wearing totally fatalistic expressions. All of this plus a pack of what I suspected were probably rabid dogs hunting for food. The announcements were of course in Russian, the notices in Cyrillic. Vicky shrugged her shoulders in a hopeless gesture, sat down on our pile of luggage, demanded a vodka from my hip flask and lit a cigarette, upon which to my own amazement and despair I lit my first cigarette for thirty years and emptied the flask.

I eventually found the train and approached a man hitting the wheels with a long hammer, like a scene out of Anna Karenina. I pointed forward and shouted "Petersburg" loudly, to which he nodded with his hammer. I fetched Vicky plus our luggage, and we were shown to our comfortable compartment by the carriage 'wardress' who refused my investment of a $20 tip. Some forty hours journey later she proved her hidden capitalist instincts by gratefully accepting the money.

The journey was very comfortable, if very hot in the overheated carriages, with heavenly plastic flowers everywhere, a clean loo and a samovar of boiling water for tea or coffee at the end of each carriage. In view of the heat the other passengers day and night appeared to spend their time in either pyjamas or underwear. We were slightly surprised to meet a burly man proudly holding up his toothbrush, parading down the corridor in very saggy undies, with a lozenge peeping out of one of the legs. By the end of the journey Vicky had acquired a full working knowledge of Russian male physiognomy.

The restaurant car was run by a chain-smoking waiter who never left his seat, a busy waitress who did all the work, and a young chef in a permanently grubby vest. It was not well patronised as most passengers ate in their compartments topping up their supplies of gherkins and shiny fat sausages with victuals sold through the windows by crowds of 'babushkas' at every station we stopped at. We patronised the dining car by pointing at the food in the kitchen, and passed a pleasant journey in a haze of vodka and staring at the endless birch forests passing by.

On our arrival, St. Petersburg was bathed in light and quite beautiful. So much had been restored since I was last there. We had a charming driver for a change and a sweet guide, Julia Korn, who took us to my grandfather's house near St. Isaac's cathedral. There was a guard outside as it is now the Court of Arbitration (previously the more sinister Public Prosecutor's office.) It was a very large building with a square inner courtyard, with two storeys added to the original. I do not imagine the family had any use for a large courtroom in their day. We managed to talk our way in, and had a good look around. The ballroom has been left exactly as it was, perfectly recognisable from a photograph of a 1909 fancy dress ball that I possess: pillars, chandeliers and all. The rest was all offices. We then went on to my great uncle Stanislaw's house, number 24 on the Fontanka canal. It was quite vast, and Vicky described it as, "Just like Harrods, only green." Just to prove that it is ours the two pediments carry a large 'P' and a large 'K' in Cyrillic letters. It now houses two hundred people in tiny apartments, so there was no point – or chance – of getting in. At the end of our visit we drove past them again, and

I imagined the fashionable crowds of guests arriving in sleighs and coaches for receptions. Oh well, back to London, only this time in 'coach class' on the plane.

WHEN GREAT GRANDFATHER Alfons Poklewski Koziell died in 1890, he left his vast fortune to his sons, but I gather that the main part was left to my grandfather Vincent, being considered the most steady and efficient of the family. Although he lived a calmer and more sober life than some of his brothers, he also enjoyed life and giving parties. One of his favourite tricks was to show off the local 'Pop' (Orthodox priest) who could open a bottle of champagne and empty it without taking the neck out of his mouth. The mind boggles as to what went on under the reverend's soutane.

On the subject of excesses, I remember my two grandmothers lunching with us in Katowice, Poland in 1939 when my paternal one, Maria, remarked on the whipped cream with the sweet dish. "How delicious, we never had cream like this in Talica." My maternal grandmother Agnes asked, "Why ever not?" Maria replied, "Well we had forty milking cows for the house, and considered more would be excessive," (here it must be explained that 'the house' in Russia, meant all the internal and outdoor staff plus their families) to which Agnes who was descended from an equally rich family who simply spent the lot, rather than losing it in twenty-four hours in a revolution, said, "Why not have another forty for the cream?" The answer did not go down too well with granny Maria.

All of this lavish lifestyle finished in twenty-four hours during the Russian revolution. The immediate family escaped through Japan to France and England, and my father went off with his regiment in the White Army, and when the fighting was finally lost, managed to make his way to England where he eventually met my mother, equally a refugee, and married, both fortunes being lost: hers through lavish spending, and his through revolution.

A Siberian Summer

CHAPTER THIRTEEN
Picanniny Bilong Big Masta

IN 1998 I decided to join my daughter Eliza in Australia, and for us to make an expedition to Papua New Guinea. No tourists, package tours, or towns were the pluses, but mosquitoes the size of pigeons, 800 separate languages (not dialects even), not to mention the diet, were the minuses. Cannibalism is supposedly extinct, although the odd, preferably young morsel was unlikely to be turned down. In 2008 the Italian photographer Iago Corazza travelled there to meet some of the last cannibals, who informed him that Japanese people taste best. In any case we firmly stuck to tinned spaghetti and tinned cheese, and avoided the local delicacy, which was grilled bat.

Our host and guide in this extraordinary country, the second biggest island in the world after Greenland, was a Polish Missionary, Father Jan, whom I had made friends with in the Maynooth seminary in Ireland where he was learning English prior to his 'posting' by the Divine Word Missionaries to Papua. There, in fact, the predominant and only language is 'Pidgin' English, consisting I think of about 800 words, some of which we learned like "neck belong me dry" (I am thirsty), and "tyre belong car me – he bugger up" (we have a puncture). Some of the more amusing phrases in *Tok Pisin* – my book on Pidgin English – were "slip im one" for any sexual activity and "down beelow" for any sexual organ or orifice – male or female. I have often thought how economic and useful such a confined language can be, and have occasionally referred to people as "a pain in me down beelow" without being accused of vulgarity.

We flew to a town near Father Jan's house on the bend of the great Sepik river, which runs through the country for over a thousand kilometres. The communications in Papua are dire, and a trip of one hour in a plane to a landing strip would take two weeks overland, as there are basically no connecting roads and the only quick connection is the river. Father Jan's parish was the size of Wales, so he could only visit some of the more distant churches twice a year. All visits were made in dug-out canoes, which were fitted with 75-horsepower engines. It was all very nerve-racking trying to avoid little local canoes being paddled by standing men, not to mention floating logs and crocodiles. The 'churches' were open barns with thatched roofs and low straw walls to let the air through. During Mass the babies, when they were not being breast-fed, were put into hanging net baskets called 'beelums' hung on hooks. The altars, beautifully carved, were a mixture of the iconography of their native traditions – for instance crocodiles (the great emblem of the Sepik) and various figures illustrating fecundity – not unlike the erotic sculpture to be found in India and the Far East. All this, plus the amazing ear and nose piercings and other body decorations were rather distracting for a Catholic chap brought up in the calm peace of a Benedictine Abbey and Gregorian chant. However as we attended a church every day, we managed to get in a few prayers.

So our journey proceeded, visiting churches or other Polish priests. I often wondered "Why all these Poles?" But then I worked out that they would go anywhere on the Earth, or beyond, to get the hell out of Communist Poland. Not that the comforts were capitalist. No air conditioning and 33 degrees all the time, night and day, with unbelievable humidity and little washing. I soon worked out that washing was a pointless pursuit after hanging out a T-shirt to dry in the blazing sun and finding that it was just as wet when I fetched it some hours later. In some of the outlying parishes we slept in the huts for the visiting priest, which looked exactly like those in a Japanese prisoner of war camp. I slept on a raised board on a blanket, and poor Eliza on the earthen floor. I fear that women are very second class there, and I was never, like the other men, allowed to carry any luggage, which was heaved along our marches by the women, on long straps attached to their foreheads, with poor Eliza bent double under her burden. Unfortunately there was nothing I could do about it as I felt I had to conform to the local practices, although I am not quite sure that my daughter concurred.

My two main horrors were the stream/river crossings, and the primitive loos. Instead of a bridge over high water crossings there was simply a round log, which the locals crossed with ease using their prehensile toes. My toes in the meantime, never having wandered much outside narrow hand-made leather shoes were useless, and I had to be held back and front as I slithered over these moist logs shouting terrified instructions, much to the amusement of the locals who immediately appeared in their numbers out of the rainforest. As for some of the loos in the primitive parishes reserved for Father Jan, I found myself perched in the open on four crossed logs, over a malodourous pit, and when enthroned suddenly found a giggling audience of children hanging out of an adjoining tree.

One of our excursions took us to stay with another Polish Father Jan on a beautiful bit of the coast. Setting out in a shaky borrowed car (ours having been "bugger up"), down a track which the driver described quite correctly as "road bugger up", we reached the sea; by which time I announced in Pidgin that "me down beelow bloody sore." When we arrived I took them out to dinner in the hotel in the tiny town, which made Graham Green's hotel in Haiti seem like Claridges in comparison. I had a chicken which had clearly been discarded after a voodoo ceremony as being unfit for the spirits. Eliza had something called "a mackerel steak" which was the size of a middle cut from one of the local whales, and tasted like it too. Oceans to drink – thank God – and interesting chats with the priests. We learned that marriage customs had not changed over the centuries. The bride has to be paid for in cash, and if there is not sufficient cash, a sister is added to the transaction and given to the tribe that the husband comes from. If there is no cash or sister available and the couple get on with it anyway (a practice which seems to be increasingly accepted in England these days), then the litter of children is divided equally between the two tribes in the best farming tradition. On death the body is buried and exhumed after a year. Half the bones – by that time well-picked – are destined for odd places in an ancient ritual, and the other half are reburied, and money placed on the grave for the relatives.

Father Jan was bothered by a problem in one of his parishes: a row had broken out among a family as to exactly who was to get the bridal price when she took her vows, and who would collect the burial price when she died. Rather him than me to give the advice, I thought, but I became convinced that unlike some of the other missionaries – like the Seventh Day Adventists, Protestants, and Word of God – the Catholics tend to go along with the local culture where possible and I am certain that even the odd extra wife is benignly ignored.

The other Polish priest, Father Stan, was running a parish consisting of six islands, hours by sea away from the coast and so small that we could not even find them on the map. These he reached in a small boat given to him by some worthy people in Poland, which was called 'The Black Madonna' after the famous and much revered picture in the shrine in Czestochowa. The combination of Father Stan's black beard, and the black boat, only needed the Jolly Roger on the main mast to complete the picture. I could only hope that he did not jolly well roger all the island girls who, I was told, were much more attractive than the mainland ones. When I mentioned to one of the other missionary fathers that I did not think that the female population of Papua New Guinea presented a dangerous temptation, he agreed with me, but after a long pause he said that on the whole it depended on how long one had been there.

I left Father Stan's accompanied by Father Jan and Eliza (who by that time was known as "Picanniny bilong big masta") on an incredible track mendaciously described as a road. We drove at 50 miles per hour regardless of giant potholes, so I had to hang on with both hands for dear life. The scenery was incredibly beautiful: wooded hills and vast expanses of grass. One thing that struck me was that there was no sign of cultivation, until I realised that it was not really called for in that permanently damp and hot climate, with wild food including bananas growing round them, and plenty of wild animals. It's very hot, so why work if you can just reach out for a banana and trap a bat for the main course? The fact is that the land is communally owned which in effect militates against one person developing anything. The missionaries tried to introduce cattle, and smallholdings, but failed due to jealously and indolence, leaving them to continue their stone-age existence and customs. We passed through several dangerous districts where the 'rascals' (a local term for bandits) operated, but without any problems. Due to the giant potholes and the prospect of being robbed and raped by the 'rascals', one did not tend to nod off – despite the suffocating temperature.

Talking of ancient practices like cannibalism, which I am told still existed in certain remote districts in the country, I am reminded of a joke which much amused me at the time. A father decides to take his sixteen-year old son and show him how to catch someone from a neighbouring tribe for dinner, as it was time for him to learn. They set out, and came across a beautiful young naked maiden in a clearing. They chased her in a long pursuit through the rainforest and eventually captured the unfortunate creature and bound her in trailing vines. The father looked at the captive with joy and pride, and turned to his son who was contemplating the victim with pity, and asked, "What do you think son?" The son replied, "Oh dear, I really don't think I could face it." The father was shocked and surprised, but after carefully inspecting her says, "I think you have a point son, let's take her home and eat your mother."

Father Stan had a housekeeper called Calista, who'd had a terrible experience: some time ago she had woken in a pool of blood, having been given a 'potion' and raped. Subsequently she realised she was pregnant. Had she come from the local clan, her situation – whilst devastating for her – would not have mattered much to the community as virginity before marriage was not regarded as too important. However in the village she came from virginity was all-important, and the custom was that either she or the baby must die. Her sister had met the same fate, and the mother had killed the baby and buried it. It seemed quite surreal to be sitting and discussing the problem over a drink. Father Stan was going to her village to try and save a life, but I never discovered the end result, as he disappeared out of our lives before the situation was resolved, and in fact we had no idea whether he himself survived in that unearthly place.

So the trips to far-flung villages in Father Jan's parish took place, with incredibly uncomfortable nights. I remember being ill from heat stroke, and trying to sleep on a plank bed with a thin under-blanket pretending to be a mattress. Before lying down each night, I would down my daily prescription with a large mouthful of warm whiskey: two Rennies, two malaria pills, two Panadol for raging fever, two Lomotil for squitters, a gout pill, and a sleeping pill. Then I would lie listening to the permanent scurry of the curious rats. Each morning we would join a large congregation of locals in church, where the Masses started off with the sign of the cross, "Father, picanniny, and holy spirit." Invariably we would be squeezed between ladies with immense naked breasts, which proved distracting for my prayers. Me and my picanniny Eliza would get the giggles as "bugger up" appeared frequently in the sermons, as well as "Jesus Christ he penis" but I forget what exactly that meant, although needless to say it was not rude in Pidgin. We usually had to shake hands with the entire congregation because of the excitement our presence and colour caused. Father Jan appeared exhausted after endless confessions, and once mentioned that one of his penitents was suckling two babies, one on each breast, throughout the process.

The local body decorations were incredible. Many of the women have the middle of their ear lobes cut out and stretched into an enormous loop. The men mostly sport cuts meant to resemble crocodile bites. We saw a man with a pierced nose which you could stick a pen through, and an old woman who had a long leather thong strung through her nose resting on her shoulder. I wondered what it was used for – perhaps to lead her? One woman on my right had her nose covered with pierced open holes. I sat quietly and prayed that she would not have a sneezing fit.

On one of our final excursions we visited a mission clinic and found a total lack of medicines. The tiny fridge had run out of kerosene, hence the three remaining phials of penicillin were useless, and they were out of malaria drugs. I always thought of tuberculosis as attacking the lungs only, but there was a man there with it above his groin, a woman with it on her head, and a small child with a grotesque swelling in the neck, an open sore and loss of hair as it was commencing to attack the brain. One's heart really went out to these people as they stood there pathetically hoping that we could do something. In fact the only chance they would have would be to fly them to the hospital on the coast, but who would persuade the authorities here to have the local airstrip mown and opened, and who would pay for the plane? It all seemed so hopeless.

Even in Ambunti which was the capital of the upper Sepik, and where we were based, the local hospital consisted of concrete sheds, and there were no beds or doctor. Technically it was under the management and supervision of the Indian doctor in Wewak, who had not been there for three years.

In all, it was a fascinating if heartbreaking, trip and one can only hope that things are better by now, but somehow I doubt it.

CHAPTER FOURTEEN
Embalming Fluid at the Boar's Head

THE ONLY THING that faintly clouded Vicky's horizon was my later life obsession to own and run a bar in a French village, and to end my life happily leaning on a zinc bar, Gauloise dangling from my lip, and a glass of pastis nestling in my hand. I was faintly encouraged in this idea by my old friend Mark Birley who had founded the famous Annabel's nightclub. He had declared that he was keen to become co-owner and we could call it 'Bar des Sports Polonais'. Much as I adored the idea, I knew of his exquisite taste and highly demanding standards and couldn't quite imagine how the idea of highly polished Baccarat glasses, and a ban on sweaty armless vests would go down in a French country village. I let him get on with his other world-renowned clubs and decided to search myself.

Vicky and I set out for France, together with our friends Galen and Hilary Weston who decided to join us in the search and venture. There was the usual slight difference in league, for while I was looking at clapped out bars in tiny villages Hilary kept her eye out for magnificent chateaux – clearly with something like Cliveden in mind. In the meantime Vicky sat in the back of the car with a tortured look, wanting neither. I finally overcame my bar passion and we settled for looking for a small house in the non-posh area of the South of France. Vicky had gone to Washington to settle her son Ivor in the university there, and I took my son Sasha and daughter Sophie to France for the hunt. I, in the meantime, had been introduced to an estate agent in Montelimar called Jean Pierre Fougeriol, who has become one of our closest friends in France, but who at first was quite suspicious of us – in fact he started by asking whether I had the necessary cash, although he since denies this. It was full summer and unbelievably hot and I was not wearing my Savile Row outfit, but some ragged jeans and ancient T-shirt. He was naturally suspicious because very often foreigners pretend to want to look at houses with no real intention of buying, but only to enjoy a day out in the countryside in a comfortable air-conditioned car driven by him – all for free.

We visited six or eight properties, all very charming from the outside, mostly old and of the Provençal farmhouse type. The trouble as far as I was concerned was French provincial interior decoration, an example being of a newly done up bathroom with carpet going from the floor up the side of the bath in a mocha colour, and the most elaborate tap machinery – not at the end of the bath but near the floor, with controls like a helicopter. I fear that I found similar problems with them all, some with 'water features' consisting of permanently vomiting gnomes, and one with a swimming pool in the shape of a bidet and not much bigger. Our friend tired and fed up, at the end of the day said, "Would you like a house in a village?" I replied, "Why not?" "I have one for sale in the most beautiful old hill village in the whole of France!" he replied. "Really, why are you so sure?" said I. "Because I live there and I was the mayor!" he shouted. "Let's go," said I.

We arrived in a truly spectacular and beautiful walled village called Mirmande – mostly seventeenth century with just over a hundred houses and ruins within the ramparts. First we stopped in the main street outside the only bistro and sat down with a drink amongst pots of geraniums. Such was the atmosphere of the village that I clearly felt that I was going to buy the house before I had even seen it. The house was in fact halfway up the incredibly steep 'Grande Rue', which had been constructed in the time of donkey transport and not cars. We walked up as you can only get something like an old Renault 4 up it, and then only with a shoe horn and a pot of Vaseline, with the side mirrors pulled in. Absolute heaven, with a terrace on the rampart, a sycamore tree, and a thirty-mile view over the river Rhône to the hills of the Massif Central.

Like all the houses in the street it is part of a crazy terrace with very thick walls, all built in the mid-seventeenth century. There was a basement down winding stone stairs, a ground floor and first floor with large living room, two bedrooms and two bathrooms reached by an outside stone staircase with more wonderful views. I immediately wanted to buy it, as my, by now, unsuspicious friend assured me that the little orchard terrace up some further steps could be converted into a swimming pool. All this subject to the agreement of Madame, who was still in America, nervous and suspicious of our enthusiasm.

Vicky came out immediately on her return, and had the same reaction as me. There followed a long procession of notaries, bankers and architects meetings, much prolonged à la Francaise with lots of raised eyebrows, shrugs, inking, stamping and endless handshaking. At last it was ours, and we could negotiate the wiring and plumbing that appeared also to have been installed in the seventeenth century. The process was all very relaxed, and took place mostly in the bistro at the end of the street. Even the smallest gatherings involved handshakes, not only with the people we were dealing with, but also with anybody passing by as well. We learned that one kissed cheeks three times, which was easy to forget at first, thinking that plopping a firm kiss on each cheek sufficed (especially as one had seen the person the evening before). But not at all, one was faced with an expectant protruding cheek offered for number three. The other thing we had to deal with was the stuck out elbow proffered by the baker, builder or any other individual with soiled hands, and we soon learnt how to shake a flour-covered elbow correctly. I am sure that the Masonic handshake, whatever it is, is nothing compared to what we had to learn.

Michel, the baker laboured in a tiny overheated kitchen, his vest much stretched from holding in his overflowing stomach strewn with the crumbs from croissants. I remember two of our guests returning rather anxiously from the bakery where they had seen one of his cats lying cosily between two loaves on the rutted tray that had just been taken out of the oven. "What about it?" I said, "the loaves had already been taken out of the oven, Michel would never bake his pussy, it was very cold and the cat very clean." He has now sadly retired, worn out by oven strain, and I suspect a certain amount of corkscrew canker. We have however one tiny general store in the village which stocks fresh bread amongst other goodies.

The villagers, like in most French villages, are divided and one half does not talk to the other, but talks ill about them. We, on the other hand, talk to all and sundry and have avoided rows with either side. As a result, we have been quite helpful in diplomatic problems that have occurred between the clans from time to time. They are all very dear if sometimes eccentric. The ladies live to extreme ages; in fact we have attended three hundredth-birthday parties there. I think the precipitous streets, stairs and passages, and the fact that most houses are unapproachable by cars, keep them fit and healthy.

As I mentioned, our Grande Rue is just about descendable in the right sort of car, but one has to pass through a very narrow arch to get out. Shortly after we bought it, I was out there alone for a couple of days to struggle with the local craftsmen, or craftymen, as I called some of them. Not being as yet trained in how to descend the street, I drove down the street in a hire car of the wrong size, and got completely jammed in the dreaded arch. It was impossible to move forward or back, or get out, as the doors were also firmly stuck. Being winter, there was no one in sight, and there was nothing I could do but give out blasts on the horn. This brought out a group of heavy drinkers from the bistro, who duly stood examining the situation with a series of hopeless Gallic shrugs and open questioning arms. I equally opened my arms in despair, whereupon a debate commenced about the situation, with a great amount of what I call French mouth farts with showers of beery spit, indicating the hopelessness of the situation. I waited in despondent despair, until the first group eventually called out two or three more immensely built men from the bar, and they all commenced rocking the car and trying to push it up the hill with me inside. Eventually, with loud sounds of scratching metal, they succeeded, although the car must have halved its value in the process. They then reversed it up the un-reversible street, out of its stone embrace, writing off the tyres in the process. Thanking God that I had taken out full insurance on the car, I was then able to thank my saviours with copious glasses of pastis, beer and wine, while receiving many instructions on how to navigate a medieval French village – ie: better *à pied*.

Fortunately the house did not require a vast amount of structural alteration, but of course French plumbing and drains are something else and bringing it up to the minimum British standards required much imagination, time, patience, skill and expense. Eventually everything worked more or less, with splendid central heating which was already there. The locals may not have had excessive addiction to baths, but you could not beat them on heat, which was perfect, with the addition of a large fireplace that burned enormous logs. We then built a swimming pool in the terrace above which we had to reinforce with enormous steel rods, drilled into the ramparts to prevent a tsunami descending on to our dining terrace, washing us and our *foie gras* onto our neighbour's terrace below. All has been more or less structurally sound since, except when the mediaeval village drains were being rebuilt, resulting in a blockage followed by a blowback. We found our dear friend and caretaker Georges, standing in the hall knee-deep in sewage. His only remark was, "Maintenant je suis vraiement dans la merde."

The country around Mirmande is lovely: rolling hills down to the Rhône with peaches, necatarines, plums, kiwis and grapes covering all. Behind the village is a national park of forests and hills into which we can walk from the village without crossing a road, and from the top of which one can see the sub-alps. The only slight snag is an enormous atomic power station about four miles as the crow flies from us, but we cannot see it from the village. The French, being faithfully cynical, issue the local inhabitants with a box of pills every two years, which we are meant to take if there is "un petit accident" at the power station. The pills are meant to help us with thyroid cancer. I keep on losing the pills, but comfort myself with the thought that in view of our proximity, we would be powder before we had managed to reach the pill drawer.

The nearest village on the brow of the next hill, 2.5 kilometres away is called Cliousclat, and it is lovely but flat and somewhat smaller than Mirmande. It's charming, with a famous pottery run by two eccentric brothers who are great friends of ours. There are two good restaurants; one in a charming little hotel, and a splendid bar come bistro on top of a wine shop with simple good food – *frites* with everything – excellent and cheap wine and a great line in international chat, gossip and live music on occasion. The village is remarkable for its sexual practices.

There is nothing kinky about them, except they seem to exchange husbands, wives or partners once a year. We have now learned not to ask how the other half is, because he or she is someone else's half by then. It is only after we have made discreet enquiries as to the winter moves on the village sexual chessboard that have taken place, do we venture to ask. However everyone appears to continue talking to each other in a friendly manner, and the practice appears to keep all and sundry on the "qui vive" apart from providing endless amusing gossip for rainy days.

IN 1989 OUR friend Galen Weston and his polo-playing colleague, Geoffrey Kent, the owner and chairman of the upper class travel business, Abercrombie & Kent, decided to establish an exclusive residential club in America. It was to be near to the delightful little beach resort of Vero Beach on 450 acres between the ocean and the inland waterway in Florida. The club was established as the Windsor Polo, Golf and Tennis Club. For some reason Galen and Hilary Weston invited us to help in the establishment of it, and build a house there, although I had never indulged in polo, golf or tennis in my life. Vicky at least had ridden horses all her life – I on the other hand, had only been astride a bicycle, and the odd girl in my wild youth. I was to help however with the chatting-up of new and prospective members, make cocktails, and to work on people's imaginations in the midst of a grapefruit plantation. Vicky looked elegant and rode out with what I believe is called an excellent 'seat' in hunting circles (although there was nothing more than squirrels and raccoons to hunt), and added much panache together with Hilary Weston at polo matches. From these humble beginnings a tremendously successful and beautiful club has been established. The Kents eventually departed to England and devoted their energies in Europe, Africa and the rest of the world.

Polo, unlike golf and drinking, appears to be a sport that is wise to be given up at a certain age, while the other two can be continued as long as the swing and the swill can be maintained, not to mention the liver. Vicky and I immediately assented to help with great enthusiasm, and camped with the Westons in a sort of hotel called the Guest

Suites downtown, while the first three houses were being built. The general plan was drawn up by the internationally-famous town planner, Andrés Duany and his team. It was in a way totally un-American in appearance, banishing the American obsession with motorcars, which were all concealed in garages, which were in turn concealed in a wealth of green vegetation, bouganvilia and Confederate jasmine. The houses were all white, or a very pale beige or blue, with lovely gardens and concealed pools. Although each house had to conform to the rules of the architectural committee, they all had their own individual style and look.

However, back to the grapefruit plantation, our imagination, plans and promises. The golf course designed by Bobby Trent-Jones came first and the golf club was erected by assembling a number of trailers together, decorated by numerous illustrations of things to come. While the builders were occupied with bricks and mortar, we were occupied with atmosphere created out of thin air, strong cocktails and jolly music. Galen and Hilary brought lots of their Canadian and North American friends down to visit, which they were only too happy to do – shedding their furs, mittens and thermal underwear *en route*. When three houses had been built we started to take visitors to the odd (some very odd) parties, in as then still unowned but decorated houses. One in particular comes to mind, designed by an architect called Clem Schaub. We would pretend that Mrs Schaub owned the house and being the Florida version of Elsa Maxwell, was totally addicted to giving unending parties. We had to pretend that poor Mrs Schaub, who was totally unaware of what was being done in her name, was indisposed that particular evening and would not be able to appear, but had asked the Westons and Poklewski Koziells to greet guests in her place and carry on the jollities. Jollities they certainly were. Sexy clothes, very sexy drinks and what is called in Florida 'heavy *hors d'ouvres*', plus rousing music. Hilary had usually imported an ancient bewigged trio from Miami or Palm Beach who were excellent musicians (especially when suitably lubricated), and got the parties going good-oh. We often ended in the pool with the younger guests splashing around not encumbered by too many clothes. The parties were a great success and established a sort of tradition that has endured to this day.

Some of the gatherings consisted of fabulous picnics on the beach –

at least we did not have to pretend that that was going to change. Little did I imagine that in years to come I would attend Mass at daybreak on Easter Sunday celebrated on the beach with at least two hundred people attending, plus a choir.

In the early days when the beach and golf clubs were not fully developed we decided to create a sort of informal and chaotic bar in a deserted and tumbledown bungalow on the inland waterway adjoining what is now the fully developed Orchid Island Club. I persuaded my friend, the head maintenance man, to build a long bar out of massive packing cases. It had to be massive to hold all the drink and the various people who took to dancing on it, having consumed a number of cocktails originally known as 'Vincent's Pink Specials' but then renamed by the gilded youth as the 'Knickerdropper Glory'. I never discovered why. Vicky and I furnished it with the most tacky bits and pieces we could find from rubbish dumps, pawn shops, thrift shops and so on; the sole rule being that they had to be in poor condition and in bad taste. It gained immediate popularity with one and all. No money changed hands; it was a sort of permanent bottle party with everyone contributing fiery liquor of some sort. We received some splendid contributions of furniture from members, including two old double bus seats with broken springs, and a splendid old wooden case, abandoned by an undertaker stencilled with 'Embalming Fluid' on the outside. The final touch was added when Neil and Pixie Shaw gave us a stuffed wild boar's head that they had found in some pawn shop. This was hung above the bar, as a result of which the establishment was always known as the Boar's Head pub from then on. The usually post-3am returns to Windsor through the trees and sand lanes were pretty hairy and there was much noise of colliding golf trolleys as the younger set returned 'off their trolleys'. The morning after breakfasts were rather solemn and conversation was limited to a series of "How could you have?" from parents facing large bills for golf trolley repairs. I remember one even ending up in one of the ponds on the golf club. All great fun, pretty young barmaids, including a trio of young sisters who were known as 'the sprinklers' because they never really got turned on till 4am – like the golf course ones.

Those were the days, after which we built and sold two houses, as it did not really make financial sense to maintain a big house at that distance from Europe, although we remain emotionally attached to the club, and all our friends there. We see them most years when we are invited to stay with the Westons in their magnificent mansion on the beach, on condition that we don't dance on the furniture. We have actually decided to confine ourselves to the floor at our age. Every time we come, we have to wipe our eyes in disbelief. There are now nearly 230 houses there and 273 members; a tennis centre, golf club, beach club with big pool; an ecumenical church, sports gym with the latest torture machines (avoided by me), village store, riding stables and so on. All discretely laid-out, and peaceful, in spite of having up to a thousand people staying at Christmas. Just the quiet purr of the odd golf trolley and bike.

Fin

IN CONCLUSION, FOR those readers who've had the patience to reach it, all I can say is that life continues, even if one's hair fails to do so. I have now reached the age of eighty-four in fair shape, due to the heroic efforts of my medical advisers, and when asked by the less educated, "What do you do?" I simply reply, "Retired" – upon hearing which, my disloyal children tend to annunciate quite unnecessarily loudly, "But from what, Daddy?" Let them buy this book, I say.

At any rate, I feel certain that with the efforts of my beloved, if sometimes tactless children, the line will continue with the same ups and downs – tears sometimes, but laughter more often.

My 'final resting place' is Harrington Gardens, Kensington, with its two-acre communal garden. It's ideal for us as Vicky's had a lifetime obsession with gardening, and it's also ideal for 'walkies' for the most important inhabitant of our home – Florence the pug.

My stepson Rupert is a jet captain and flies a 'Mr. Big' around the USA and South America, and he lives with his children in sunny Florida. My daughter Eliza owns a wonderful and idiosyncratic shop in Chelsea Green – Felt – where she deals in modern and antique jewellery. She lives two streets away with her architect husband Philip

Gumuchdjian and their son Oscar.

My other stepson, Ivor, and his beautiful Latvian wife Ieva, accidentally live the other side of the gardens with a delightful addition to our family – granddaughter Greta Charlotte. Ivor is a musical gent – a successful producer (of Grace Jones amongst others) and composer of film music.

Sasha, my son, is a dealer in old classic books, as well as being a serial entrepreneur and showing more than an increasing interest in younger ladies.

My daughter Sophie, her husband William – a successful sculptor – and my three other grandchildren, Sacha, Robin and Zoisa live in rural bliss in Cornwall, a place we love to visit. Sophie has been instrumental in creating a free school – Route 39 Academy – which made me very proud and happy until I discovered that the synonym 'free' included the fact that she is entirely unpaid.

Vicky, having dabbled as a painter on and off all her life has now become highly successful, especially with painting what she describes as 'vegetables with attitude'. Carrots, cabbages, potatoes, you name it… She boasts that her models cost under a pound and then she eats them when she's done. She puts up with me with loyal laughter at my old and much-repeated jokes. So life goes on. The only thing I have been forced to give up is bicycling in London, as a result of an unsuccessful encounter with a motorcar in the King's Road, when I went sprawling off my bike, fracturing my shoulder.

According to the actuaries – and also my doctor, who rather tactlessly said not to worry when I mentioned that we only had a 33-year lease left on our flat – Shakespeare's 'mortal shuffle' will be clearly unwound sooner rather than later. I have always been a believer, and on the whole a reasonable practitioner of my religion. The world population on the whole believes in God, or gods, or for lack of religious definition – the unknown. The unknown is where – let's face it – we are all equal, and I have no quarrel with most beliefs. However, being Christian, I have a slight disquiet with those who believe in reincarnation.

What a worry being reincarnated 'below stairs'. I have always been upwardly mobile most of my life, but the thought of carrying breakfasts up four storeys, day after day – and if it was the wrong century, the end product of the said breakfasts down four storeys – fills me with gloom. I suppose one could reappear as rich, glamorous and successful on the stock exchange and mattress, but I fear it more likely I'd be a mahout. Can you imagine spending one's days on an elephant's neck? Just imagine the noise and smell – not to mention vertigo and motion sickness? No point in speculating further. I'll stick to my own religion, and if I do avoid the boiler room, I hope I will not be sitting next to too many souls that I might have upset unintentionally in this life, or more importantly the more numerous ones that have bored me rigid.

As far as I am concerned, I can only finish with a well-known quotation: "That money talks, I won't deny – I heard it once, it said goodbye!"

1▲ 3▼   2▲

1. Annabel and Vincent on their wedding day, 1962
2. Alik & Zoia Poklewski Koziell and Agnes de Stoeckl outside church
3. Vincent and Annabel on their honeymoon, Sardinia

1 ▲ 2 ▼   3 ▼

1. Porto Raphael, Sardinia
2. Raphael Neville and Vincent
3. Vincent and Raphael

1 ▲ 3 ▼

2 ▲ 4 ▼

5 ▼

6 ▼

234

1. Luttrelstown Castle
2. Aileen Plunkett
3. Doon Granville and Aileen Plunket
4. Aileen and Vincent at a fancy dress party
5. Oonagh Oranmore and Browne
6. Aileen and Annabel learning the twist from a Parisian instructor
7. Annabel
8. Vincent and Aileen at Ballyconneely, Connemara
9. Eamonn Andrews and Eileen Mount Charles, Stacumny
10. Vincent and Annabel

1▲ 3▼   2▲ 4▼

1. Vincent and Sasha, Oakley Road
2. Vincent on his way to the office
3. Father Christmas at Brown Thomas with Eliza, Sasha and Rupert
4. Christmas at IMCO
5. Annabel, Susan and Tony O'Reilly
6. Gerry Albertini, Annabel, Vincent and friends
7. Sasha, Sophie, Eliza, Rupert and pets

5 ▲ 6 ▼

7 ▼

1 ▲ 1a ▼

2 ▼

1. Dolly's Cottage, Mullinacoe on Lough Erne…
   and later burnt down by the IRA
2. Vincent and Harry Erne
3. The Kent children arriving to stay in Dublin
4. Vincent, Eliza, Sasha and Sophie visiting Rupert at the Carlton Hotel, Cannes
5. Stas, Vincent and Lucy Poklewski Koziell, Warsaw
6. Vincent and Stas Poklewski Koziell, Stacumny

3 ▲ 4 ▼   5 ▼

6 ▼

1 ▲ 2 ▼   3 ▼

1. Vincent and Vicky getting married, 1982
2. Vicky, Pug and Pimms
3. Ivor and Vicky
4. Ivor, Sophie, Vicky, Vincent, Eliza and Sasha on Vincent's 60th
5. Vincent, Vicky, Rupert, Eliza, Sasha and Sophie, Christmas at Stacumny, 1990
6. Family and household at Stacumny wearing some of the hat collection, 1989

4 ▲ 5 ▼

6 ▼

1 ▲   2 ▲

3 ▲ 4 ▼

*Vincent Poklewski-Koziell is a man who insists on the best. We also show some of the designs recently available at Pinks, where you will find a **constantly changing** selection of plain colours, stripes and checks, with up to fifty different patterns at any one time.*

242

5 ▲ 6 ▼   7 ▼

1. Part of the Stacumny hat collection
2. Vincent and Polly the dog featured in 'The Hat Book' (© Rodney Smith & Leslie Smolan)
3. Stacumny House
4. Advertising Thomas Pink shirts: "I wear Thomas Pink shirts for the luxury of pure cotton poplin" – says Vincent Poklewski Koziell, international wit, raconteur and well-dressed man.
5. Vincent, Vicky and Jerry Hall
6. Ronnie Wood and Vicky
7. Vincent in party mode

1 ▲ 2 ▼

1. Family house in Yekaterinburg (now the city museum), Siberia
2. Great Uncle Stas' house on the Fontanka canal, St. Petersburg
3. Vicky and Vincent with descendants of Poklewski family household retainers, Siberia
4. One of the family distilleries, Siberia
5. Picture of Vincent's great-grandfather, the founder of the Poklewski distilleries, on a vodka bottle

3 ▲ 4 ▼   5 ▼

1 ▲ 2 ▼

1. Missionary father with some of his congregation
2. Eliza with villagers
3. Inside of missionary church
4. Outside of missionary church
5. Travelling down the Sepik river
6. Crossing a river
7. Vincent

3 ▲ 5 ▼   4 ▲

6 ▼   7 ▼

 1 ▲ 3 ▼   2 ▲

1. Hilary Weston and Vicky on polo ponies at The Windsor Club, Florida
2. Vincent posing as a decorator
3. Galen Weston and Vincent
4. Galen and Hilary Weston with Vincent and Vicky
5. Vicky, Galen and James Abercorn at a polo match
6. Columbus O'Donnell, Eartha Kitt and Vincent

4 ▲ 5 ▼

6 ▼

1 ▲ 3 ▼   2 ▲ 4 ▼

1. Vincent and Vicky dressed for 'hunting'
2. Andrea O'Donnell and Vincent
3. Vincent and Vicky
4. Blowing for dinner
5. Vincent and Vicky in a bicycle rickshaw, Florida
6. Mirmande (© Office de Tourisme Livron-Loriol-Mirmande / J. Labanne – L. Leblanc)
7. Family on Vincent's 80th birthday in Scotland
8. Next page — Vincent and Vicky in bed (© Herlinde Koelbl)

5 ▲ 6 ▼

7 ▼

From left to right, top row: Ieva Imsa, Ivor Wimborne, Rupert de las Casas, William Peers, Arran de las Casas, Vincent, Vicky, Zoisa Peers, Eliza Poklewski Koziell, Philip Gumuchdjian, Annabella de las Casas. Bottom row: Sasha Poklewski Koziell, Sacha Peers, Robin Peers, Sophie Poklewski Koziell, Oscar Gumuchdjian